AMERICAN EDUCATION

Its Men,

Ideas,

and

Institutions

Advisory Editor

Lawrence A. Cremin
Frederick A. P. Barnard Professor of Education
Teachers College, Columbia University

A MERICAN EDUCATION: *Its Men, Ideas, and Institutions*
presents selected works of thought and scholarship that have
long been out of print or otherwise unavailable. Inevitably, such
works will include particular ideas and doctrines that have been
outmoded or superseded by more recent research. Nevertheless,
all retain their place in the literature, having influenced educational thought and practice in their own time and having provided
the basis for subsequent scholarship.

Curriculum Construction

by

W. W. CHARTERS

ARNO PRESS & THE NEW YORK TIMES
*New York * 1971*

Reprint Edition 1971 by Arno Press Inc.

Reprinted from a copy in
  The Wesleyan University Library

American Education:
  Its Men, Ideas, and Institutions - Series II
ISBN for complete set: 0-405-03600-0
See last pages of this volume for titles.

Manufactured in the United States of America

Library of Congress Cataloging in Publication Data

Charters, Werrett Wallace, 1875-1952.
    Curriculum construction.
    (American education: its men, ideas, and
institutions. Series II)
    1. Education--Curricula. I. Title.
II. Series.
LB1570.C45 1971   372.1'9   74-165713
ISBN 0-405-03702-3

CURRICULUM CONSTRUCTION

THE MACMILLAN COMPANY
NEW YORK · BOSTON · CHICAGO · DALLAS
ATLANTA · SAN FRANCISCO

MACMILLAN & CO., LIMITED
LONDON · BOMBAY · CALCUTTA
MELBOURNE

THE MACMILLAN CO. OF CANADA, LTD.
TORONTO

Curriculum Construction

by

W. W. CHARTERS

Professor of Education, Carnegie Institute
of Technology

New York
THE MACMILLAN COMPANY
1923

TO MY WIFE
JESSIE ALLEN CHARTERS

PREFACE

The school curriculum is the latest great social agency to feel the effect of the theory of evolution. Biology for sixty years has recognized the fact that living structure is modified to serve the functions of plants and animals. Sociology, economics, and history accept the fact that the forms of institutions are determined by the attempts of man to make his environment minister to his needs. Psychology has developed a functional and behavioristic point of view, and in philosophy pragmatism has achieved a permanent place.

While all these revolutionary changes have been under way, the theory of the formation of the curriculum has been slow to react to them. The curriculum builder has felt, like his pre-evolutionary prototype who clung to the theory of epigenesis, that the specialists who organize the subjects to meet the needs of their groups have developed the best possible curriculum. The force of evolutionary theory has been negatived by the strength of the doctrine of the transfer of training and by the prestige of the scientist. It has been held that the training of the faculties could be secured by already existing forms of subject matter and that change in structure should therefore be resisted. To add to this conviction, the prestige of the scientist induced the lowly school teacher to believe that a structure built in conformity with his needs was equally suitable and satisfactory for the needs of the layman.

Long before Darwin formulated his theories there was much intense, destructive criticism of the subject matter taught in the elementary schools. Particularly from the time of Rousseau educational theorists and an innumerable number of laymen and teachers have contended that the content of school subjects does not fulfill the functions of popular education. This criticism has resulted in some modification by the elimination and addition of some subjects and parts of subjects, as is seen when we note the differences in the content of the school curriculum during the last fifty years. But these have been changes in detail; the cedar roof has been changed to slate, the veranda has been changed into a sleeping porch, a sun parlor has been added, a wing built on, and the outside painted: but the house still stands essentially as it came from the architect and the builder.

In the last ten years, however, the criticism has begun to take constructive shape and a number of pioneer studies have been made from the functional point of view. Functions for subjects have been set up and the structures which will realize the functions have been derived. This has resulted in a considerable body of knowledge which can be collected and interpreted in terms of the functional theory of curriculum construction. To this task the present volume addresses itself.

The author wishes to acknowledge his appreciation for the services rendered him by many educators, including Bonser, Bobbitt, Coursault, Dewey, Meriam, and Yocum. Particularly does he wish to express his appreciation of the assistance of his former colleague, B. H. Bode, whose criticism of the theoretical principles underlying the treatment has been a stimulus to clarifying analysis, especially in the field of ideals and activities.

W. W. C

July, 1922.

CONTENTS

PART I

ix

CONTENTS

PART I

PRINCIPLES OF CURRICULUM
CONSTRUCTION

CHAPTER I

THE THEORY OF CURRICULUM CONSTRUCTION

§1—INTRODUCTION

The tardiness of change. — One would expect that those profound changes in the aims of education which follow revolutions in world thought would be reflected in equally fundamental changes in the curriculum of the school; but in practice the changes have always been tardy and have seldom been complete. For instance, it would be expected that with the wholesale acceptance of Christianity by the people of Europe, the quadrivium and trivium of Greek civilization would have been supplanted by books which more directly taught the rudiments of Christian culture. In this case the expected did happen to the extent that the administrators of the Christian church caused the establishment of the catechetical and catechumenal schools. But as soon as instruction in the practices of the Christian church had been taught to those who so recently had been pagans, then the quadrivium and the trivium regained ascendancy and long remained the basis of school instruction in Christian Europe.

The same fact is noticeable in the cultural revolution of the Renaissance, and in the period which followed. During the period of the Renaissance the ideal of ancient culture dominated the schools of Europe and led to the inclusion of the classics in the courses of study. Aristotle, who had been forgotten for many centuries, again came into importance, and the classical group which he dominated furnished the content of the curriculum.

As time went on, the individual was discovered, and thus was initiated a great world movement which was reflected in the statement of the aims of education by Rousseau and those who amplified and refined his point of view. But, through all these changes in

3

theory concerning the aim of education, the actual curriculum in operation in the schools changed comparatively little. Again in the present period, when world thought has been turning to a consideration of social factors and ideals, the theory of the aims of education has been modified but the changes in the curriculum in actual operation are still quite inconsiderable.

The causes. — The cause for this tardiness lies partly in the fact that the mechanics of such an institution as the public schools are so complicated that an appreciable time must elapse before changes are felt; but the cause lies much more truly in other factors, of which three are of enough importance to bear elaboration.

Briefly stated, the curriculum has been slow to respond to the changing statements of the aim of education because (1) those who have formulated the aims of education have not taken into account the activities which individuals carry on. Rather have they laid stress merely upon ideals from which a curriculum can be derived. As the result of this failure, (2) the curriculum has been under the domination of the idea that the youth should be given a bird's-eye view of the knowledge of the world rather than a compendium of useful information. Furthermore, (3) when the material in this curriculum has been criticised as lacking practicalness, the school administrators, with whom the defence of the curriculum rests, have until quite recently justified it by an appeal to the doctrines of formal discipline and the transfer of training.

The standards of our day demand that our courses of study be derived from objectives which include both ideals and activities, that we should frankly accept *usefulness* as our aim rather than *comprehensive knowledge*, and that no fictitious emphasis should be placed upon the value of formal discipline.

A description of the effect of these demands upon curriculum construction constitutes the purpose of the author in the preparation of this text. We shall first of all elaborate and criticize the theories of curriculum construction as observed in the history of education, then analyze and describe the recent technique of curriculum construction, and finally present a body of the more significant studies which have been made within the last decade.

§2—AIMS, IDEALS, AND ACTIVITIES

Aims precede curriculum change. — Changes in the curriculum are always preceded by modifications in our conception of the aim of education. In the organized writings of educators, fundamental changes in the curriculum have been advocated only after the writers have brought forward a statement of aim differing from the current idea. Among these writers we find Plato describing the qualities of the perfect warrior guardian of the state, before determining what the training of such an individual should be. Similarly, Comenius presents the aims of virtue, piety, and learning before describing his well-known curriculum. Rousseau likewise justified his course of study by an appeal to certain assumptions concerning the development of the "nature" of the child.

In the less formal and more fluid movements of thought of any generation, including our own, at the time when the curriculum is in the making, we find that only after such aims as social efficiency have been discussed for a number of years in the educational press and forum do changes in the curriculum begin to appear. No wholesale change occurs, but bit by bit additions are proposed or eliminations advocated. Indeed it may be said that a change in the curriculum runs on the average ten years behind the advocating of a change in the aim of education. And for the curriculum change to become large enough to be noticed, a much longer period of incubation is necessary. It is rather generally the case that most of the theoretical discussions among educators as to changing the statement of aim fail to modify the practical curriculum as it is taught in the schoolroom. But even though a change comes slowly and sometimes seems infinitesimal, it is always preceded by a new statement of the aim of education.

Uses of the aim. — This preliminary statement of aim is a prerequisite to both selection and use. The inheritance handed down through the schools to the young is so massive that it can never be completely assimilated. Selection is, therefore, necessary, and a basis of selection must be determined. This is obtained through the statement of aim. For instance, if piety is to be the aim of education, then it is necessary that the course of study should contain an adequate amount of religious material. If, on the other hand, social efficiency is set up as the aim of education, it is obvious that the activities with which people are engaged in conjunction with other people should receive primary emphasis. If the earning of a living through a vocation be set up as the primary aim of education in any school, then it is natural that vocational technique should be included in the course of study. These illustrations make clear the fact that an aim is prerequisite to selection.

Moreover, the aim is necessary for use. Information has no value considered apart from its function. For different purposes it must be used in different ways, and thus assumes various forms. If topics are studied with the outstanding purpose of teaching morality, the moral implications will be stressed; while if training in social efficiency is the aim of the curriculum, then the topics will be considered from the point of view of their usefulness in assisting the individual to become the servant or the leader of others. Facts in the special subjects, as in chemistry, are essentially different facts when taught in the vocational course in agriculture from what they are in a course for pharmacists. Though the facts concerning carbon may seem to be the same facts irrespective of use, fundamentally carbon presents a different body of subject matter in relation to dietetics from carbon as studied for mineralogy; only a few elementary facts are the same.

This idea may perhaps be stated more clearly if we look upon subject matter as containing not only facts but also the uses of those facts. For instance, the study of carbon gives us a few elementary facts about carbon, and in addition to these it gives us what we call the applications of those facts to other fields; and both the elementary facts and their applications are essentially parts of the subject matter to be taught.

The failure of investigators. — While writers on the curriculum have begun with the statement of aim, none has been able to derive a curriculum logically from his statement of aim. In every case he has made an arbitrary mental leap from the *aim* to the *subject matter*, without providing us with adequate principles such as would bridge the gap—without presenting steps which irresistibly lead us from aim to selection of material. This may seem to be a sweeping statement, but a few illustrations will demonstrate its accuracy.

Plato. — In Plato's *Republic* the author states his aim clearly as follows: "Then in our judgment the man whose natural gifts promise to make him the perfect guardian of the state will be philosophical, high-spirited, swift-footed, and strong." Proceeding with his dialectic he says: "This, then, will be the original character of our guardians, but in what way shall we rear and educate them?" This query he treats as follows: "What, then, is the education to be? Perhaps we could find hardly a better than that which the experience of the past has already discovered, which consists, I believe, in gymnastics for the body and music for the mind." Subsequently he analyzes gymnastics and music into their different divisions, and argues for the inclusion of such narratives, fables, and poetry as present certain ideals in the proper form, and adds to these certain types of melodies and songs. After analyzing his course in music in this way he gives a slight description of the course in gymnastics, while paying little attention to the content but emphasizing the ideals of temperateness, happiness, and health of body.

The mental leap occurs at the point between his characterization of the ideal guardian ("philosophical, high-spirited, swift-footed, and strong") and his prescription of "music and gymnastics." Plato has not taken us into his confidence and let us see why he thinks that the "philosophical" disposition can be best trained through "music and gymnastics." He has not indicated what particular part of the censored literature is to be selected, nor has he shown what gymnastic exercises should be included in the curriculum. Is there no other material through which the guardian may be made "high-spirited"? Should not Plato specify some of the exercises which will best promote the "swift-footed" athlete? Moreover, we are tempted to ask whether such a group of ideals might not also hold for the youthful citizens of America, and whether—if so—the same ideals would call for an identical course of study.

Plato's curriculum is not an adequate system of instruction for warriors. Within the last few years we have seen the spectacle of "a million men springing to arms" who were high-spirited and strong, but certainly were not perfect soldiers. Before they could become "perfect guardians of the state" their curriculum was made to include much besides "fables and poetry, melodies, song, and gymnastics." They had to learn to march, to shoot, to thrust with the bayonet, to fly in airplanes, and to sail the seas. Nor was Plato's curriculum any more adequate for the warriors of ancient Athens. When his men were trained in music and gymnastics they still had much to learn before they could become perfect guardians of the state: they needed to be able to carry on all the forms of ancient warfare.

Comenius.—The aims and the curriculum of Comenius present the same deficiency. This great educator assumes the aim of education to be that of bringing to maturity the seeds of learning, virtue, and piety planted within us by Nature. He then outlines his course for the vernacular school as follows (after Quick): "In this school the children should learn—first, to read and write the mother-tongue well, both with writing and printing letters; second, to compose grammatically; third, to cipher; fourth, to measure and weigh; fifth, to sing, at first popular airs, then from music; sixth, to say by heart sacred psalms and hymns; seventh, catechism, Bible history, and texts; eighth, moral rules with examples; ninth, economics and politics, as far as they could be understood; tenth, general history of the world; eleventh, figure of the earth and motion of the stars, etc., physics and geography, especially of native land; twelfth, general knowledge of arts and handicrafts."

This curriculum of Comenius cannot be derived logically from his three-fold aim of "learning, virtue, and piety." *Learning* as an aim will give no basis of selection unless one could expect to learn everything. The interest of Comenius in his "pansophy" indicates his belief that in a general way one might encompass all knowledge, but only in a general way. The details of knowledge could not be learned, because that task would be too great for the time of any individual. Selection is therefore necessary, even in a "pansophy," and *learning* as such will not provide the basis for selection. Nor do *virtue* and *piety* provide this basis. Will ciphering, singing, or economics assist in any particularly valuable way in promoting these two ends? Or, to carry the question farther, what details of ciphering or physics will be most valuable in promoting *virtue* and *piety?* Clearly, since one fact is as virtuous as another, subject matter cannot be derived from *virtue* as the aim of education.

The cause of their failure. — The impossibility of deriving subject matter from the aims of Plato and Comenius is due to the fact that their aims are statements of *ideals isolated from activities.* For the curriculum is properly concerned not only with the ideals which govern life, but also with the things which a person does and thinks about. A virtuous carpenter does not perform the same actions, nor does he meet the same problems, as a virtuous blacksmith. A pious business man receives a different education from a pious doctor. A virtuous and pious Chinaman thinks and acts upon matters different from those which engage the attention of a similarly virtuous and pious American. The ideals are the same; the lives are widely different. It would be futile to teach the Chinaman the same curriculum as the American unless the intention were to Americanize him.

The ideals are the same, but the curriculum is different; and it is different because *it is derived from both ideals and activities.* Some ideals, such as virtue, or swift-footedness, piety, or social efficiency, must be set up in the system of education; but in order to determine the curriculum it is absolutely essential for a teacher to know the activities, problems, thoughts, or needs which these ideals are to influence and control.

Plato had a golden opportunity to set a new style in curriculum construction when he described the education of the perfect warrior. If instead of resting content with enumerating the *qualities* of his "perfect guardians," he had analyzed their *duties* and had decided to teach swift-footedness, strength, and the high-spirited mind *through these activities*, he would most powerfully have influenced the education of the next two thousand years. But when he had stated as his aim *an ideal*, he was compelled to slip back into the rut of the traditional subjects of his day as the best agencies for developing this aim. And similarly, if Comenius had inquired into the *activities* of the French or the English citizenry, if he had found out the daily problems they had to meet, and had sought to make them "virtuous" and "pious" in *their perfo. mance of these duties*, he would have had a curriculum of demonstrable validity. Only then would he have known what ciphering and economics, what music, sacred songs, and Biblical passages to include. In other words, he would have been able to determine not only what subjects, but what parts of subjects to include in his curriculum. In the absence of a statement of *activities* there is no possible way of deriving a curriculum from *ideals*.

Spencer. — One notable attempt has been made in the past to analyze activities as the basis for curriculum organization, and in addition several current attempts have been made. Spencer, having set up the aim of education as complete living, analyzed it not by showing what qualities were necessary for complete living, but by indicating what activities were to be carried on. The analysis led him to class the activities in five divisions, having to do with (1) self-preservation; (2) the earning of a living; (3) the duties of parenthood; (4) the activities of citizenship; (5) occupations for leisure.

Having interest only in the broader outlines of the subject, Spencer did not sub-classify these activities, but proceeded at once to show that the curriculum should consist of the natural sciences. Undoubtedly if he had taken time to analyze the activities more thoroughly he could have come much nearer to determining subject matter than the others have been able to come who have set up ideals and qualities as the aim of education. His failure to prove that the natural sciences are the proper material for the curriculum is due primarily to his failure to analyze the activities. His position is open to yet another criticism, of a more fundamental sort, to the effect that he paid no conscious attention to the ideals which were necessary for complete living. "Self-preservation" may be secured at the expense of very important ideals; it is frequently of less importance than the ideal of unselfishness. Without taking ideals into consideration, we cannot determine the form in which activities shall be carried on. The same criticism can be leveled against an activity-analysis such as that of Bonser, who, in *The Elementary School Curriculum*, specifies job analysis as the method to be used in determining what shall be taught, but fails to give equal emphasis to the ideals which shall dominate the activities.

Summary. — Summarizing, we may say that in order to determine the content of the curriculum the aim of education must be stated in terms both of ideals and of activities. When the aim is stated in terms of ideals only, there is always a gap between the aim as stated and the curriculum as ostensibly derived from such a statement. Conversely, when the activities are stated without the ideals which dominate them, there is no means of selecting the proper method of performing the activities.

Chapter II

FACTORS OPPOSED TO CHANGE

§1—The Prestige of Systematic Knowledge

The result of failure to analyze. — In the absence of a combination of activities and ideals to be used as the basis for analysis, the investigator who includes in his aim only a statement of ideals unconsciously falls back upon the traditional course of study, which he may modify slightly or extensively, depending upon many factors that influence his decision. Plato, as noted above, accepted the conventional course of study of his time and made some slight modifications. Comenius made numerous modifications of the course of study found in institutions of learning in his generation, the wide variety of his changes being due to his belief in the practicability of acquiring all learning, and in the wisdom of providing universal education. His curriculum was not derived from his ideals of "learning, virtue, and piety." Rousseau, having stated his idea of the aim of education as being the free development of the "nature" of the child, selected his subject matter largely, it would seem to the careful reader, upon the basis of his own experiences as a child. That he derived it thus, rather than logically from his statement of aim, is due to the fact that the medium through which the nature of the child is developed varies with the child's activities, and these depend partly on the surroundings in which the child is placed.

The reason for this reversion to the conventional subjects in the curriculum of the day, with supplementary modifications, is the prestige of systematic knowledge and the value attached to formal discipline. The first of these we shall discuss somewhat more fully in this section.

The prestige of brilliance. — Education was for many centuries an undifferentiated social activity, carried on as a by-

12

product of the home. As the fathers and mothers earned their living they trained their children to perform tasks which were intended primarily to help the father and mother and secondarily to give training to the children. However, as conditions of living became more complex and schooling became more and more desirable in the equipment of the young, parents began to realize that they lacked the time and knowledge necessary to teach their children. The need for the school having been demonstrated, it was to be expected that men who knew the information to be taught should be selected to teach, and this led naturally to the ranks of scholarly men as a source of supply. In the beginning, when only the children of the very wealthy were taught, the teachers selected were those who knew to the fullest extent what had been gathered together by the scholars, and in many cases those who were themselves engaged in research. As greater interest in schooling developed, the law of supply and demand operated in such a way that the level of scholarly attainments was lowered. Yet in no case was a man employed who was not in some degree acquainted with the scholarship of his day.

When such a man was selected the problem of developing the young became his problem, and his also became the problem of selecting the proper subject matter by which such development could be obtained. It is a very significant fact that in their search for materials of instruction such teachers turned to the most brilliant and most highly organized material that had been evolved by scholars. The works of the masters became the textbooks of the children; no other course was easily possible. The lowly teacher was an admiring worshiper of the scholarship of the masters; no other kind seemed to be of so much worth to him, or therefore of so much potential value to his students. In such manner the method of curriculum construction which may be called specialistic determination came to be accepted.

Brilliance *versus* use. — We should have had quite different curricula through the ages had the early teachers decided to use activity analysis as the basis and to teach the material most useful to the young in coping with the humble problems of their lives. Vocational education would not have been delayed until the present half-century. Hygiene would probably have been included to a greater extent, and other items closely related to the life of the common people would have been inserted.

It was, however, too much to expect that this could be done in the beginning, because admiration for the brilliance of the human mind working upon erudite problems has always been a dominating force in the minds of scholars, and the early teachers had neither the ability nor the desire to hold opinions about what constitutes valuable knowledge other than that contained in the works of the master minds. And when, at a later time, teachers began to be carefully prepared for their vocation, particularly through the development of scientific methods, the idea that what is most brilliant is also most useful for education held and still holds a firm position in the pedagogic mind. Indeed even to-day it verges upon bad taste to assert that many very brilliant products of genius ought not to be included in the course of study for the first twelve grades. The organized fields of knowledge have attained positions of almost unassailable strength.

The evolution of the sciences. — These organized bodies of knowledge were born in very humble surroundings. Botany was first studied by the women of the tribe, who sought for simple herbs to cure common diseases. Zoölogy began with observation of the habits of wild and domesticated animals, and the subject of astronomy was first studied by the dwellers in open spaces who guided their steps by the sun, the moon, and the stars. When to these pursuits were added the ingredients of curiosity and wonder it came to pass after many centuries that men of leisure devoted all their time to the investigation of one or another of these fields, with the result that they detached the material from its practical relations and divested it of the concrete situations which fettered investigation. The abstraction of the material from concrete situations gave free play to curiosity, which, guided by the logical machinery of the human mind, could therefore make spectacular discoveries. So it was only when number became an abstract science that the brilliant discoveries of arithmetic, algebra, and the calculi became possible; and it was only after botany, zoölogy, and chemistry became abstracted from their practical beginnings that it was possible for the human mind, following its own untrammeled urgings, to produce the amazing results which are now incorporated as parts of the tissue of these romantic subjects.

Mental morale. — That such subjects, so developed, should possess unusual importance is to be expected. The *first* value of these systematic fields of knowledge as subjects of schooling lies in the fact that they undoubtedly add to human morale by calling to the attention of youth the brilliance of the intellectual achievements of genius. One can hardly fail to be filled with enthusiasm for the possibilities of the human mind when one studies the stupendous intellectual achievements exhibited in the findings of history, literature, art, and science. Even those stolid or cynical high school students who treat their studies with matter-of-factness or flippancy have been touched by the magnificence of human genius.

Applications of knowledge. — The *second* value, of greater importance in human progress, is the influence of the great fields of organized knowledge upon the practices of civilization. The discoveries in electricity which have made possible such conveniences as electric lighting and electric power, gasoline engines, and rapid transportation were made by men who had no idea (or, at least, little interest in the idea) that electricity could be used for practical purposes. The X-ray was discovered and developed by people who, as far as we know, saw none of its applications to medicine or its relations to radio-activity as a revolutionary concept in chemistry and physics.

Consequently much has been said in favor of the position that if youth can be put into possession of the principles of the arts and sciences it can be trusted to apply these to practical life. This is appealing because of the thousands of instances which can be mustered in which applications of the pure sciences have been made to engineering, to industry, to agriculture, and to social welfare. The scientist, whether physical, biological, or social, has demonstrated, and perhaps never more spectacularly than to-day, that pure science is the greatest single practical force in the modern development of civilization.

Ease of instruction. — A *third* value of systematic knowledge lies in the claim that because it *is* highly organized it is easy to teach. The great fields of knowledge are for the most part based upon the principles which have settled as precipitates after years of study, during which the organization of the field has been in a state of fluidity. When (to change the figure) after the passage of a few years or generations, the contents of the field can be seen in perspective, the divisions and subdivisions are obvious; and it is then possible to select from the principles and facts in each field those items which, thrown into relief in elementary text-books, will give a well organized, bird's-eye view of the whole field.

Criticisms. — It would seem that with such an array of advantages there should be no considerable weakness in the position that youth can best be trained by a curriculum consisting of a compendium of the organized fields of knowledge. But in the minds of many thoughtful students the case against it seems also to be strong. Criticism centers around such questions as the ability of youth to use the material in the organized fields of knowledge, and the disposition that is to be made of the unorganized fields of knowledge. Those who question the superlative value of such organized fields as the social and physical sciences, history, art, and literature, as subjects of the course of study, raise objections to the items included. They take the position that some elements of the organized fields will necessarily be included, but they believe, also, that many items from the unorganized fields must likewise be inserted. They assert that it is a mistake to select material from the organized field upon the basis of providing a miniature model of the systematic organization. They maintain that the material to be used from each field should be selected because of its practical usefulness. They are less concerned with giving some acquaintance with all the subdivisions of each field than with including only such parts of the subdivisions as will function in practical life.

What is practical? — By practical life is meant not alone—or even primarily—the earning of a living. The practical man must, to be sure, have a vocation, but besides vocation he has many other interests. He has, for instance, problems of art, such as the decoration of his home, the selection of his clothes, and the beautification of his city. He is confronted with the need of choosing books to read, music to appreciate, and pictures to enjoy. He must in addition perform the duties of citizenship, of religion, of morals, and of manners. Practical life consists in the dealings and activities embraced in the conduct of well-rounded members of society.

Organized knowledge constantly changes. — When it is claimed that a compendium of the great fields of organized knowledge does not necessarily provide the best training for such an individual, the claim is based upon four considerations. It is pointed out in the *first* place that the organized fields of knowledge are constantly changing. They are organized and reorganized from different points of view as the problems of one generation of scientists give way to the problems of the succeeding generation. In the popular mind the facts of the sciences have a metaphysical finality and a corresponding sanctity, but in the minds of scientists no such illusion exists. They know that the sciences are the product of the human mind, and that among investigators fashions rule with definite power. The problems which one generation works upon are not those which will stimulate their successors. For instance, while systematic botany prior to 1860 was concerned with the classifying of plants, a new science of botany was developed after Darwin; and this differed from its predecessors much more markedly than the hoop skirt and bustle of the same period differed from the attenuated skirts of to-day. Again, as late as 1890, the problems of the anatomy of plants were in the foreground, and the systematic high school texts were anatomical in content; but by 1900 the problems found in the textbooks were physiological, so that instead of finding the high school botany systematizing the parts of plants we find it dealing with the physiological functions. What has happened in botany happens in every science. Any science is the product of the intellectual energy of alert men who, because they are in love with the game, are always open to new suggestions and very frequently leave one part of their field for another part before all the problems of the first are solved. Obviously, then, the problems of the organized fields change, as is right and proper and natural; and as the problems change the structure of the field changes so that the compendium of to-day does not have the same content as that of yesterday.

This line of reasoning inevitably leads one to this question: If scientists select from their fields that material which solves their problems, why may not the layman ask them to select for him that part of their material which will be of use to him in solving his problems? The scientist organizes his field around his own problems, and therefore ought to be willing to organize the contributing parts of his field around the problems of other people.

Acquisition and application. — In the *second* place, it is claimed that the application of knowledge is more difficult than its acquisition. The applications of chemistry and physics, taken in the large, have been made by a multitude of investigators, each working on a specific application. But it is to be noted that this has been accomplished by a group of individuals working upon specific problems. To this they devoted their major energies for an extended time, and by singleness of devotion were able to accomplish remarkable results. But it is one thing to say that one person is able to make one application, and quite a different thing to assert that one person can make all the applications, particularly when he has not specialized narrowly upon any phase of the problem. It may be granted that one application can be made by one specialist, and still be contended with force that a single specialist cannot make all the applications; still more strongly can it be contended that all the applications could not be made by one layman, no matter how brilliant he might be. Both principles and their applications must be taught.

Motivation. — It is claimed in the *third* place that when knowledge is divorced from the consciousness of usefulness it is extremely difficult to motivate. While it is acknowledged that there is a small proportion of individuals who are natively endowed with such an electric alertness that their curiosity will stimulate them to the study of everything that is new, yet anyone who will make an inventory of his acquaintances will readily agree that the number of such people is small, and that universality of curiosity is not typical of the great mass of people.

The critics of the public school lay the blame for this narrowness of curiosity upon the methods of instruction in the school, but this criticism is not well founded. The lack is based rather upon the psychology of the individual. Certainly the high school student has a broader range of interest than the adult, but even among such students there is continual criticism of their subjects of study on the ground of lack of vitality. This cannot be dismissed with the statement that they ought to be interested, or that the teaching is inadequate. It is rather due to the fact that people are chiefly curious about matters which affect them closely, and are not normally curious about the things for which they see no use.

Usefulness. — It is not claimed that the material contained in the sciences is not useful. Every product of human effort has been developed in an effort to assist in the solution of some problem, and the materials of the scientist are not an exception to this rule. But they are the solutions of the problems of the scientist and not of those of the layman. Consequently we often find that the high school student, even though he possess a wider range of interest than the adult, does not appreciate the problems of pure science, whatever latent or active interest he may have in their popular phases. It follows, therefore, that we are not so much concerned with the differences between use and non-use as we are with differences in the uses which may be made of the specialists' material. It frequently happens, as has been said, that while youthful students have little interest in the specialists' problems they may be keenly interested in practical, lay problems connected with the field. If there is any appreciation of the use of the material, they will recognize its value; but if the problems which the material solves are not appreciated, motivation will be lacking. While it is one of the duties of the school to increase the range of curiosity, a widened range of interest can be secured as a social measure not by presenting a wide range of material to learn, but by making the student more keenly sensitive to the use and application of the facts which are presented to him for acquisition.

Unorganized fields. — The thoughtful student of education sees a *fourth* weakness in the course of study composed of the systematized fields of knowledge. He feels that to equip youth properly for the problems of maturity, instruction must be given in the current, unorganized social problems of the day. For instance, we have facing us now the problems of labor, direct action, governmental control, and the participation of workers in the profits and administration of business, but the facts concerning these are not usually taught in the grades or in the high school. Whether they can be taught with complete adequacy or not is beside the point; the student must face the problems either with inadequate information or with none.

The chief reason why they are not taught is that they are not organized sufficiently to be easily placed in textbooks. A textbook writer hesitates to insert problems in his text, no matter how pressing, unless they have been under discussion sufficiently long to have the material organized for their solution. There seems to be a strong bias against including anything that has not been systematically arranged. To be sure, this material might be placed in the books in the form of current problems, the arguments of both sides of the controversy being presented as an aid toward solution; but it is almost bad form for an author to present a collection of these rather than a system, even though the problems be vital and pressing for action, when no person is yet able to systematize it. Such tragedies fill the pages of the history of the curriculum, for often by the time the material has become systematized the "psychological moment" for its practical use has gone forever.

Possibly the most serious criticism of the systematized fields of knowledge as the sole material for the curriculum is found in the fact that they do not contain solutions for many important problems which confront the layman. This is particularly noticeable in connection with the field of "applied" psychology. To students of this subject it is no new information that the problems which have been most fully investigated in psychology are those which deal with cognition and habit, while comparatively little has been done with the feelings and emotions. As soon, however, as we study the practical problems of the management of men, for instance, we find that the most important element of control is the feelings, and that men are swayed less by intellect than they are by emotion. Yet when the practical psychologist goes to his major field for solutions to his problems, he obtains no assistance, for the reason already stated: that psychology has not investigated the problems with which he is concerned. It is therefore apparent to him, and through him to all of us, that since the organized field is inadequate it must be supplemented by material taken from other sources.

Required and elective courses. — The foregoing statements will not be subject to such severe criticism if a distinction be made between required and elective courses. Through the latter, the high school student who possesses the interests of the specialist finds it possible to pursue his study in any field, to the full limits of the opportunities offered in his school. Concerning such elective, independent courses, no criticism is raised in this connection. The problems which are investigated appeal to the mind of the specialist as being worthy. His judgment is not subject to review by men outside the field.

Required courses, on the other hand, since they are imposed on all students, irrespective of individual differences in interest, have to be considered from another point of view. They are studied not because of the scientific problems which they solve; their inclusion in the course of study is dependent upon their usefulness to laymen outside of the field of specialists. Were they not required of everybody, criticisms could not be raised upon the points just mentioned. But once they become required, then they have to show, item by item, that their content is directly useful for the conduct of the layman.

However, even in the case of these elective high school subjects which are studied to prepare for future specialization in college and university, some objections are encountered. Science teachers in colleges often say that they prefer to have the student come to them without high school training in their subject; that they find his technique faulty, and that instead of their having a *tabula rasa* to work on when the student enters, they must erase many false impressions. But the common answer—that the earlier teaching is to blame—is not correct. More properly, the difficulty lies in the fact that the student has had laboratory methods imposed on him before he has the necessary mental interest and physical skill to master them. And it is possibly better, in view of this immaturity, that high school students should have only general science courses—even those students who later become specialists—and that these general courses be based upon practical use.

Summary. —Systematized knowledge has been made the subject of instruction in the schools from the beginning because the teachers selected on the grounds of scholarship, considered that the brilliant products of the human mind provided the best equipment for youth. The great fields of knowledge have spectacular prestige because they throw into relief the naked brilliance of the human mind, because they are responsible for many advances of civilization, and because they are easy to present in systematized form. Doubt has been expressed from time to time as to their adequacy in training for practical life, because of the difficulty of applying the principles and facts of the abstract sciences to concrete situations, and because many of the principal facts contained in these fields do not apply to the everyday problems of the layman. As a substitute for a bird's-eye view of the fields of knowledge it is proposed that the selection be made from both the systematized and the unsystematized fields of knowledge, upon the basis of practical use—by which is meant usefulness in performing the activities and inculcating the ideals necessary for living a well-rounded life.

§2—FORMAL DISCIPLINE

Its acceptance. — When schoolmen fell back upon traditional material after their failures to derive a curriculum from ideals, they met from time to time a heavy bombardment of criticism and censure. There have always been objectors who have claimed that such a curriculum does not meet the needs of youth. At this point the forces of conservatism produced the defense provided by the doctrine of formal discipline.

The doctrine of formal discipline met with general acceptance at the close of the seventeenth and the beginning of the eighteenth centuries. At this time the course of study was encountering severe criticism on the ground that the narrow humanitarian curriculum which had been enthusiastically introduced a few centuries before as a result of the influence of the Renaissance did not adequately prepare for life. It was at this time that Locke, the philosopher and psychologist, crystallized the idea, germs of which are found scattered throughout the writings of the great educators before his day, that mental training could be transferred wholesale from one subject to another. It was asserted, for instance, that memory is a faculty which, when trained by the study of one subject, such as Latin, will function adequately in the remembering of names and faces; and that reasoning when developed in mathematics will work equally well in trade.

Its record. — This principle of the transfer of training has occupied an unenviable position in modern education. It has added no subject to the course of study. It has probably added no new methods of instruction, because the age at whose close it was elaborated is notable in education for its technique in obtaining thoroughness of instruction. The principle has been merely the bulwark of conservatism, the last argument—after others have failed—upon which to base the retention of subjects in the course of study or to oppose changes within the subject. It is an educational eddy in which many items of instruction have been held, which, in the ordinary course of educational progress, would long since have floated down into the ocean of oblivion. For it has appeared to be obvious that, if training is the end of education, and if it can be obtained in certain subjects, then, no matter how far removed they are from practical usefulness, it would be unwise to invite trouble and unrest by changing.

Its present status. — At the beginning of the twentieth century the first serious attack upon the claim of wholesale transfer was made by Thorndike, and his criticism has since been elaborated by many investigators. Since that time the educational world has been superficially divided into three classes. Naturally there are those who view any attack upon the transfer of training with suspicion and in some cases with alarm. There is a second group, of very large proportions, that maintains essentially that there is no transfer. And there is a third group, the most constructive and powerful of the three, which is endeavoring to find just how much can be salvaged from the remains of this once magnificent structure, and be put to use. Thorndike says that there is transfer where there is identity of substance and procedure; Bagley claims that ideals may be transferred, and Ruediger adds that this is particularly true if the ideals are made conscious; Colvin shows that many general habits can be transferred, when habits which are called general are really specific habits of general application; Judd holds that generalizations may be transferred; and other writers have made other additions.

But whatever may finally be saved from the wreck—and at present the process of salvaging occupies the attention of those engaged in studying the subject—there is no doubt that wholesale transfer as the *sole* principle of selection of subject matter is permanently discarded. Fortunately, even if it were ultimately reinstated in its former commanding position, the attacks delivered against it have already produced excellent results. The last ten years have shown that when those subjects which have been resting in lassitude beneath the shadow of formal discipline have been brought out into the sunlight of constructive thought in an effort to find and utilize the functions which they conserve, they have been enriched and vitalized through fusion with practical values generated by investigation.

A conservative position. — The safe position for investigators to take in matters concerning the curriculum is that the training of abilities should be carried on in connection with material as close to normal situations as is possible. If memory is to be trained for use in practical situations, then it should be trained in material as nearly practical as possible. If discrimination in color is to be trained, exercises should deal with color and not be confined to the learning of discrimination through the study of technical points of language and grammar. The training should be given in situations as nearly normal as possible, and the supporters of any subject are wise when they assume that formal discipline is not one of the arguments in favor of retention of their subject. If this position is taken, other functions will be found which have an enriching influence upon the subject, and if by any chance there should be a large degree of transfer of training, it will be added as a value supplementary to the other values.

The foregoing description of the influences which have handicapped the modification of the curriculum to meet the changing demands of succeeding ages prepares the way for a statement of the methods which may be utilized in obtaining more thoroughgoing and rapid results. The query is: What will the curriculum be like if one starts with ideals and activities and proceeds by logical processes, taking into account the developmental stages of youth and the individual differences of children in each stage, together with a consideration of the environment in which the school is situated? The answer to this is found partly in the realm of theory and partly in results obtained from specific studies which have been carried on during the last decade.

If we may state briefly the proposed plan of the text, we shall attempt to show that the following rules may be laid down for the construction of the curriculum: *First*, determine the ideals and activities which constitute the major objectives; *second*, analyze these and continue the analysis until working units are obtained; *third*, arrange them in order of importance; *fourth*, raise to positions of high rank in these lists those ideals and activities which are of great value for children even though low in value for adults; *fifth*, determine the number of most important ideals and activities which can be mastered in the time allotted to school, after eliminating those which can be learned outside of school; *sixth*, collect the best practices of the race in teaching these ideals and activities; and *seventh*, arrange the material in proper instructional order, according to the psychological nature of children and the texture of the material.

CHAPTER III

IDEALS

Satisfaction is subjective. — All men strive to secure satisfaction through the performance of activities under the control of their ideals. This is the great formal objective of life and as such determines the aim of education. For education is the social agency which trains youth so that it may secure satisfaction through activities which are governed by the ideals that society thinks are valuable. This statement resolves itself into three concepts: satisfaction, ideals, and activities.

Satisfaction is psychological in the sense that it is the tag which we place upon successful activity. If the activity is satisfying, then so far as the individual is concerned it is successful. Conversely, dissatisfaction is the sign of failure in the sense that for the individual no activity which produces dissatisfaction is by him considered to be successful.

Dissatisfaction is the motive for the performance of activities, and satisfaction is the goal sought through activity. When the individual is entirely satisfied with the performance of an activity there is no reason for a change. Change in activities occurs only when the individual is dissatisfied with their present form, and his purpose in making a change is to replace dissatisfaction by later satisfaction.

Satisfaction possesses the peculiarity of being subjective. The activity which satisfies one person may not satisfy another. We can say whether one action produces more satisfaction than another for no one save ourselves. Nor can we affirm for another individual that one act produces a higher or more intense sort of satisfaction than another, though there may be such distinctions. So we can classify the actions upon the basis of satisfaction, which is subjective, only when we translate it into approximate equivalents which are objective.

Ideals are objective. — This has led the race through the ages to rationalize satisfaction and to make broad judgments concerning the kinds of actions which produce in general more of satisfaction than of dissatisfaction. Thinking men have observed that certain classes of action are, on the testimony of many people, more likely to satisfy than to lead to dissatisfaction, and these actions they have described as honest, loyal, or generous. At the same time, others which produce, in the long run, more of dissatisfaction than of satisfaction they have classified as dishonest, disloyal, or selfish actions. So honesty, loyalty, and generosity have come to be called good ideals, or high ideals, and their opposites bad or low ideals. They are the objective equivalents of satisfaction or dissatisfaction.

"Ideals" is a more convenient term to use than "satisfaction." This can be seen quite clearly in the light of one or two illustrations. For instance, in a discussion an individual may say either "That action satisfies me" or "That action is honest." It is quite clear that I, as an observer, cannot know nearly so surely the objective value of the action when the individual says that it is satisfying as when he says that it is honest. Satisfaction is subjective, so this action may satisfy him and still not be socially desirable, or desirable for him if he were to take the long view of his life and actions; but as soon as he says that it is honest, then I have—as an observer—a clear idea of the objective value of the action. I know that in the long run it will be an action that is satisfactory to many people and is most likely to be eventually satisfactory to the individual who made the statement. So, ideals are efficient devices for the discussion and handling of activities in relation to their capacity for providing satisfaction.

Satisfaction *versus* ideals. — It must be noted in passing that there is not always complete harmony between satisfaction and ideals, for since satisfaction is immediate and individual (while ideals are based upon long-term percentages and upon social consensus) it often happens that the action with a low ideal may be immediately satisfying, while one with a high ideal is quite the opposite. For instance, it may be much more satisfying at the moment to steal than to be honest, but we know that in the long run thievery will produce a higher percentage of dissatisfaction. We can get a consensus of opinion upon the relative value of ideals and so can readily distinguish one from another. We know that honesty is better than dishonesty and that these are different from generosity or loyalty. We know this because ideals are objective and because the race has been thinking about them from the beginning as means for attaining satisfaction.

Because ideals are more objective than satisfaction and therefore more easily studied, it is preferable to use them as materials for the construction of the curriculum. This is true because in recognizing them we do not discard the factor of satisfaction, since in making the assumption that efficient ideals are satisfying, and inefficient ideals are dissatisfying, we keep the connection by implication.

Activities and ideals. — Activities are the means through which dissatisfaction is eliminated and satisfaction is obtained. The term so used includes both physical actions and mental activity. The range of activities is broader than the popular conception, which confines the definition to the physical field. Such an interpretation gives only a superficial idea of activity, since it is just as accurate to speak of moral, social, religious, or aesthetic activities as of physical actions. Unless we give activity this breadth of content it is not possible for us to claim that men strive to secure satisfaction through activities under the domination of ideals.

Activities partly independent. — From the point of view of the construction of the curriculum, it is important to understand the relationship between ideals and activities. In the *first* place, ideals are not the sole source of activities. The normal behavior of man consists of activities which produce satisfaction and destroy dissatisfaction. They are based upon his instincts and impulses. They are dependent partly upon his original nature and partly upon his environment. What sort of actions he will perform is determined not only by his ideals but also by his original nature and by his geography. His actions are therefore limited by many factors. The structure of his body, the capacities of his mind, and his instincts are determinants of his action; so also is his environment, physical and social.

At the beginning of a day's work the individual does not normally set out with the objective of attaining any ideals. Only occasionally does he say to himself, "To-day I shall do those things which will make me honest and generous and efficient." Rather he starts out with problems which are couched in terms of activity. He plans for himself the eating of his meals, the transaction of business with his associates, and the performance of personal duties. He has problems to solve and needs to satisfy which are not primarily concerned with ideals. The presence of dissatisfaction merely impels him to strike out toward new actions, so that he may be rid of his dissatisfaction and somewhere obtain satisfaction. His actions do not originate in satisfaction or in ideals. Satisfaction is only the sign that he has arrived.

Ideals are standards. — Ideals are standards of action rather than originators of activity. They are the belated products of the human race, formulated by long-continued thought. They enable us to judge of the efficiency of action in producing satisfaction. We do not usually perform actions to show that we are honest, but rather we solve some problem and, before accepting one solution in preference to another, we apply the standard of honesty. What we have in view at any moment is a line of action which is censored by our ideals. If, when judged by the ideal, an action is below standard, we seek for some other line of action which will satisfy the demands made upon it, or we modify the present solution so as to make it conform to our standards. In some cases, we may discard the high standard in favor of immediate satisfaction and take chances on the future outcome.

Motivation. — In the *second* place the failure to realize ideals, which results in feelings of difficulty, pain, and inferiority, produces a motive for the performance of activity. We have just seen that activities are not prompted by ideals alone, and that they are dependent upon other factors as well. We are now laying stress upon the fact that when activity of any sort has been initiated, the method of motivation is through some form of dissatisfaction in connection with the ideals. If the ideals are satisfying, the activity will continue unchanged. If the ideals are not satisfying, then the activities will be modified. The motive for change is the obtaining of an activity which will conform to the ideals.

Ideals are fluent. — In the *third* place, activities are less fluid than ideals. In the formation of the curriculum we can determine with considerable exactness what the activities are which are carried on by the individual. This can be done with some degree of scientific precision; but when it comes to the determination of what ideals shall operate we have no standards so precise as those by which we measure activities; whether honesty or courtesy shall be the ideals of the student or the school, whether open-mindedness or artistic taste shall dominate as the controlling ideals, cannot be settled by scientific measurement. We have to fall back upon individual opinion or upon the consensus of the group, and this results in wide divergence of opinion.

This fact, which is dependent upon the individuality of human nature, is rich in significance. We have never been able to get all men to agree upon the relative importance of ideals, and as a consequence of this we have the widest possibilities of divergence in individual development, carrying in its train a richness of individual and social life. If all men held exactly the same ideals, we should long ago have been reduced to the level of machines, without the power of adaptation and change; but because different men in different localities and in different generations have held different ideals and have, with intensity of purpose, sought to realize them, enriching contributions have been made to our civilization from generation to generation.

Individuality. — It is, therefore, entirely defensible for a faculty by vote of its members to set up for instruction any ideals which it believes to be most valuable. There is a place in a growing democracy for people whose faith rests in the values of academic education alongside of institutions which have vocational ideals. It is fortunate that certain institutions and men stress the religious ideals, and that others stress physical ideals—fortunate because each group can make its contribution to the total social life of the nation.

But, though the relative importance of ideals for a school may be determined by the faculty, their judgment must not be lightly or arbitrarily formed. The social demand must be studied so as to enable the faculty to interpret the spirit of the age. To this end, the opinions of thoughtful men and women in public and private life, as expressed in speech or writing, need to be carefully weighed. Not only so, but a thoroughgoing investigation of the needs of the students who are to be instructed must be followed through. From all sources, the faculty must gather data upon which to base their judgment.

Ideals and activities. — Ideals cannot be abstracted from activities. When they are so abstracted they fail to function in conduct. Honesty as an ideal will function in conduct only when it is made concrete in action. The Golden Rule is inoperative in behavior unless it be carried out in unselfish actions. No man can be said to possess an ideal unless he can exemplify it in terms of conduct.

Courtesy means nothing except as translated into action. Only as courtesy means, for a boy, allowing older people to precede, lifting the hat to a lady, and running an errand for a friend, is it significant at all. Stated positively, ideals must be made concrete in order to function. The task of the teacher who wishes to inculcate ideals in the lives of children must necessarily be to analyze type activities to which an ideal applies, and see that the selected ideal is applied in connection with such selected actions. Not otherwise is it possible to develop standards which will forcefully function in the minds and hearts of men.

Summary. — In this section we have endeavored to show that ideals are the objective forms of satisfaction, and that as such it is possible to apply them as standards to actions. Activities are the outgrowth of the rich inheritance of the individual and his environment, carried on under the censorship of ideals. As such, the ideal is fluid, while the activity is objectively definite. Since this is the case, there is no concrete separation between the ideal and the activity. Activities are not carried on without ideals to govern, and ideals will not operate except through activities.

CHAPTER IV

ANALYSIS OF ACTIVITIES

Job analysis is familiar. — Analysis of activities is not an unfamiliar operation. It has long been used as a method of instruction, but its application has not been wide and the present emphasis upon analysis is an effort not so much to use a new method as to make wide application of a method which has been used for a long time in a few situations.

The recipe one type. — One of the simplest forms in which the analysis of activities is used is in recipes for cooking. The recipe shows the items in the order of their performance and supposedly in terms of the working units of the cook. As an illustration of a recipe we have the following:

French Dressing

$\frac{1}{2}$ cup olive oil
5 tablespoons vinegar
$\frac{1}{2}$ teaspoon powdered sugar
1 tablespoon finely chopped Bermuda onion
2 tablespoons finely chopped parsley
4 red peppers
8 green peppers
1 teaspoon salt
Mix ingredients in the order given.
Let stand one hour.
Then stir vigorously for five minutes.

In this recipe we have an implied problem; superficially it is to make a salad dressing. Presumably a cook who understands the terms could use this as a textbook, or course of study, and produce a more or less satisfactory salad dressing.

All directions for doing anything are based upon job analyses. Courses in cooking (as just suggested), in sewing, in embroidery, swimming, and all forms of physical exercise, are examples of analysis thrown into the form of directions.

A formal job analysis. — A somewhat more formal sort of analysis is that which is known as the job analysis. Used at first in the vocations as a device in the employment offices of organizations which were too large for the employment officer to be familiar with the duties of all the jobs in the organization, it spread very rapidly and came to have its greatest usefulness and largest amount of publicity in connection with the Army during the World War. While its widest use in the vocations has been in connection with employment, its most valuable use is in connection with training programs.

Another example of the analysis of a simple job is that of the position of application clerk in a department store, which is given as follows:

1. Meets people who desire to open accounts.
2. Asks them for the information to fill out blank.
3. Writes form letters or telephones for references.
4. Fills out Mercantile Agency blanks.
5. Looks up rating in Dunn's, etc.
6. Files applications temporarily till references come in.
7. Makes notes of references on blanks and hands to Credit Chief, who passes on them.
8. Enters name, address, and number of applications in index.
9. Answers requests from other firms for references.

In this table are shown nine duties which the application clerk has to perform, and clearly the course of study needed to train such a clerk will deal with the nine topics. It should teach him how to meet people who desire to open accounts, how to ask them for information with which to fill out blanks, how to write form letters, how to get information over the telephone, etc. When the student has been taught each of these topics according to ideals which would necessarily be included, all the theory needed by him has been presented.

Other cases. — The foregoing analyses of the tasks of cook and of clerk are two very simple analyses. In both we see that it is possible to make a minute analysis of the operations to be performed in carrying on a job and we infer that it would be possible to list the ideals governing the performance of each activity. This will be demonstrated later. These are simple cases of analysis, but in more complex operations the same methods are involved. Noel (p. 278)* has made a more complicated analysis, in which he lists machine operations involving the computation of revolutions per minute, and this presents a tiny curriculum requiring considerable skill and a somewhat difficult course of study. Allen (p. 274) likewise analyzes many operations in machine drilling and shows not only the processes involved in these operations but derives from them the fundamental mechanical science and art necessary to understand them. Greene (p. 287) enumerates the processes involved in sheep-raising and presents all the available experimental information to explain the basis for the accepted methods. Rising to a still more complicated level, Strong (p. 292) makes an analysis of the duties of executives in forty plants, and after classifying them derives, with the aid of his associates, a complete curriculum for the commercial engineering department of a technical school.

Informational analysis. — In each of the foregoing illustrations the analysis has had to do with processes which are carried on step after step, but the same method is used with some modifications in the gathering of information. In this case the function which the collected material is to serve is subjected to a preliminary analysis in order that it may become the controlling element of the investigation.

An illustration. — For instance, in connection with retail selling curricula, when the problem is that of collecting information

*Page references in parentheses appearing after proper names are citations of studies found in Part II.

useful to shoe salesmen, the first step is to determine and analyze the purpose for which shoes are purchased. The analysis yields a list of five values in which customers are conceivably interested. Perhaps not all customers are interested in all the values, yet each value will interest some customers, and the salesman must accordingly have information covering each. These five values are the durability of the merchandise; its serviceability for different occasions; the perfection of its fit; the up-to-dateness of its fashion; and the comfort or ease derived from wearing it. As will be shown later, such an analysis enables the collectors of information to select those facts in connection with leathers and their preparation, manufacture, and production which explain how differences in the enumerated values are obtained. For instance, it is possible to select from the manufacturing processes those facts which explain why one shoe is more durable than another and, in terms of the structure of the foot and the shoe, why one is a better fit than another.

In a similar way values which customers seek in the purchase of textiles are analyzed for assistance in collecting information for the textile salesman. There are added to the list of values in shoes, just quoted, such values as the becomingness of garments, the launderability of materials, the fineness of materials and of garments, and the satisfaction that comes from knowing that the article is exclusive or hand-made or antique.

Duties *versus* performance. — To avoid confusion at this point or later, it is advisable to remark that an analysis may result either in a list of duties or in a list of methods of performing duties. There is no line of demarcation between duties and their performance, because the methods of performing any duty are simply the details constituting a larger activity called the duty. For instance, in the case of the application clerk, a number of duties are listed such as meeting customers and asking for information. But this list does not state the detailed activities utilized in performing such a duty—it does not show what one would actually do in "meeting customers." If, however, we should analyze the duty of meeting a customer, we would obtain yet another list of component duties, such as greeting her courteously, asking her to take a seat, inquiring into the object of her visit, etc.   This, then, would be a *duty* analysis, its units combining to constitute the method of performing the duty of "meeting customers."

Methods of making job analyses. — There are at least four methods of making a job analysis:

(1) **Introspection.** — This is the method used by the person who is already familiar with the job whose duties are to be analyzed.   To make a job analysis of the duties of a Sunday School teacher, a person who has taught a Sunday School class would naturally begin by listing all the duties that have come within his experience. The printer who purposes making an analysis of his occupation will likewise list all the duties of which he can think.   The public school teacher will list the duties met in the classroom.

But it is probably not sufficient—at any rate it is neither safe nor economical of time—to trust to one's own unassisted analysis. Even if one is familiar with the job, it is better to supplement introspection.   If one is not familiar with it, it is better to begin with interviewing.

(2) **Interviewing.** — By this second method the interviewer asks the individual on the job to give a list of his duties; after the list has been jotted down by the interviewer and typewritten, it is returned to the worker for correction.   Other workers on the same job are also interviewed independently, and later the lists of the workers are compared in order to get a composite group. In every case a man in authority who knows the job is asked to check the list and add whatever items have been left out.

(3) **Working on the job.** — The foregoing method is perhaps most convenient because it takes the least time, but in some cases a third method is used by the analyst.   He works on the job and carries through the operations himself.   The advantage of this method is that the investigator comes to the job with scant knowledge of its processes, and therefore is better able to analyze it than are old-timers, since with him none of the duties has become

habitual; but its weakness is that it requires a great deal of time, so that investigators generally feel that better results are secured by many very careful interviews than by having one individual work upon the job until he knows it thoroughly.

(4) **Questionnaire.** — The written questionnaire is sometimes used as a method of analysis, but for reasons which will be noted later (Chap. XIII, Sec. 6) it is not satisfactory in yielding more than a preliminary list, and even for this it is so inferior to the interview that its use is not recommended except in extreme cases.

Complete analysis. — The aim in all of this work is to make the list of duties as nearly complete as possible. This is particularly difficult to do, especially in mental operations, where one cannot see the steps carried out in connection with material. To analyze, for instance, the activities of a woman during a day is no simple task. It is comparatively easy to make a list of the things she does with her hands, because an observer can see these; but to list the things she thinks about no one can do save herself, and even she is unable to make a complete list of them. To illustrate this difficulty, and the care needed in meeting it, reference may be made to the collection of three hundred diaries (p. 328) gathered for the purpose of securing analyses of women's activities, and contributing to a composite more representative than could be obtained from one woman. Much of the material which must be analyzed is of the same intangible sort; the utmost care and the highest degree of patience are necessary in order that accurate lists may be obtained.

Duty analysis and difficulty analysis. — Not only may an analysis of duties be made, but in addition an analysis of difficulties can be carried out, which frequently adds to the list items which might otherwise be missed. For instance, when a small group of teachers were asked to name their duties as classroom teachers, a list of twenty items was secured; and then, when they were asked what difficulties they met in teaching, fifteen additional items were discovered. Theoretically the difficulties will be identical with the duties when every duty presents a difficulty, but the critical task in a job analysis of this sort is to induce the person being interviewed to recall duties which he has been performing more or less unconsciously; and in this process of extraction the duties with which he has had difficulty will stand out more clearly because of the amount of attention they have claimed from him. When he is asked to recall these as duties, he is not so likely to think of them as when they come to the surface of his memory in the guise of difficulties.

Errors and use. — The same distinction is found in informational material when a contrast is drawn between analysis of errors and analysis of use. For instance, if we attempt to determine what the course of study in grammar should be when based upon use, we can get better results by collecting the observed errors in grammar as a starting-point and then determining what grammar will be necessary to correct these errors, than we can by deciding what laws of grammar are used in practical speech. Not only can we get more leads, but in addition, in this particular case, we get all the leads we need, since the grammatical rules which are followed and not broken do not need to be called to the attention of the student.

Summary. — In determining the activities upon which instruction is to be given, analysis is necessary. This may be done by the use of job analysis in certain types of situation, or by setting up control elements in informational analysis. Difficulty analysis indicates the duties and information upon which special emphasis must be laid in the curriculum. Without such analysis we are entirely at a loss to know how to proceed in building the curriculum.

CHAPTER V

THE DETERMINATION OF MAJOR OBJECTIVES

§1—INTRODUCTION

Emphasis, not definition. — No writer on the aims of education is able, or has been able, to encompass the totality of the aim of education in a single phrase. There is no one statement into which the full range of ideals and desires of the human mind can be compressed. Morality, the most frequently mentioned of all aims, does not express this totality, for health and beauty are also important and have elements of significance which are neither moral nor immoral. Social efficiency, our most recent aim, offers no provision for the performance by the individual of acts which have no social significance.

In all statements of aim the emphasis has been placed upon one ideal or more, and the others have been relegated to a secondary position or have been ignored entirely. Certain aims, as for instance, physical health, have for centuries been included in many statements. And from time to time such aims as morality and love of the beautiful have been made subordinate to social efficiency, as when it is asserted that to be socially efficient one needs to be moral, healthy, and beauty-loving. Writers in each generation have seemed to think it necessary to stress one aim or another, sometimes because the tendency of the day favored that special aim, and at other times because the age appeared to be so lacking in the spirit of a certain aim that it became desirable to stress it.

An historical definition. — In such a treatise as Monroe's *History of Education* it is to be observed that this group of aims, of which one or another has been exalted to a position of highest importance by writers during the last score of centuries, is comparatively small—probably not more than eight in number: practical efficiency, morality, piety, learning, obedience, individual development, social efficiency, and mental discipline.   These, with their modifications arising from the peculiarity of the individual writer or from the peculiarities of his age, constitute the more important of the group of major aims and objectives which have been given positions of commanding importance; and, as has been said, any writer who selects one of these would assert— if the question were put to him directly, that in so far as the others are of importance their significance is due to their subordinate relationship to the one which he has selected as his premier aim.

The aim of the present age. — Whether this group which the history of education has separated for us into its constituent items is or is not sufficiently inclusive cannot be decided by history alone, for some of the objectives of the past, such as the mistreatment of the body by the ascetics, clearly do not represent ideals which the race to-day considers to be of value.   Rather do we need to examine into the spirit of our own age and try to discover, by analysis of ideals and of activities constituting conduct, what are the ideals which we consider important.   We are living a life to-day whose fundamental objectives are in many respects identical with those of past generations.   Morality and the intelligent rearing of children concern us now as always. Emotions and instincts have to be inhibited and guided, but probably not more so than in any century in the past.   Yet the activities in which moral acts are clothed, the behavior of children of this generation, and the conduct which controls the emotions, differ quite significantly from those of any age which has preceded this.   It therefore becomes necessary for every generation to take stock of its ideals and of the activities of its people, to the end that the young may live the life which will prepare them best for participation in the work and play of the world.

Building the future on the present. — The best of this generation must be taught to the next, even though we recognize that the ideals and activities of the next generation will differ in part from those of our own.   The weight and importance of social ideals shift with comparative slowness, and the changes can be taken care of if to instruction in the activities and ideals of our generation is added training in methods of clear thinking. With the ability to think their problems through for themselves we can trust the new generation to face their own problems with their feet solidly placed upon the structure of the past. If the new generation is sufficiently trained in methods of intelligent thinking upon practical problems, it cannot fail to develop new solutions to meet new situations.

Varieties of objectives. — The variations in objectives may be caused by variations of ideals or by variations of activities. The moral aim of education is one in which one ideal, that of morality, is selected from many other ideals and emphasized. The æsthetic aim, which seeks to develop love of beauty, is one which is obtained by emphasizing that ideal over others.

Through emphasizing different activities we get different kinds of schools; for instance, vocational schools, in which the activities of the vocation are given primary attention. This emphasis also produces medical schools, engineering schools, colleges, and a wide range of professional institutions. The difference between women's education and that of men is less a contrast of ideals than of activities for which the training is to be given.

This change in emphasis, which we find running through the history of the evolution of educational aims, pointedly raises the question of methods of determining objectives. Is it possible to determine scientifically the major objectives of this generation, and if it is possible, is it advisable to have a national set of major objectives? This leads to a consideration of the method of determining the objectives.

§2—DETERMINING IDEALS

Determining the ideals. — As has been seen, ideals are fluid and cannot be scientifically evaluated. Consequently, the one thing that can be done is to have either an individual decision or a faculty decision concerning the ideals which are to dominate in each specific situation. The individual teacher may accept or decide, either consciously or unconsciously, what seem to him to be the important ideals which shall dominate in the instruction which he gives to his students. This is the normal situation in the schools to-day. To each teacher is left the decision as to what ideals, if any, he will emphasize. If he happens to be a man of strong feelings he may have a very effective influence upon the molding of the ideals of his students. If, on the other hand, he is of a neutral personality, his students may not be affected by contacts with him.

Ideals, however, are found to be a matter of group consensus in such cases as those where we speak of the spirit of a school, or of the outstanding characteristics of the graduates. Students in one institution may have a different set of ideals from those in another, which in a conscious or unconscious way have been developed during their four years of college life. This is the result of the influence of an individual instructor, of faculty consensus concerning ideals, or of the ideals of the student body. Perhaps it is most often a combination of all three; and as to which is the dominating force it is difficult to say. Sometimes the administration has ideals of such strength that it selects faculties which will carry out its ideals, and the administration and the faculty mold the student body. At other times the student body has its own ideals, and the faculty has comparatively little influence upon it.

It is quite clear to the writer that it is not necessary to leave the emphasis of ideals to chance. There is every reason why a faculty should decide for itself what will be the dominant ideals of the institution, after taking into account the individuality of the students and of the members of the faculty.

Three methods. — There are three methods of arriving at the ideals which dominate instruction in any subject matter. The *first* of these is listing the activities and determining which ideals are the most efficient in carrying out the duties. To return

to our example of the training of an application clerk, we find
that such a job analysis falls into two divisions, as follows:

Duties	*Personal Qualifications*
1. Meets people who desire to open accounts	Friendliness
2. Asks them for the information to fill out blank	Ability to question tactfully
3. Writes form letters or telephones for references	Discrimination in using blanks
4. Fills out Mercantile Agency blanks	
5. Looks up rating in Dun's, etc.	
6. Files applications temporarily till references come in	Spirit of "follow-up"
7. Makes notes of references on blanks and hands to Credit Chief who passes on them	Ability to summarize references
8. Enters name, address, and number of application in index	Copying skill
9. Answers requests from other firms for references	Keen judgment in answering credit questions

On the left-hand side are the duties, and on the right the
personal qualifications which are thought to be necessary in
carrying out these duties effectively. For instance, when the application clerk meets people who desire to open accounts, it is very
important that the ideal of friendliness should dominate his
actions. If his acting be controlled instead by indifference or surli-
ness, they will differ radically from those performed under the
ideal of friendliness, and will be quite inefficient. Similarly, in
connection with obtaining the information for the application
blank, the quality of tactfulness is very necessary.

Qualities or qualifications for the *job* are ideals for the holder
of the position. Traits already possessed may be termed qualities;
when they are not possessed, but are striven for, they are termed
ideals. The ideals for an application clerk are the qualities neces-

sary to the efficient performance of his job. So, by this method, the activities are first listed, and the dominating ideal is then attached to each.

Faculty action. — A *second* method of determining the relationship between ideals and activities in any training school is for the faculty to choose the ideals by consensus and then select the activities with which to connect them. For instance, in a faculty of thirty people connected with a women's college, it was decided that the following ideals should dominate the instruction given to the students: love of beauty, health, service, forcefulness, discipline, honesty, courtesy, scholarliness, cheerfulness, and spirituality. Then, when these ideals had been decided upon, each instructor took upon himself the task of deciding upon the activities connected with his own class to which each of these ideals should be particularly applied, and the dean of women and the dormitory staff likewise drew up a list of extracurricular activities which should be governed by each of the ideals selected by the faculty for emphasis.

The difference between this method and the preceding one should be clearly noted. In the one case, the activities are first determined, and then the ideals which dominate each are selected. In the other case the ideals are determined first, and then from the activities carried on by the students those are selected to which the determined ideals should particularly apply.

Individual character analysis. — In the selection of ideals by the faculty an interesting method can be used which is particularly applicable to the elementary school. The difficulty in determining the ideals to be emphasized in each grade lies in the fact that it is almost impossible to obtain an accurate statement from teachers. If, for instance, we ask them what ideals should dominate, they are unable to recall all the ideals that might be emphasized, and might not even have a very clear idea of the exact nature of the problem which they are trying to solve. To meet this difficulty the following device can be used with considerable success. A list of ideals may be prepared, of sufficient breadth to cover all those ordinarily accepted by people as being of importance. Then submit this list to the teachers of the public school system, and ask each teacher to think of one pupil and decide which of the ideals needs to be stressed with him. Then, when this has been checked, the task may be continued until the ideals which need to be stressed for all the pupils in the grades have been indicated. When this has been done we can obtain through frequency of mention some indication as to which ideals, in the opinion of teachers, need to be stressed in the first grade, in the second, in the third, and so on for all grades.

In this study the points that need particular attention are the preparation of the original list of ideals and the exercise of careful judgment by the teachers as they check.

Desired qualities *versus* emphasized qualities. — The query may be raised as to whether the ideals to be stressed in a school are identical with those which it is desirable for its graduates to have. When a faculty is asked to indicate the ideals which graduates should possess when they leave school, is it influenced by remembering the ideals which need to be stressed in the instruction of the students whom they know? Can they distinguish between the qualities needing to be stressed and the qualities which it is desirable for people to have? The difference between the two alternatives lies in the possibility that some children may have ideals so strongly developed that they do not need to be stressed. For instance, the well-bred child may be quite obedient, while children with different home training may need to be taught obedience above all other ideals.

To throw light upon this point, a study has been made in which a faculty was asked to give two lists, one of the desirable qualities which college women should possess, and another of the ideals which should be stressed in a woman's college. Among the ten ideals receiving the highest mention in each list, there was a difference in only one case. In other words, for practical purposes, the ideals which this group of teachers marked as being desirable are identical with those which they considered most necessary for emphasis.

§3—Types of Objectives

Vocational objectives. — As regards major objectives there are two important types to be analyzed: vocational and non-vocational.

At present we have two types of institutions of higher learning, the vocational school and the cultural or academic school. In the first of these, instruction is given in the subject matter pertaining to learning a vocation. In the second, attention is only secondarily paid to vocation, while primary emphasis is placed upon the kind of training which a person is supposed to have irrespective of his vocation. The tendency in the vocational type of school is to lay comparatively little stress upon the type of information found in the "cultural" school, in whose course of study the vocation is not directly included. These facts lead to constant controversy between the supporters of the two types of schools, as to which constitutes the better type of education, and as to the real definition and nature of culture.

Extra-vocational objectives. — But it is admitted by all that the man who follows a vocation has in addition as a citizen of community and nation, many extra-vocational interests and activities: æsthetic interests not connected with his vocation; social relations independent of what he does to earn his living; intellectual interests; and physical recreations which need have nothing to do with his profession. It follows that when a vocational school determines its objectives and from them derives its curriculum, two types of major objectives must be taken into account, the vocational and the extra-vocational. In the construction of the curriculum an analysis needs to be made not only of the duties of the vocation but likewise of the interests and activities found in extra-vocational life. The material derived from the first constitutes the vocational part of the vocational curriculum, and the material derived from an analysis of the extra-vocational activities would constitute the cultural part of the vocational curriculum.

This implies that the cultural elements of the vocational curriculum are those relating to the individual's life and his interests irrespective of his vocation. As to whether or not such material should be strongly tinged with æsthetic ideals is a question, and perhaps the term "cultural" is not entirely satisfactory for the material described. But whatever the term, it is an essential principle of curriculum construction that all professional or vocational curricula designed to prepare for earning a living must include also an extra-vocational core which will be mastered by all people regardless of the vocation which they follow. The extra-vocational material for a school of engineering will be essentially the same as that for a school of law or a school of medicine; obtained by an analysis of extra-vocational life, it will deal with the problems which people meet no matter what vocation they may choose. That these problems are not only political and social, but also æsthetic, intellectual, and physical, makes it all the more necessary that such a core should be determined for all vocations.

The "cultural" core of a vocational curriculum. — This presents a constructive program for the determination of the extra-vocational content of vocational curricula, and is contrasted with the usual negative attitude of those who make up vocational curricula in that the latter know definitely what should be included in the *vocational* elements but are very much in doubt as to what should be included in the *extra-vocational*. Consequently we encounter heated arguments as to whether the extra hours not used in the vocation should be filled with such extra-vocational subjects as foreign languages, history, English, or sociology. In the absence of definite methods for prescribing the extra-vocational material the tendency is always to fall back upon those traditional subjects which appeal to any particular faculty. The difficulty is very well illustrated by the inquiry from a professional faculty as follows: "We have arranged for all our professional curriculum except nine hours, which we have left for cultural subjects, and we should like to know what these should be." In this case consensus of opinion was used. But it is generally much better to analyze extra-vocational activities, and make eventual selection on the ground not of how many or how few hours a subject will require, but rather of how essential it will be in the students' extra-vocational life.

§4—Current Studies

Studies. — One of the most interesting studies that has been made in the analysis of vocational objectives is that of Strong (p. 292) at Carnegie Institute of Technology assisted by committees of the faculty. As is described in the second part of the text (p. 292) it was decided that certain units in the institution should be utilized in the training of executives for building and construction firms and for production and printing plants. With the field of the graduates so defined, it then followed naturally that a job analysis should be made of the positions of executives in concerns of these three kinds. Ultimately the executive positions in forty concerns were analyzed and their duties listed. These duties were classified into large groups corresponding in a general way to the different types of subjects which might be taught, and these groups, under committee action, were worked out in considerable detail.

Job analysis revealed the duties, but no particular attention was paid to the qualifications which were necessary, or the ideals which should dominate in the performance of the duties (though in a few cases such qualifications were collected as were considered important by the executives interviewed). In this respect the study was incomplete, since neither by analysis nor by faculty consensus were the dominating ideals decided upon.

A second study is that made by Jones (p. 334) as Chairman of a committee of the college teachers of education. In this case it appears that the analysis was produced in conference with a number of teachers in the neighborhood of Philadelphia, and from this source a list of 170 items was obtained. Then, to obtain frequency, the total list was presented to a large number of teachers to check. An examination of the list suggests two shortcomings: that some important duties were not mentioned at all in its compilation, and that many of those mentioned were made too general to elicit definite replies.

A third study is that being made of the organization of women's education in Stephens College (p. 328). In this study the faculty decided upon the ideals through consensus of opinion, and the ten selected were to be so stressed in the curriculum that every student should, during her four years, be given adequate appreciation of their value and control of their use.

This analysis of the activities of women is an extensive rather than intensive study. The diary method has been used, to obtain a record of what women do and think about during the day. Each of a large number of women kept for a week a diary as intensive as possible, then, by throwing all the diaries together, a cumulative picture was obtained of the women's activities. There has also been made a long check-list of all sorts of activities discovered both in the diaries and outside, and this was submitted to a large number of college women, who were asked to indicate the presence or absence of these interests in their lives.

However, not enough studies have been made to explore adequately the field of the analysis of major objectives and more such studies must undoubtedly follow as their technique is better understood.

Scant attention to major objectives. — The reason that so little attention is paid to the major objectives is that they are so difficult to determine, and so relatively indefinite in content, that the time of attack must necessarily be delayed until an adequate body of data as to method has been obtained under less difficult conditions in the study of similar problems in the field. The situation, therefore, results in a series of pioneer studies which are of interest rather because of the methods utilized than because of the content of the curriculum.

Recent investigations. — In selecting problems for study of the curriculum the investigators have been concerned for the most part with the subjects of the course of study, such as spelling, mathematics, and English, rather than with the major functions of the curriculum. This is partly because the subjects have been under continuous and general attack due to alleged weaknesses in content, and partly because criticism of the curriculum has been conducted in terms of the subjects, the claim being made that certain elements of a subject should be omitted and certain other elements added. Consequently the investigators have been interested in studying the subjects, to see to what extent the traditional content of any one would be modified if certain functions of the subject were accepted. They have assumed that these subjects were of such importance that they will always be retained in the course of study, no matter what the analysis of major objectives may develop.

One may challenge the validity of this assumption, of course, but equally one must realize that such an assumption exists, if one is to get a clear understanding of the significance of the studies reported upon in the text. In all of these, with the exceptions noted, the determination and analysis of major objectives are left open. The subjects, as at present named and delimited, are accepted as units in the course of study, and attempts are made in the investigation to determine the amount and nature of the modifications which arise when certain functions of these subjects are accepted.

Objectives. — Statements of objectives of education and of subjects of the curriculum lead to confusion unless they are analyzed into *ideal objectives* and *activity objectives*. Social efficiency as an objective becomes easily analyzed if we see that it means *social ideals* and *social activities*. Social ideals are determined by one method, social activities by another. Good citizenship must likewise be analyzed into the *ideals* of the good citizen and the *activities* of the good citizen. A curriculum in moral education requires the *ideal of morality* on the one hand, and a list of *moral actions* on the other. Good health, in a similar manner, is differentiated into certain ideals and certain actions or habits, hygienic rules, and information. Once the analysis of objectives into ideal objectives and activity objectives has been made, the process of deriving the curriculum presents no serious difficulty. But if the investigator confuses the two, and at one time talks of ideals and at another of activities, without sensing the difference, his efforts will not carry him through to a curriculum. He will remain in the field of theory.

An analysis chart. — In order to clarify the relations between ideals and activities the familiar form of the graph can be used. What is needed in order to derive the curriculum from objectives is, as we have seen, an analysis of ideals so as to make them easy to handle, and an analysis of activities to the level where they also may be handled efficiently. For instance, in the case of Herbart's objective we may say that the individual should lead a life "which is ethical." In this there are obviously two elements, ethical ideals and living a life. In living a life the individual performs series and groups of activities which are controlled by ethical ideals. It is necessary, then, to analyze ethical ideals on the one hand into such items as honesty, sympathy, etc., and similarly to analyze the activities involved in living a life.

The resulting situation may be represented by a graph, along the top of which are run the ideals, while along the side are listed the activities, and in the squares are checked the ideals which dominate the performance of each activity. In the following chart the ethical ideals are analyzed into five classes, let us say, indicated by the figures from one to five. Other classes and subclasses of ideals extend to the right. The group of activities (A) is analyzed and sub-classified as shown on the left. The checks

Activities	Ethical Ideals						Social Ideals, Etc.		
	1	**2**	**3**	**4**	**5**	Etc.	**1**	**2**	Etc.
A									
1.									
(1)									
(a)									
i	X		X						
ii	X	X					X		
iii									

indicate that in performing activity A 1 (1) (a) i, the ethical ideals 1 and 3 dominate, while in performing activity A 1 (1) (a) ii, the ethical ideals marked 1 and 2 and the social ideal, 1, control.

Considering the vertical column it will be found that an ideal along the top adheres to the many activities along the side. A housewife might conceivably seek to perform many actions in conformity with the ideal of neatness. She might, for instance, wish to be neat in dressing in the morning, in preparing breakfast, in mixing a mash for the chickens, in clearing the table, in making beds, etc. Or, if we consider an activity along the side, it may happen that one of these will be dominated by a number of ideals, not only ethical, but social, æsthetic, etc. In serving breakfast, for instance, the housewife may be dominated by the ideals of neatness, health, and sociability. Viewed from either top or side we may either teach ideals through activities, or teach activities under the domination of ideals, depending upon our philosophy of life.

The effect of adding other ideals is merely to increase the width of the graph. The activities do not change. They are determined by an analysis of the physical and mental experiences of the individual. This widening of the range of ideals would merely result in the control of the activity by more ideals. In that case instead of the person's merely attempting to turn out an honest piece of work, he might also attempt to make it beautiful and perform it as a service to humanity.

The public school curriculum. — In the reorganization of the course of study in the elementary schools we have now considered three points. We must, first of all, determine the size of the unit for which the curriculum is to be organized. This unit may be the individual school, as in the case of a private school or an institution of higher learning. It may be a city system of schools; possibly the unit might be considered to be the state, and conceivably it might be a national unit. In deciding upon the size of the unit, due regard must be had to the complexities of the situation. The probabilities are that our nation is a unit too large for any sort of coherent similarity. The school system of the state is more nearly workable because it is possible to get the teachers together. The city system, because of its geographic compactness, would be a desirable unit.

But in any case, after the unit has been selected, it is necessary, in the second place, for the faculties of the schools, the school boards, and public-spirited citizens generally, to decide upon the ideals which shall dominate the instruction of the youth in the schools. Then, in the third place, an analysis must be made of the important activities of laymen, irrespective of the vocation which they may enter; this involves making an extra-vocational analysis; and, finally, determining after the analysis the essential elements of learning common to all vocations.

In collecting material for a course of study for vocational schools we have thus covered three steps. The dominant ideals must first be decided upon by interested parties such as the faculty, the board, and the students, if mature enough. In the second place, a job analysis must be made of the vocation. And in the third place, an analysis must be made of extra-vocational life in order to determine what the extra-vocational elements of the curriculum should be.

Summary. — In this chapter we have sought to show the place of ideals and activities in relation to the major objectives of education. We have shown the work which analysis has to perform in picking these objectives and deriving from them the topics for the curriculum. In the succeeding chapter we shall examine the elements of the analysis, and the determination of the relative importance of materials to be used in the practical curriculum of the school.

Chapter VI

THE LIMITS OF ANALYSIS

The limits to which an analysis should be carried are determined by the working units of human accomplishment.

The mental stride. — Man has a mental stride with which he marches from one goal of civilization to another. We are familiar with his physical stride; the male adult normally steps about thirty inches, with some variation. Outside of the realm of magic carpets and seven-league boots there is no way of greatly increasing the length of his step beyond this, because the stride is determined by the length of the human leg. The Mohammedan pilgrim, when he sets out for Mecca, knows that he must travel by paces thirty inches long and that only by adding one step to another can he reach his goal. Not for him is it sufficient to know merely that he must arrive at the tomb of the Prophet. If he is to reach his religious objective he must translate the Holy City into a general direction plus careful attention to each of the intervening paces.

Units of achievement. — In a manner exactly analogous the human mind has a mental stride by which it has come up from savagery to civilization. It has used small working units whose size is determined by the structure of the human mind. It has grown from savagery to civilization, and is growing from infancy to maturity, by units of achievement whose sizes are determined by mental ability. There is no way of rubbing a ring and summoning a genie to help us cross the gap from one achievement to another. Even in such a small matter as the attaining of neatness in the home the objective is reached only by little steps. One's clothes must be picked up in the morning and put away in the evening. The hair must be combed; the coat must be brushed and the clothes pressed; the pencils must be placed in a row; the ashes shaken into the tray. It is entirely futile to expect neatness to come merely at the call of deep desire. The task of accomplishing ideals and of performing activities is so large that it is absolutely necessary for them to be broken down into working units of the size of human ability, so that these may be mastered one by one.

Every teacher who instructs children in such a way as to see his teaching influence conduct knows that this is the only way to reach objectives. It is only those who write and do not teach who say that it is sufficient to set up the final objective, and that by some divine alchemy, some hit-or-miss endeavor, the end will be attained. Exhortation will not produce correct speech; the errors must be mastered one by one. In spelling, the field is covered by teaching word after word. Geography and history are acquired fact by fact, and grammar, definition by definition. Skill in addition clearly is obtained only by the mastery of the forty-five combinations, and skill in reasoning is secured only by considering simple problems first and proceeding to more complex ones later. A moral life is the cumulation of a great mass of single moral acts, and social service results from the performance of specific social duties.

Zones. — In stating that working units of achievement lie at the lower limits of analysis, we have for clarity avoided discussion of individual differences in the size of these units. Within limits differences exist. Just as the physical pace of the infant toddler is less than twelve inches in length, while some very tall adults normally step a yard, so the mental stride of the little child is shorter than the pace of the adult who has grown in mental stature. Whereas the novice takes but a small pace in his field, the initiate proceeds with giant paces when working under normal conditions.

There is no geometric point at which analysis ends. Working units fall into zones whose breadth depends upon the ability and experience of the individual who is to be instructed. For instance, when, during the War, the Federal Government advocated the canning of tomatoes by the cold-pack method, for some women no further information was necessary. Stimulated by the patriotic appeal to can tomatoes they were able to do so at once because they had the experience and knew how to use that method. But other women, who accepted this objective and desired to conserve food, did not know how to can by the cold-pack method and for them a job analysis was necessary. They were told that the steps in performing this operation consisted of: collecting canning utensils, cleansing them, testing jars, rings, and lids, grading the tomatoes, scalding them, etc. These directions were stated in sufficient detail for a part of the women, who possessed some experience but less in amount than the group first mentioned.

It was found, however, that the demonstrators in their canning campaigns had to make a supplementary job analysis of each of the foregoing items so as to break them up into smaller steps in order to reach the working units of many practical housewives. For instance, instead of saying merely, "Collect canning utensils and cleanse them," the demonstrators found it necessary to give these steps: "Secure a well screened, light, airy room, protected from dust and drafts, containing a good stove, a supply of good fresh water, a table, dish-pan, kettle with a lid, tea-kettle, paring knife, a sack of salt, teaspoon, tablespoon, and a supply of glass jars. Wash the hands thoroughly, clean the fingernails, don a clean apron and cap, etc."

This analysis of duties was found to be sufficient for even the least experienced cooks; but, if the same process were by any chance to be taught to little children, some of these steps would need to be analyzed again. For instance, the methods of washing the hands thoroughly would need to be analyzed for little children. It may be stated parenthetically that this is one of the operations which has to be taught to young medical students, who have long since passed the age of infancy.

The working units into which material has to be broken are dependent upon the learner rather than upon the subject matter. If he is young and immature, the steps into which the material has to be broken must be smaller, whereas if he has greater maturity detailed explanations are not so necessary. Similarly the limits of analysis of objectives are dependent upon the ability of the learner rather than upon the nature of the objectives. Morality is morality, but the directions given to little children about how to be moral are much more definite than those which are given to adults, because the adult has already learned the little things which the child has not, and is able to perform a greater task.

But in making this statement we must avoid the common danger of failing to carry analysis far enough even for adults. A principle of conduct will not be accepted unless it is supplemented by many illustrations which are expressed in terms of the experience of the learner. The great principles of the New Testament have carried over with especial success largely because of the parables and specific illustrations which show the followers of Christianity how to apply the principles to tasks which are quite within their experience.

Spencer's analysis. — Spencer realized that analysis was needed when he defined complete living as consisting of self-preservation, the earning of a living, parenthood, citizenship, and "culture." From that point he proceeded at once to show to his own satisfaction that the sciences could provide the whole curriculum, and he specified physiology, chemistry, physics, mathematics, biology, æsthetics, astronomy, history, and the science of society. But his analysis did not proceed far enough to enable him to determine what facts in each of these sciences should be selected. What he should have done in order to accomplish this, if he had desired to do so, was to analyze each of the five groups of activities mentioned down to the limits of working units.

He should, for instance, have asked what are the actions which good citizens perform, and finding them, he should have taken up the supplementary analysis of each until, step by step, he had reached the zone of working units of those to be instructed. Good citizenship, he might have said, consists of many elements, one of which is the paying of taxes promptly, and another the intelligent voting for city officers. The first duty, that of paying taxes promptly, would not need to be analyzed if the student knew how to pay them promptly, but if he did not it would be necessary to continue the analysis and divide the paying of taxes into methods of ascertaining the amount, learning the place of payment, the days upon which they should be paid, etc. When this has been carried to sufficient detail to meet the capacities of the student, then all that is left to be done is to state how to perform each of the duties finally arrived at. In a similar way voting intelligently for city officials would need to be analyzed until the idea had been carried down to the point where those to be instructed could follow the directions without assistance. When this had been done for all his five activities he would then have known what sciences and what specific items of each science were necessary for complete living.

The perfect analysis. — The perfect analysis is one which is carried to the point where the student can learn without assistance. If it is put into the form of a book, the ideal text is one which teaches itself. In it the material is so expertly presented that the student understands everything, can follow it through to its end, incorporate it in his experience, and use it in his life of action.

Approximations. — Theoretically, this would mean a different curriculum for every learner, since each student has capacities different from those of every other student, and to meet these a curriculum would need to be carried to different levels of working units. But since this is obviously impracticable two approximations are made. The first is secured by the use of a "general level." With this in mind the curriculum is constructed for grades, and as a result we have primary texts, intermediate books, and high school and college curricula. In each case the author more or less arbitrarily sets up an assumed standard of what—in general—are the capacities of the students at the level for which he writes. In writing for this group he endeavors to strike an average and make a compilation which is neither too easy nor too difficult. By careful attention to these matters he hopes to construct a book which will largely teach itself.

But in case it does not teach itself completely he has recourse to the second method of approximation. The teacher out of his scholarship, on the one hand, and his knowledge of the working units of the student, on the other, will help to translate into terms of the experience of the students what the writer fails clearly to present. In other words, the teacher takes the analysis which the author has made, carries it beyond the point to which the author carried it, and bridges the gap between the limits of the author's analysis and the student's ability.

Under ideal conditions, as has been stated, there should be no necessity for work of this sort by the teacher; but unfortunately the determining of the level of experience is so difficult for those who at present prepare curricula and texts, and the differences in the abilities of students in the same class are so marked, that the teacher is compelled to devote broad scholarship and profound pedagogic thought to the task of bringing the curriculum down to the level of the working units of the class.

Authorship. — In the absence of these ideal conditions three methods are possible. In the first place the curricula and textbooks for any grade might be prepared by teachers of that grade. In this case the difficulty lies with the teachers, who are frequently not sufficiently scholarly or expert to satisfy the demands of accuracy in formulating new material or in reorganizing old.

A second possibility is for the scholar who contemplates writing a textbook to teach the material to the grade of students for whom it is to be prepared. The disadvantage in this arises from the fact that scholars are unwilling to go to this trouble, or do not have the facilities to do it. But it must be definitely urged that any person who, unaided, attempts to write textbooks for any grade of the elementary school or the high school should not do so unless he has had actual teaching experience with the grade of students for whom he attempts to write.

The third method of approximation to ideal conditions is joint authorship. In this case the scholar in the combination guarantees the accuracy of the subject matter, and the teacher of the grade who coöperates with him in preparing the material will provide the pedagogic adaptations. For many reasons this method is not so satisfactory as is either of the others, but it is more readily carried out and has more advantages than disadvantages.

Current studies. — Some of the studies that have been made have reduced their material to working units. The spelling vocabulary is derived from children's themes and composed of words already used by children and is, therefore, theoretically within the zone of working units. Sometimes these words are listed by grades, which makes the list still more certain of practical usefulness. Such lists come close to teaching themselves. Similarly the lists derived from adults' correspondence are all within the ability of high school students. Particularly, Greene (p. 287) taught his material on sheep husbandry to ninth-grade boys for the explicit purpose of testing his attempt to reduce his material to the level of the students, and found that with few exceptions his material was quite intelligible. Most of the other studies are, however, not concerned with any analysis beyond the first step. Miss Camerer's material would hardly teach itself to high school students. Horn, Bassett, Bagley, Wilson, Monroe, and many others list topics which demand further analysis, but they can be defended by the fact that analysis to the level of working units was not part of their problems.

Chapter VII

RELATIVE IMPORTANCE

§1—The Problem

The reason for selection. — Because the units of achievement which are available for instruction are so numerous that even if progress ceased no one person could hope to learn them all in a millennium, it is necessary to select the units which shall be included in that roll of honor and usefulness which constitutes the curriculum of the schools. So great is the importance that thus attaches to the chosen items of the course of study that the selection must be made with extreme care. Those vested interests, the traditional subjects with their conventional content, whose position is established so strongly in the schools, must be temporarily disregarded in the process of reconstruction, until by analysis of the objectives of this generation it can be determined which parts of them should be retained. They may, as at present constituted, be the best possible units that could be included in the course of study, or they may not. Their retention depends upon their usefulness. But certainly they have no greater basic right to be included in this Hall of Fame than have some more recently discovered products of the human mind.

Home *versus* school. — There are three specific conditions which make this selection imperative. The *first* of these is the fact that some units are taught better outside the school than within its confines. What these are is the subject of argument, but the tendency is to add more and more of them to the school course when they seem to be neglected outside of the school. To be specific, it is generally agreed in this country that religion is not a subject for public school instruction. There is less unanimity about personal habits such as the care of the teeth and proper food. Practice here seems to depend upon what the schools are driven to. As a practical matter, it has become apparent that the decision as to what should be included must be left to the school staff, the school board, and the public, so that we may discover which home duties should be included in the school curriculum, and the extent to which the school shall withstand that outside pressure which leads to the overcrowding of the curriculum.

The time limit. — The *second* reason for selection is the existence of different time limits. Children have, in most states, to attend school until they are fourteen to sixteen years of age or until they have finished the first eight grades. This means that their school education may cease at the end of the sixth grade, or at any time from that up through the twelve grades of the public school, or at any time during the sixteen- to nineteen-year period which the doctor's degree ends. This range in time limit forms a problem in selection. Particularly since the majority of children have completed their education when they have finished the sixth grade, should they be given the minimum essentials of the curriculum during those six years, or should eight grades be taken as the minimum limit of education? In any case, the limits of time make it necessary to determine the relative importance of material in the course of study, since if selection must be made the least important should be omitted.

Learning. — Determination of relative importance is necessary also in the *third* place because items need attention not only on the basis of their intrinsic importance but also on the basis of the relative difficulty of learning them. Some items of very great importance can be learned very easily, while on the other hand items of relatively less importance may be much more difficult of acquisition. Clearly, then, the amount of time which shall be spent upon any item is dependent not only upon use but upon difficulty.

§2—How to Determine Relative Importance

Use. — Importance is determined in the last analysis by use. An electric washer is better than a tub and boiler if it cleanses the clothes as well in less time or better in an equal time. Lime is a better fertilizer than phosphorus for some soils if it produces more corn to the acre. And honesty is preferable to dishonesty because its results in terms of human well-being are better. All values are in the last analysis determined by the effect they have upon desires and needs.

No ultimate aim. — There is no ultimate objective which stands out as the measuring stick of all the others. Spencer gives self-preservation such a position of final importance, but there are times in which the sacrificing of a man's life is of less importance than the safety of women and children. Yet, in turn, the safety of women and children cannot be regarded as the ultimate objective of life, since they are saved only because their safety is of importance for other objectives. What we really have is a great nexus of values bound together, each serving both as means and as ends to the others. No one is superior, but all are inferior to the welfare of the whole. People may differ as to which of these are of greater value. The advocates of a certain value may seek to prove the supremacy of that one; and it often happens that such proof is sufficiently convincing for one community or one generation. But viewed in the large what appears most clearly is that no one is paramount—but rather that a great cluster of objectives are mutually interdependent.

Quantitative results. — In certain fields, however, it is easily possible to measure results. For instance: one farmer uses lime; thousands of others do not; and a majority vote declares that lime is not a satisfactory fertilizer. But when finally we look toward results, these show that lime raises more bushels of corn per acre—and its superiority is indisputably demonstrated. Methods of salesmanship can be measured in terms of dollars, and machines in terms of output. Close attention to business may be proved superior to laziness by contrasting the sizes of the institutions employing these two principles. In all fields where quantitative measures may be definitely applied, values are easily determined.

The verdict of history. — The vast majority of our values, however, cannot be so exactly measured. In the field of politics there is no such measurement for immediate use. Shall we consider peace as better than war? Is high tariff superior to free trade? Shall we mingle with others or remain in isolation? Is government ownership preferable to private ownership?

There is no political micrometer to measure the answers in fractional terms. Frankly, we do not know. Certain individuals may think they know, but certain others hold opposite views, so that the correct answer hangs in suspense, perhaps forever. Frequently the answer cannot be given until history passes its tardy verdict, which is determined by results, and even then is only more or less accurately determined.

Consensus. — To meet a situation of this sort democracies have hit upon the device of the majority rule, and have agreed that so far as civic conduct is concerned that policy is considered better which can muster a majority. In the absence of absolute measurement, consensus determines superiority.

But even in this case we find that the minority may hold that the judgment so determined is wrong. They may attempt to defend this by appeal to results which will appear in the future. "In future years," they say, "the minority will be shown to have been correct in this contention, when results of a distressing nature follow from the majority action." The majority on the other hand make the same appeal to results. Both minority and majority recognize the fact that consensus is not the final arbiter. They merely accept it as a convenient method of decision until the results shall have been evaluated before the final tribunal of history.

Expert opinion. — In certain cases it is found to be more reliable to substitute expert consensus for common opinion. Even in the political affairs of democracy some selections of men and decisions of fact are left to expert opinion without recourse to popular review. In questions of law there is no immediate popular recourse from the decisions of the Supreme Court. The relative value of technical points is frequently left to the opinion of groups of experts selected because of their special training and experience. Even in matters upon which the final decision is made by popular consent the opinions of experts have weight, especially when such opinions are quite or almost unanimous.

In fields other than political, expert opinion is wisely used. The ranking of poets is not determined by the votes of the majority of people. The most popular music is not always the best music; it is considered the best only when musical experts so decide. In all matters of art the consensus of experts is accepted. Grammatical forms are likewise viewed in the order of their preference by masters of English rather than by common usage; at least they are so accepted in most cases, with an occasional exception when universal usage of some term originally considered incorrect by experts ultimately authorizes the wrong form by sheer weight of volume.

§3—CURRENT STUDIES

In the studies reported upon in the latter part of the text, expert opinion has been used to a very considerable extent. Several types of appeal have been made to experts. They have been asked to give their opinion upon the relative importance of items in the curriculum. Wooters (p. 245) obtained from seventy-three members of the American Historical Association their opinions concerning the relative importance of dates selected from Bourne's "The Teaching of History." The heads of the university departments of political science, economics, and sociology were asked by Horn (p. 251) and Bassett (p. 251) to select twelve books which present "the more crucial activities, conditions, and problems of present-day life." Bank cashiers gave Miss Camerer "opinions about banking information for depositors." Business men were questioned by Wilson (p. 213) concerning the relative importance of arithmetical topics taught in the elementary school. Coffman and Jessup (p. 216) requested superintendents to give information upon the same subject. The cumulative opinion of politicians concerning the importance of political issues by reference to political platforms was obtained by Bassett (p. 308).

The limitations of expert opinion. — Expert opinion is of great value but it must not be made a fetish. Bagley (p. 262) noted that some members of the American Historical Association failed to understand the conditions of elementary education and so gave relatively inexpert opinion. The business men questioned by Wilson (p. 213) undoubtedly gave snap judgments on what arithmetic is used in business. It can be safely assumed that they answered the questionnaire with the same speed used in transacting business, notwithstanding the fact that the subject of the questionnaire was one on which they did not have sufficient data to make their opinion of great value as to the topics which should be either emphasized or omitted. Coffman and Jessup's (p. 216) superintendents were handicapped by the lack of sufficient knowledge as to what arithmetic and how much is used by people outside of schools. As a matter of fact, all the analytic studies show that much less arithmetic is used than the superintendents mention. For instance, they think that more attention should be paid to interest, yet in the 14,000 problems collected by Wilson (p. 223) interest does not have a single appearance. The opinions of parents to whom Miss Camerer appealed correlated only to the extent of .32 with the opinions of the bank cashiers.

The use of expert opinion, even when all the facts are available, is merely an approximation. The most substantial basis for the determination of relative importance is the objective measurement of the material concerned. Lacking this, expert opinion has its value, but the validity of this opinion is in direct ratio to the familiarity of the expert with all the conditions involved. No mere opinion of business men or of highly trained experts is necessarily of value. As soon as they answer questions outside of their own field of specialization, they are almost as liable to error in judgment as is any other layman.

Expert classification. — In several instances the investigators have made use of expert classification. Horn (p. 251) used the outlines of Langlois and Seignobos in classifying his historical facts by periods. He also checked thirty-eight items against the *International Encyclopedia*. Monroe (p. 219) followed the Federal Census in classifying arithmetic problems by the occupations represented. Bagley and Rugg (p. 246) compared their items of history found in textbooks with the findings of the Committee of Eight. Bassett (p. 251) followed Small's classification of social activities. He also compared some of his findings with the amount of space devoted to certain items in the *Encyclopedia of American Government*. Mrs. Dodd (p. 255) determined historical characters by reference to the *Century Dictionary of Names* and Brewer's *Reader's Handbook*.

To those may be added numerous instances of accepted classifications within subjects, such as the classification of arithmetic problems according to the operations involved, of grammar according to the parts of speech and rules of syntax, and of the related subjects in the machinists' trade. The classifications so followed were those accepted by all experts, those used by individual authorities, or those found in specific books of reference.

The textbook, used in such studies as Bagley and Rugg's (p. 246), where common elements are observed, may also be considered as an expert source, though frequently textbooks have been written by men who held no claim to expertness of a high order. However, the texts are expert in the sense that the authors have at least consulted authorities and provided a body of fact which has been generally accepted. But the validity of using the common elements in textbooks as a norm rests entirely upon the degree to which they contain the material which has been derived by either an unconscious or a conscious analysis of objectives. If their content has been unduly influenced by tradition or other disturbing factors, it is obvious that the composite picture of the common elements will be as reliable as the original material and no more so.

Units of mention. — In such a widely variant mass of material as has been subjected to study, the units used as a basis for compilation are varied. In some cases topics are counted; in other cases words, errors, or inches.

Topics. — Coffman and Jessup (p. 216) and Wilson (p. 213) submitted lists of topics to superintendents and business men and computed the number of votes given per topic. Miss Camerer (p. 326) submitted to bank cashiers and parents of children a list of topics concerning which depositors might well have information. Fuller (p. 300) obtained a list of home repairs by survey and interview and submitted them to high school students and their parents.

Words. — Obviously in spelling the basis must be the word; some spelling studies list the words used while others list the errors. Most of these studies include all the forms of the word, in contradistinction to the vocabulary study, which may list only the root form. Not only is the root word "write" included, but also its derived forms, "writing" and "written."

Errors. — All the studies in language and grammar make the error the unit. Sometimes this is the word, at other times a phrase, clause, or sentence.

Specific mention. — In arithmetic a variety of units appears. Coffman and Jessup (p. 216) and Wilson (p. 213 and p. 223) tabulate operations, as noted above, while Mitchell (p. 236), Williams (p. 238), Callaway (p. 238), and Charters (p. 231) list specific processes and quantities. For instance, Mitchell records the number of times one-fourth, one-half, etc., occur, while Coffman and Jessup refer only to fractions without mentioning the size of the fractions specifically. In addition, Williams and Charters list specific operations and show their complexity, while Wilson describes the complexity without presenting all the material in detail.

Inches. — Bassett (p. 308) uses the inch as the unit in measuring the importance of items in political platforms: that is most important to which the greatest amount of space is given. This is a variant of the method of using the number of words used in describing the item and gives the same sort of information because we are in the habit of estimating so many words to a page and when we know the number of inches to the page we can tell the number of words per inch.

Single mention. — Several studies have not been concerned with frequency and have paid attention only to occurrence. For instance, Allen (p. 274) includes all items in "related subjects" without regard to frequency. So also do Greene (p. 287) in sheep husbandry, Todd (p. 324) in physical education, and others. Frequency is not necessary if the limits of time are not narrow or if the items are equally important, but if this is not the case, some method of selection is necessary.

Short-cuts. — An interesting problem arises in counting the frequency of mention in such subjects as history and geography. It was found in the geographical study (p. 270) based on *The Literary Digest*, that the mention of countries such as the "United States" presented no difficulty in scoring in place geography. If, however, one is scoring to find the importance of the country by means of frequency of mention, the term "Americans" should also be scored, since if the reference appeared as "the people of the United States" the meaning would be the same and the score would naturally be counted. Again, if the Americans were referred to as "the Yanks" the nickname necessarily ought to be noted. Still further, if one is counting all references, pronouns could not be omitted since "they" refers to the names of people and "these" to countries. Finally the term "the Allies" would need to be distributed and each country scored, since it is by implication of enough importance to be one of the great political powers.

This illustration shows quite clearly that there are a number of problems to be considered in determining the scoring unit. In this particular case we show that if only geographical names (the United States), names of people (the Americans), distributed terms (the Allies), were included, the coefficient of correlation with the list obtained by the complete mention of all items, including pronouns and nicknames, was about .96. Consequently it was clearly unnecessary to score nicknames and pronouns in the study.

Scoring each item. — The problem takes another form when a decision is to be reached about scoring each item. Shall we score every mention, one mention per paragraph, or one mention per selection? In the geography study just mentioned, each item was scored, but Mrs. Dodd (p. 255) scored only one mention of an historical item for each poem, on the grounds that in determining how frequently an item was used in poetry it was important to determine the number of poems which included the item. This would indicate how widely the item was used and would be of more importance than to know how many times it was used in one poem. The use of "Alexander" in six poems is thus much wider than six uses of the word in one poem. Bagley (p. 262) in his studies with his students in geography and history scored each item of reference once for each article. (If reference were made to London as a commercial center and as an art center in an article, the city would be scored once for each, but not more than one reference to each in the same article.) He states, without giving reasons, that this method of scoring was found to be clearly superior to that of counting each individual mention.

On the other hand, Horn (p. 251) and Bassett (p. 251) used the paragraph as the unit so that if an item occurs more than once in the paragraph it is still scored only once.

It would make an interesting study to rank the items after scoring all mentions and then correlate this ranking with that found after scoring one mention per selection, per paragraph, and per article. This would be of value because if it can be shown that the larger unit presents a ranking of high correlation with the smaller units, the saving of time is considerable.

All these methods have assumed that frequency will give some approximate idea of the relative importance of items and in the absence of any better method of approximation they must be used.

Limitations. — In using them, certain limitations must be borne in mind. The *first* is that if the item is used often enough, little attention needs to be paid to it in the curriculum: it will be learned incidentally. The words "a" and "the" have a very high frequency in spelling but they do not demand attention in the course of study because they take care of themselves. If, in a list consisting of a thousand words, maximum efficiency is desired, it is for this reason more important to pay attention to the less common words than to the most frequent.

Again in language, when an error becomes very frequent it ceases to be an error and becomes correct form. There is, for instance, evidence to show that in the judgment of experts the most common language errors are not the worst.

The *second* limitation lies in the fact that items less frequently used are sometimes more important than their quantitative ranking would indicate. Adverbs are used much less frequently than verbs, but they are just as important. Fractions are used only occasionally, but they are quite as important when they are used as are the fundamental operations.

Yet, on the other hand, if we are not concerned with absolute perfection and have to choose between the largest number of mistakes and a smaller number, it is clear that fewer mistakes will be made if the more frequently used items are learned. Upon this fact rest the strongest claims for quantitative determination of items. If verbs are used more frequently than adverbs it is obvious that fewer mistakes will be made per hour by one who uses only verbs correctly than by one who uses only adverbs correctly.

Specifically, in utilizing the common elements in textbooks as the basis of minimum essentials some items included by only a few authors may be much more important than the commoner ones used by many authors, because the less frequent items may be of later insertion. They may just be beginning to appear, while some of the more common items may be of little current value because their usefulness may be waning. Frequency, therefore, as a basis for determining importance has both values and limitations and is to be used when nothing better is available.

Chapter VIII

CURRICULUM MATERIAL

§1—The Curriculum as Method

We have been concerned up to the present point with the topics of the curriculum. We have theoretically learned how to determine the ideals and activities which shall be taught and we have now arrived at a place where we are able to discuss the methods by which the activities may be carried on.

Ideals are a part of the curriculum. — At the outset it must be insisted that the curriculum consists of both ideals and activities on the one hand and their methods of realization and performance on the other hand. In a very real sense, education has not only to show youth how to control objectives but also how to want to control them. It is quite one thing to teach a pupil how to wash his hands and tell the truth, and quite another to arouse in him the desire for clean hands and honest speech.

The method of instilling ideals is in particular a pedagogical problem for teachers and parents. It is also a matter of direct youthful concern and therefore belongs to the curriculum content.

Curriculum content is method. — In propagating interest in the control of ideals it is evident that the curriculum consists of methods of achieving objectives, but it is not so evident, though equally true, that all the content of the curriculum is methodic. Everything taught or discovered, recorded or achieved, has been a method. Ideals were first formulated and used as means of realizing older desires. In childhood they are first understood as means to other ends. Loyalty, for instance, originally was and still is being developed as a means of attaining group solidarity. The moral ideals, such as honesty, have been accepted by the race only after it was demonstrated that

74

they constitute superior methods for obtaining the satisfaction of a whole range of objectives.

Facts are methods. — In like manner facts are methods of control. In spelling, for instance, it is a fact that *pencil* is spelled p-e-n-c-i-l, but this combination of letters is meaningless except as it is a means of putting on paper some characters which will describe, or bring to the writer's mind, or help the reader to understand, the object of value for which it stands. *Four and four equals eight* is a fact which is learned because it is a part of the method of measuring objects of value. The statement *Charles Dickens was an English prose writer* is the method by which we learn that the character was a writer, that he was an Englishman, and that he was a writer of prose rather than poetry. The statement is found in the school reader because one or another of these minute objectives is thought to be valuable. At the beginning of Volume II of a certain treatise on economics is found an introductory statement: "We have defined private economics as that portion of the science which deals with private enterprise." As it stands this is the method of recalling to the reader's mind what has gone before, with the very necessary purpose in the mind of the author of giving the reader a running start in the perusal of subsequent pages. Moreover, if we omit the first three words of the statement and substitute "is" for "as" the sentence is amended as a statement of fact from the author's point of view, and as such is the method of defining the term "private economics." Even the fact *Bombay is in India* is a statement by which to locate a city.

Art is method. — If we consider painting, sculpture, architecture, or literature, the same principle holds. Every product of the brush, the chisel, and the mallet, the draughting board, and the pen is a means of achieving some function. *The Bells* expressed the feelings of Poe about the sounds described. The Venus de Milo, the Parthenon, and *Cymbeline*, each is a medium through which an idea is put into concrete form by its creator.

Not only are they media for the creator, they are in like manner methods by which the observer can build up in his experience the ideal embodied in them by the artist. They are not raw material to be catalogued by those who encounter them; they were brought into being because they furthered the achieving of an objective. They are retained by the race and imparted to the young because they assist the rising generation to realize the same or similar ends.

A practical difficulty. — This point of view, presenting the material of the curriculum as a method, may not seem to explain the feeling that instructors have about teaching information to students. It may seem quite far-fetched to assert that all the facts in history are methods of achieving ideals or that the facts of physiology and chemistry are similarly methodic in their nature. It would seem quite useless for the teacher to call all these facts methods of control. Yet if we take the longer view we know that we collect information chiefly for the purpose of using it. The evolutionary function of memory has been that of recalling useful experience for later application. The beginnings of history have lain in the value of the resurrected experience of the tribe. All facts are primarily retained because of their use.

The difficulty which we have just mentioned will clear up if we state in addition that the memory often accepts a fact for which it, at the time, sees no particular use. It takes it on faith. If there is no feeling of faith that some time it will be useful, the retention is explained by the fact that the memory, which has been trained to retain useful facts, gets into the habit of retaining facts whether or not they seem immediately useful. This, however, does not absolve the instructor from blame if he presents bodies of facts which have no utility so far as he or the students can see. There are so many useful facts which can be learned and so short a time in which to learn them, that it is a waste of time to require students to learn useless facts.

Information and conduct. — The relation between information and use may be viewed from another angle. Until quite recent years the school has been chiefly concerned with a statement of methods and only incidentally with putting the methods into practice. This distinction has been partially described in the aims of education by the terms "information" and "conduct." As a matter of common procedure the schools have sought to give information upon the assumption that the mere giving of information will influence conduct. But a different idea is now gaining ground: that in practice as well as in theory, the function of instruction is not fulfilled until the information has actually modified conduct.

New material added. — From this distinction arises a new mass of subject matter heretofore implied in our discussion. This material deals not merely with a statement of the methods by which an objective is obtained but also with the methods by which this method is put into operation. For instance, in the department store a merchandise manual may be prepared to provide salespeople with information about how to advise customers intelligently about purchasing. But since the task is not completed until they actually use the information in conversation with customers, it is a necessary part of the operation that they be supervised in their selling until it is apparent that the information is being so used. The old view considered that the information alone was a valid part of the curriculum. The new behavioristic view of information includes also in the curriculum the methods by which the information may be properly used. In department stores at least, where salespeople have no exaggerated idea of the value of knowledge, the merchandise manual would be ignored as a source of information in the midst of more pressing duties if the methods of using it were not included.

In school the same thing holds true. We were formerly concerned primarily with giving information about how to develop ideals, for instance; but to this we are now adding a statement of the means by which the methods for realizing ideals are to be put into effect. The idea that education must modify conduct has enlarged the range of the material of the curriculum.

§2—THE SELECTION OF METHODS

Evaluating methods.—In achieving the ends mentioned, the race has not always been fortunate enough to devise the best methods upon first trial. Later effort has sometimes brought better results. Facts which were true become false when "true facts" are discovered. Art which was good is superseded by better, and machines which were best become obsolete when improvements are invented.

On the other hand the best is often followed in time by inferior methods. Many poets have followed Shakespeare but perhaps none of them has been his equal. Classical music, which is superior music, is usually old. We constantly hear that the old methods are better than the new, and in some cases this is undoubtedly true since periods of decadence are familiar phenomena of history.

Not only are inferior methods followed and preceded by superior methods, but both inferior and superior methods may exist contemporaneously. Crime is handled in some cases with laxness and in other cases with firmness. Health may be preserved by exercises, sports, or patent medicines. Tonsils may be clipped or dissected. Railroads may be owned by the state and controlled by it, or owned and controlled by private interests.

Frequently two methods of equal value may be used as alternatives. The Austrian method of subtraction exists side by side with the common method. A score of life-insurance companies are about equal in the service they render. Some farmers use one method of tilling the soil while their neighbors obtain equally satisfactory results with others.

In selecting for the curriculum subject matter which will realize the objectives determined by analysis, we are confronted by the task of evaluating the material so as to provide the learner with the best or with one or more alternatives of equal value.

Empirical and scientific methods. — In realizing the objectives both empirical and scientific methods are used. The earliest stages of control have always been empirical. For generations agriculture was unscientific because the machinery for quantitative testing was unavailable. Moral action is necessarily empirical because no quantitative methods would ever be available.

Every art begins in empiricism, and the reputation for superiority is determined by consensus of opinion.

When an art emerges into the second stage of scientific measurement it is obvious that at first the number of scientifically determined methods is small and the disappearance of empirical methods will be slow. The rate of disappearance of these methods depends upon the rapidity with which the scientists can test them out and upon the facility with which they lend themselves to testing. In sheep husbandry, for instance, Greene found that nearly fifty per cent of the expert methods now in use are still empirical although it is one of the oldest of agricultural sciences. Indeed, almost all the activities in which men engage have only a small fraction of their procedure measured. A few highly specialized fields, such as the applications of electricity, have a larger proportion of scientifically determined facts; but even in these fields the more nearly they approach operation under normal conditions, the more closely must they rely upon actual experience.

As the result of this the problem of selecting the methods by which ideals are realized and activities are performed becomes very complicated and requires the highest degree of scholarship and of wisdom in knowing which materials will best apply in practical situations. If by any miracle the schools could start afresh, and the children be taught only by the most efficient methods, the sudden rise of the level of civilization would be almost unbelievable.

The dissemination of better and better methods amongst the population is the most important of all social agencies. It is also one of the most difficult of achievement; this is partly because the methods of determining superiority are not always well developed, and partly because people are slow to give up familiar ways — even though they are inferior — for new and strange methods which are patently superior.

The problem of the schools is theoretically quite simple. The best methods of realizing ideals and performing activities must be collected. But practically the problem is difficult for the reasons mentioned. This, however, cannot be accepted as an excuse for failure to attack it with vigor and intelligence.

§3—ERROR AS CONTENT

Functional psychology has made us acquainted with the fact that problems arise only when activity is hindered in such a way that habit and instinct cannot respond effectively. At the point where these fail to function in an adequate manner, reason emerges to solve the problem which thus arises. Therefore, the very significant statement can be made that all the achievements of men have been made by reason in its effort to overcome difficulties. Dissatisfaction stimulates mental activity in order to produce better means of achieving satisfaction.

Errors. — It would therefore seem only natural that the curriculum should be constructed with the purpose of *overcoming difficulties in achieving objectives* rather than with the purpose of *achieving objectives*. That this is a very real difference can be easily shown. For instance, if we assume in spelling that the function is to promote communication we can at once see that the words most commonly used in communications are *a, the,* etc. If we concentrate our attention upon the difficulties encountered in communicating we find the most frequest errors are *which, separate,* etc. Clearly the curriculum in the second case would have a quite different arrangement, for in the first case *a* and *the* would rank high and *which* and *separate* would have low frequency, while in the second case the emphasis would be reversed.

The same difference appears in a study of language. If we list the rules most frequently used we shall have a quite different order of importance among rules from what is found when we list those most frequently broken. So, in the vocations, we assume that some of the most frequent duties need comparatively little attention because they can be learned on the job, while the most difficult need to be strongly emphasized.

Bobbitt's principle. — Bobbitt* has recognized this distinction in his differentiation between undirected experience and directed training. He holds that children should be allowed to obtain as much education as possible from undirected experience upon a play level through intellectual roving. Then he believes that when this has been gained, directed training should be centered upon observed imperfections, errors, and shortcomings found in the experience so obtained. His curriculum "is to be discovered in the shortcomings of individuals after they have had all that can be gained by the undirected training."

Qualifications. — This point of view is based upon the sound psychology just described, but it is subject to three qualifications. The *first* of these lies in the fact that the undirected experience to which Bobbitt refers is not undirected so far as the curriculum is concerned. It is undirected only so far as the learner's attitude is concerned. No child is permitted to roam where he will. Metes and bounds must be prescribed. He is not allowed to pick up experience from thieves and robbers, nor can he be permitted to read lewd and degrading books. Parents and schools prescribe the content of the areas over which he roams as he gathers his "undirected" experience. The difficulty arises from the fact that Bobbitt has confused the psychology of the child with the construction of his curriculum. It is true that while the child browses and roves on the play level he feels that he is getting what he wants without interference, but the stage has been set for him and the limits of experience have been prescribed.

These limits have not been prescribed on the basis of errors or difficulty. They are set for him so that he will be brought under the domination of the ideals and activities with which he should be brought into contact. They are prescribed not because he has failed in achieving them but because he needs to become acquainted with them.

The *second* qualification arises from the fact that in many new subjects taught in school there is no preliminary undirected ex-

*The Curriculum, Houghton Mifflin Co., 1918; pp. 41, ff.

perience and consequently everything presents a difficulty. For instance in foreign language study, all words, all phrases, and all inflections present difficulties. In such a case one might better fall back upon frequency of use, teach the commonest facts, and be done with the job. So also in piano-playing, if a child works without directed training she is likely to build up bad habits which must later be eradicated. On the other hand, if the most common stages early become the subject of directed training the possibility of inefficiency would be lessened to some degree.

But on the other hand, and in the *third* place, error is of great value in determining where emphasis should be placed in the teaching of the curriculum. When material has been inserted in the curriculum it follows that some parts of it will be mastered quickly while other parts will be learned slowly. Clearly a discriminating perception as to which parts give the greater amount of difficulty will be of great value in deciding where emphasis must be placed. It is quite important to know that *which* and *separate* require special attention in spelling, that verbs present more difficulty than nouns in grammar, and that home repairs need more attention in manual training than does house construction. In short, errors *prescribe emphasis;* they do not *provide content.* The content is determined by the duties, while the emphasis is distributed according to the difficulties.

A vocational curriculum such as that needed for retail selling or for school teaching, a curriculum based upon a difficulty analysis, is admittedly not a complete curriculum. It deals only with the difficulties, and hence could be considered a complete curriculum only in case every duty were a difficulty, for then a difficulty analysis and a duty analysis would yield identical lists.

Much use has been made of difficulty analysis in arithmetic and spelling to determine the order in which material should be taught to pupils of varying abilities and the amount of emphasis to be given to each. Such studies as those made by Halloway, Courtis, Monroe, and teachers' committees in Boston and in other cities are examples.

CHAPTER IX

COLLECTING CURRICULUM MATERIAL

§1—INTRODUCTION

When we wish to determine the methods by which activities are carried on and ideals are realized we find that they may be obtained from two sources. The recorded part of human achievement is found in books, in works of art, and in other material form. In addition there is a great mass of unrecorded material which is contained in the experience of people who have not put their methods into writing. In the first group we find books, sculpture, paintings, music, mechanical utensils, monuments, and buildings. In the second group we find material belonging to the unorganized fields of knowledge, such as those which deal with methods of developing morality, of making social contacts, and of performing man's other duties, particularly in their social relations. But it is not only in these social fields that methods go unrecorded: in all the arts there exists a great mass of material which has never been printed but has been handed down from master to apprentice and from father to son by word of mouth alone.

§2—CONTROL ELEMENTS

Functional analysis. — In collecting material upon the topics of the curriculum the laws of logic demand that certain control elements be set up and that functional analysis be made a conscious method. By "functional analysis" is meant such analysis as makes explicit the logical relations between a function and the parts of the structure developed to carry out that function. By contrast, "structural analysis" means the analysis of the structure into its parts without an explicit statement of their functions.

Functional analysis requires that after the analysis of the structure into its parts has been made, the relationship of each part to the performance of the function must be carefully scrutinized. The function in this sense becomes the standard by which a decision is made as to the value of any part of the structure. When the structure is being built up to fulfill a function, this function is the criterion by which to decide whether or not certain parts shall be added or omitted.

A "structural analysis" of the chair in which I sit yields us legs, back, seat, springs, coverings, and arms; but to make a "functional analysis" of this article we must add two steps, thus making three steps in all. First, the function of this chair must be determined: perhaps it is the providing of a comfortable, durable, and beautiful article on which to sit. Then, the structural analysis into legs, back, seat, etc., is made. In the third place, each of these parts must be sized up in terms of function, and if the structure is good, each must be justifiable in terms of that function. For instance, the springs are built into the seat for comfort and, in order to be made more comfortable, are built deep. They are built into the back for the same purpose. The quality of the leather and of the springs contributes to greater or less durability. The strength of every part of a chair can be justified in terms of the function as here laid down, if the chair is perfect; but any part that cannot be so justified is defective.

In constructing the curriculum the same three considerations enter. The objective must be set up, the items of the curriculum must be selected, and in the selection a process of evaluating each item in terms of the objectives must be constantly performed.

Control element. — Viewed as a task of outlining and collecting, the functions become the control elements which determine what shall be included and what omitted. If the function of spelling is the prescription of the order of letters in words used in communication by school children, this constitutes the control element of the investigation. Obviously one is concerned with the order of letters, and not with a mere vocabularly; consequently it is indefensible to omit *writing, written, write,* and *wrote* and cover them under the single root word, *write.* If we were studying the vocabulary of children it would be quite permissible to score each of the forms of the word *write,* but where the control elements include the order of letters in the word, each of the foregoing has different letter constituents and must therefore be included. This control element dictates also the kind of themes and letters which are to be analyzed. They are to be those of children, not adult letters, newspapers, and literary classics.

Setting up the control elements is particularly important in collecting information which must be gathered from many sources. For example, in collecting merchandise information for salespeople, the range of material is so broad that without control elements it would be impossible to know what to include and what to discard. In such a case the method to be used is to set up control elements and use them as the standard in selecting the material. Specifically, in collecting information about shoes we know that it is desirable for a salesperson to be able to discriminate between differences in durability, fit, quality, fashion, and comfort. Then, with these items set up as control elements, the compiler is able to skim through books on leather, manufacture, anatomy of the foot, foot defects, etc., and preserve any facts which will throw light upon the topics. Anything, for instance, concerning the raw materials or their manufacture which would show how or why durability was secured, and anything about the anatomy of the feet and the nature of foot defects which would have a bearing upon the fit—these would be included. Items having no bearing upon any of the control elements would be omitted.

A graph. — This idea may be made somewhat clearer by a graph. (See following page.)

We need to think of each rectangle as having relations both to the top and to the side. It is to be used as a depository for information concerning an item at the top which has a bearing upon an item at the side. In other words, in the space that is related to durability and raw materials will be inserted those facts concerning the raw leathers which have a bearing upon durability. In the space which is related to manufacture and quality will be included those items about manufacture which have a bearing upon the superior or inferior quality of the finished product.

	Raw Materials	Tanning	Findings	Manufacture	Defects and Anatomy of Foot
1. Durability					
2. Fit					
3. Fashion					
4. Quality					
5. Comfort					

While most tasks are so complicated that the material for them can hardly be graphed in this simple way, all of them can be handled graphically by the general principle here described.

"**Backgrounds.**" — The use of control elements destroys that refuge of lazy thinkers which is called the "background." There are those who seek to defend the inclusion of irrelevant material in a course by affirming that it provides a background. They fail to recognize that the background is subject to the same laws as the remainder of the content. The background of a painting, from which the term is borrowed, is not just background; its details all enhance the function and idea of the foreground. The student who has a broad background from which he gathers facts to enrich his thinking draws specific facts or feelings and not general or unfocused ideas. The curriculum maker who presents backgrounds should, likewise, be able to justify the items of which they are constituted by their logical connection with his control elements. To attempt to justify the items of which they are composed upon the basis of their being mere background is evidence of superficial thinking.

This was rather clearly brought out in connection with the merchandise study of china made by Miss Ringo. As she collected material a good deal of historical matter appeared which would interest the salespeople but would not help to explain the differences in the control elements. Rather than attempt to justify the inclusion of this as "background"— in the usual sense of the word — it was decided that a control element must be established for it; and so there was added an historical chapter illustrating the romance of the potter's art. With this new control element set up, including this mass of historical material was made logically possible.

"Introductions." — The same criticism can be made of the inclusion of the irrelevant as an "introduction." Many people who collect material for the curriculum assume that the introduction to the course or topic does not need to obey the laws of logic; they succumb to the common weakness of putting into a course something of which they are personally fond and for which they have no logical justification. But the introduction is as integral a part of the material as any other and must be subject to the same rigid laws of logic.

Current studies. — The function in spelling, stated as the determination of the order of letters in written words used in communication by children or by adults, leads naturally to the listing of all words that have different letter orders. Jones (p. 177) analyzed children's communications, Ayres (p. 171) and Cook and O'Shea (p. 173) analyzed those of adults. Capps (p. 188) lists only those words with whose letter order his high school students have difficulty.

Incidentally it may be pointed out by way of criticism that Cook and O'Shea do not follow the control elements consistently because they list *is, are, was, were, being,* and *been* as *be.* Jones (p. 177) fails in a similar manner when he lists plurals in *s* and past tenses under the singular and present forms respectively "where there was little chance of misspelling." On the other hand Eldridge is justified in using only the root forms because his is merely a vocabulary study.

In the Kansas City grammar study (p. 194) the function of grammar was assumed to be that of assisting children in the correction of errors. This made it logically necessary to analyze the errors made by children to see what rules were broken. Mitchell(p.236) assumes a very simple function for mathematics which he states to be that of being able to read a specified cookbook, a specified catalog, and two other sorts of material. In this case his task necessarily consisted of listing the mathematics found in the material examined. Bagley and Rugg (p. 246), when they collected the material found in texts, assumed no function for their material explicitly but utilized the content of the texts as their control element. Their problem was that of finding what were the common elements and the variations within the series of books. Bassett (p. 308) assumed the function of civics to be that of giving assistance in the practice of government and proceeded to analyze the practices as shown in political platforms. All of the other studies listed in the second part of this text assume or state certain control elements which are usually applied with considerable logical severity.

§3—INTERVIEWING

Unrecorded methods. — In collecting *unrecorded* material for the curriculum* intelligent care must be exercised in order to obtain accurate descriptions of the methods used. It is very apparent that the written questionnaire will not provide this information, for reasons which are stated in Chapter XIII. The recognition that the written questionnaire is inadequate has led to the development of the interview as a technical device in curriculum construction. In the social arts where people have to be handled, the two sources from which methods may be obtained are the principles of psychology and the expert but empirical methods of experienced individuals.

The methods of psychology. — By the first, the principles of psychology are formulated and then applied to solving the problems of selling, handling people, or teaching. This method has two specific weaknesses. In the first place, scientific psychology

---

*"The Collecting of Unrecorded Specifics", *Journal of Educational Research*, April, 1922.

has in certain directions not worked out principles governing fundamental problems of the applied field. Particularly, as has been said before, psychology has developed comparatively little material in connection with the feelings, yet it is precisely in the domain of the feelings that we need principles to guide us in handling people And, in the second place, principles so derived will not become valuable until they have copious specific applications. Knowledge of a principle does not guarantee wisdom in its application.

Empirical methods. — The second way to collect methods of handling difficulties in the applied field is to find out how experts work. This can be learned with more or less exactness through interviews. These constitute a fine body of suggestions which, when collected, may become the basis for a great program of scientific evaluation. For through them, concrete problems are provided with specific solutions which have stood the test of experience. It is because of these considerations that the pooled-information method (based upon duties or activities or upon difficulties) has been evolved in our laboratories.

A difficulty analysis. — We first obtained a difficulty analysis based on the compilation of a list of difficulties encountered in the operations in the field. In the case of the pooled-information method applied to teaching, instructors made a duty analysis and checked those duties with which they had difficulty. In salesmanship, salespeople were asked to state the difficulties encountered by beginners; executives were requested to give a list of difficulties encountered by salespeople; and an observer was put upon the task of watching the salespeople and diagnosing their difficulties. In the case of the handling of salespeople by managers, the salespeople were asked to state the differences between good and poor heads of departments; the heads of departments were asked the same questions; and the query was likewise put to the high executives in several stores.

In each case the difficulties were thrown into the form of questions such as, in teaching: How do you prepare your lessons? and, How do you get students interested? — In salesmanship the form was similar and as follows: How do you show interest and courtesy? How do you display merchandise effectively? — In handling people the queries ran: How do you show kindness without being easy? How do you get your people to do their work efficiently?

Interviewers. — These questions being formulated, the next problem was to train interviewers. In selecting interviewers it is important that the prospect should be a logical thinker, have a good rhetorical style, and ease of adaptability. He must be *logical*, because the people who are interviewed ramble away from the question. *Good writing* is necessary because it is important to retain the flavor of the language and the exact terminology of the person interviewed. *Adaptabilty* is necessary because it will seldom be possible to stick to a formal set of subordinate questions worked out in advance. The material will be collected best by those whose minds can nimbly follow the interview and ask the right questions at the right point.

In training the interviewer it is important that each question be gone over with him thoroughly, so that he may clearly understand how to word it to get the most satisfactory answers. He should then conduct one interview, write it up, and bring his material back to the group for criticism so that he may learn wherein he has failed or succeeded in collecting the methods. Particularly important is it to insist that in reading his write-up he shall not supplement what he has written by oral explanations: everything of importance should be down on the paper.

Several mechanical points need to be closely safeguarded to obtain the best results. The answer to each question should be written on a separate sheet or half-sheet of paper. A key sheet should be filled out by each person, bearing the name of the expert being interviewed, his location, the name of the interviewer, the length of the interview, the time spent in the write-up, and a code number. A corresponding code number should be placed upon each answer sheet to refer the compiler to the individual who gave the interview.

If the interview embraces, say, seven questions, the material turned in should consist of eight or more half-sheets of paper, the first being the key sheet, the next beneath it the answer to the first question, etc.   In all our interviews it is found that the use of not more than seven or eight questions gives the best results.   If more than eight questions are asked the last questions are less well answered.   In our interviews with two hundred and fifty experts in retail selling we found that the number of suggestions did not become appreciably greater after we had secured thirty persons' ideas; consequently the same question was not usually asked of more than thirty.   We found also that the best thirty salespeople in any retail store use practically the same methods as a similar number in another store.

Certain differences were disclosed in the ability of interviewers. About thirty per cent of our interviewers were unsatisfactory, because they lacked logical ability, or were not adaptable, or wrote up the material very poorly.   Some of them also lacked in keen interest and persistence.   They failed in some cases to ask for illustrations.   They failed to bore continually into the expert's experience and to keep asking the question: *How* do you do it?

Assembling the material. — When the interviews had been completed the material was assembled, the first step being to throw together all the answers to one question.   An illustration will make this clear.   In assembling the answers to the question, "What means do you use to show your people that you work with them as a leader rather than as a boss or driver?" we find seven different devices used:

    I. Work with them at their tasks

   II. Request rather than order

  III. Share their problems and information with them

  IV. Dismiss or transfer disturbing elements

   V. Give them responsibility and get ideas from them

  VI. Do not ridicule publicly or "bawl out"

 VII. Be friendly

Then each page is examined for material on any of these seven points.   In reply No. 3, for instance, the second and the third methods are used; in No. 6 the first, third, and fifth; in No. 11 the first is suggested; and in No. 12, the first, second, and third.

The compiler of the material runs through all of it and indicates by lines and Roman numerals in the left margin how it is to be sorted out. Then a typist sorts it, typing on a separate paper the matter relating to each method, and identifying the method by its proper Roman numeral. An assistant then separates these and puts all examples of Roman I together, all of Roman II, etc. After the material has been put into this form nothing remains except to write up the methods.

What we now have is a collection of methods. To develop the psychological *principles* that apply, it is only necessary to ask the question "Why?" after each of the seven types of method, and any answer that may be made to this in terms of psychology naturally constitutes a psychological fact. For instance, when the first method of leading people, "Work with them at their task," is followed by the question "Why?" the answer is as follows. "A leader always appears to his followers to be a member of the group." When the question is asked in the fifth method, "Why should the leader get ideas from his followers?" there are two answers: (1) In getting ideas from his followers he appeals to their self-respect; (2) the leader to maintain his leadership must lead wisely and often followers have good ideas. These two methods are therefore based upon three psychological facts. The whole 140 methods listed in the complete study of handling salespeople when submitted to the question "Why?" will give the material for a course on the psychology of handling salespeople.

Disadvantages. — The weaknesses of interviewing as a method are two. First, the material is empirical. (It can, however, be evaluated in terms of psychological principles.) Second, the person being interviewed tends to state what he thinks *ought to be done* rather than to describe what actually is done. This is not a serious objection, however; for when an expert tells us that he believes such and such a method to be the best, the fact that he himself does not always use it is negligible.

Advantages. — The advantages of pooling information are as follows. Empirical methods of controlling activities are collected as a basis for a later program of evaluation so that a decision may be made as to which methods are best. This pooled information provides a wide range of methods which can be used, at least, in the form of suggestions; it accumulates concrete solutions to concrete problems; and it furnishes connecting links between principles and practice.

The interview opens up in a thoroughgoing way a rich vein of methods which have never been recorded. For, after all the formal literature on the subject has been examined, there still exist many methods in common use that have not been recorded. Many of the latter are better than any that have been put into print, because they are more concrete and less likely to be idealized by the educational writer, who, in seeking illustrations, is sometimes tempted to mould them to fit his theory.

CHAPTER X

GRADING SUBJECT MATERIAL

§1—INTRODUCTION

The theory of curriculum construction running through the foregoing pages may be gathered together at this point, as the methods of collecting subject matter have been described, and its grading remains to be taken up.

The first step in curriculum construction is to determine the major objectives, be they citizenship, morality, social efficiency, or growth. The decisions as to what these objectives shall be rests with those who offer the instruction, and must be the product of sagacious and sensitive interpretation of the spirit of the generation.

As the objectives are being determined they must be analyzed into ideals and activities, in order to focus on the one hand the ideals which should dominate the learner and on the other the activities in which he is to engage. The ideals are to be determined after careful study of all the supporting facts by those responsible for instruction. The activities are not based upon opinion but are objectively derived from examination of the physical and mental activities in which the individual is engaging or may in the future engage.

In the case of both the ideals and the activities, analysis and sub-analysis must continue until working units are reached. In the case of ideals, the elementary forms which constitute the composite commonly used in major objectives (such as the ideals of good citizenship) must be determined by analysis to the point where they can be handled efficiently. Likewise in the case of activities (as these constitute good citizenship) the analysis must be continued until topics of sufficient minuteness are reached to enable the learner to handle them.

When this point has been reached there is spread before curriculum makers a very long list of activities and a shorter list of ideals. At this point the task of curriculum construction shifts to that of collecting the best methods of carrying on the discovered activities according to the standards of the selected ideals.

§2—THE PSYCHOLOGICAL FACTORS

Up to this point the ability and interests of the learner have not entered into the discussion except where by implication the limits of analysis set at the level of working units were discussed; but from this point forward the learner exercises an increasingly important effect on the curriculum. His effect on methods of instruction is always evident, of course; but in addition he has a profound influence upon the curriculum itself. This influence shows itself in various forms.

From earliest times teachers of the young, and parents in the rôle of instructors, have been hurled against the stone wall of children's ignorance, incapacity, and lack of interest as judged by adult standards. But only within modern times has the child been considered to be anything other than a pocket edition of the adult. During this period he has come to take an increasingly important place, although his influence has been felt more in the field of methods of teaching than in curriculum construction. The effect of increased attention to the capacities of childhood has resulted in four distinct types of theory.

The culture-epoch theory. — The first attempt to grade subject matter from the point of view of the children was a wholesale procedure adopted from the theory of recapitulation of embryological bodies. The proponents of the educational analogy applied the theory to post-natal life and divided child life into certain stages which recapitulated the racial life of man in his ascent from barbarism to civilization. From this assumption they postulated the principle that the best subject matter for a child in any stage of his development was the culture of the corresponding historic racial stage. So, in the German Folk School the children were taught folk and fairy tales in grade one, Robinson Crusoe in grade two, and the history of the patriarchs and Moses and the Thuringian Tales in grade three, with corresponding parallels in succeeding grades.

While the theory had some vogue in the field of education in this country it has left traces only in the added attention that is now given to primitive materials in the primary grades. That it did not remain as a permanent contribution at any other point in the curriculum is due to its fundamental lack of soundness as a description of fact and to a lack of detail sufficient to give definite assistance in the selection of subject matter. Specifically, it could not determine which of the folk stories or what parts of the history of Moses or of the Reformation should be studied.

Genetic stages.— More recently another attempt to grade by wholesale has been made through the division of child life into stages such as babyhood, up to the acquisition of speech; early childhood, up to second dentition; later childhood, to the advent of puberty; and adolesence, to the completion of bodily growth. The methods of curriculum organization deduced from these stages rested upon the belief that the moment of optimal ease of learning was that at which the interests and activities were strongest within the stages. The rule to be followed was to present appropriate subject matter at the psychological moment within the stage when the interest is functioning most strongly.

But these divisions have had no more than academic interest, because in the first place, like the stages of the culture-epoch theory, they lack sufficient detail to afford any practical criterion for grading. The period of later childhood, for instance, spreads over two or three grades and is, therefore, a classification too rough to be used in assigning material to a specific grade. A still more serious objection lies in the fact that children do not display the advent of interest within the stages at anything like the same chronological time. Never has any investigator been able so to dissect the stages of development of the children in a class in school to such fine detail as to provide a basis for grading the material in a manner suitable for practical classroom procedure.

Interests and needs. — The search for the psychological basis of the curriculum has of late years taken another form. As noted later in Chapter XV, there is a distinct school of educational theory which seeks to erect the curriculum upon the basis of children's interests and needs. They avoid the difficulties of genetic stages by refusing to make a genetic classification, and they strengthen their position by making a rough approximation to the interests which they believe are present in each grade. For the most part, however, the selection of subject matter to meet the needs and to conform to the interests of childhood in specific grades has been a matter of the individual opinion of the particular school in which a curriculum was constructed. Moreover, courses of study have been built without explicit acknowledgment of the necessity of directing the interests of childhood according to adult social patterns.

Current studies. — A few objective studies have been made to determine the grades during which selected units of subject matter are of maximum interest. In particular, Uhl (p. 316) has obtained the opinions of over two thousand teachers and seven hundred pupils of all grades concerning the interest shown in the material of readers in current use. Judd* similarly obtained opinions from about one thousand teachers concerning the grades of children whose interest was best met by the bulletins, "Lessons In Community and National Life."

Methods such as these illustrate the procedure which must be followed in placing subject material according to the interests of students. After determining major objectives in the form of ideals and activities, after analyzing them to the level of working units, and collecting the best procedure for carrying on the activities, the material must be tried out in the grades, and a division concerning placement must be made upon the basis of the discovered points of grade interest. If a unit is more interesting in the second grade than in the fourth, the presumption is that

---

*Vice-presidential address before the American Association for the Advancement of Science, 1921.

(other things being equal) it should be placed at the point of greatest interest.

The factor of utility. — Another method for the gradation of material is found in the concept of use. Other things being equal, the material should be taught at the moment when the use for it is apparent. Sometimes it may be the point of initial use. For instance, Jones (p.177) in grading his spelling curriculum included within the material placed in a grade those words which first occurred in two per cent of the original compositions of school children of that grade. His assumption clearly is that when words are found to enter the vocabulary of children in original themes for the first time, we have reached the point where they will be used. While at first glance this appears reasonable and may upon complete investigation be found to be sound, it is charged with one serious handicap: twenty-four hundred words would thus be taught in the second grade, and a decreasing number in each succeeding grade.

The point of greatest usefulness does not always coincide with initial appearance. It may occur at any time. The recognition of the point of usefulness lies at the basis of the theory of incidental teaching of subject matter where it is assumed that the instrumental units, at least, shall be taught at the point of use in furthering some objective for whose mastery they are the instruments.

Whether use is determined by the onset of general interest or by specific situations in which the child finds himself, there is no question that the material should in part be graded so as to synchronize with psychological moments of utility.

Difficulty. — The principle of difficulty enters in as a factor to modify the criterial factors of interest and of use. Certain subject matter may be of interest or of use, but also be so difficult to learn that if it be presented, interest will be killed and use will be prohibited.

The principle of classification by difficulty works in two directions. It may determine both the moment of initial presentation and the amount of emphasis to be given to specific units. In general, material must be so graded that a unit shall not be presented before the learner has reached the level of ability where he may reasonably hope to master it, and instruction must be continued until he has mastered it to a satisfactory degree.

Current studies. — Many results have been obtained in spelling and in arithmetic. The work of Ballou, Holloway, Rugg, Monroe, and others in arithmetic, and of Ashbaugh, Ayres, Buckingham, and others in spelling, are cases in point. In the vocational subjects Allen arranges his material in what he calls instructional order and grades the processes in any operation in order of difficulty, the simpler being taught first and the more difficult later.

The principle of difficulty has an important bearing upon the teaching of coherent subjects where units must be taught in series of which the later units are dependent upon the earlier. In amorphous subjects, the order is of minor importance. In such coherent subjects as grammar, there is no way of avoiding the teaching of definitions before rules, although the rules may be the items of greatest use, as for instance in the correction of errors. Likewise the fundamental portions of arithmetic must be learned before problems in fractions, commercial operations, or mensuration can be handled with any degree of efficiency.

§3—The Relation between the Psychological Factors

The foregoing discussion inevitably leads to the conclusion that the gradation of subject material is both complicated and empirical. In the absence of specific help from educational psychology the only method remaining is that of "fumbling and success." The subject matter is first presented in places where experience suggests that it is likely to have optimal efficiency; and after this initial placement, the opinions of teachers, the results of tests, and, occasionally, the conclusions of the pupils themselves will enter to modify and correct the original grading.

Difficulty and interest. — These criteria of interest, use, and difficulty do not necessarily conflict in actual practice. If a unit is interesting, it may be easier to acquire; if it is recognized as useful, it is more likely to be interesting, and so to be easier to acquire. But where interest does not operate strongly enough to overcome difficulty completely, then the conflict is present, and difficulty will take priority over interest. Material should, therefore, *first* be graded for *difficulty*, and *second* placed according to *interest*, in such a way that no units of excessive difficulty shall be presented to the learner at any time. If a unit is both difficult and important, it should be saved for the moment when the ability of the student is equal to mastering it.

Difficulty and use. — The principle of use has similar relationships with interest. If the material is recognized by the learner as useful, interest in it is likely to be enhanced; but it must be borne in mind, as regards certain units of subject matter, that even though the learner may not, as a child, realize their usefulness, we know that their fundamental importance warrants including them. If such a unit is simple enough to be mastered by the learner it should be taught, even though at no time during his school life can he be stimulated to take a direct interest in it. Of this sort are the fundamental operations of arithmetic, some of the facts of geography, and, with many children, some of history, and in such cases appeal must be made to generic interests of the schoolroom.

Some educators assert that any material which does not evoke the whole-hearted interest of the students would better remain untaught; but the writer believes that fundamental units which have adult value and which are not contrary to the law of difficulty ought to be taught, even where extrinsic forms of interest must be relied on exclusively. This does not mean that all reasonable pains shall not be taken to teach such material in contexts which will demonstrate utility and stimulate interest, whenever their difficulty is not too great; but it does mean that fundamentally important material must be taught, even though, to the child, intrinsic interest and evident utility be lacking.

§4—The Steps in Curriculum Construction

In the first section of this chapter we epitomized four steps in curriculum construction, viz.: selecting objectives, dividing them into ideals and activities, analyzing them to the limits of working units, and collecting methods of achievement. At this point the psychological factors enter and three additional steps may be enumerated.

In the first place the limitations of time make it necessary to rank activities and ideals in the order of importance. Clearly not all activities can be taught, since they are infinite in number. It is equally clear that some units can best be learned on the job. Still other units, such as those connected with religion, for various reasons cannot be taught in public schools. All these considerations make it necessary to arrange units in their order of importance so that those of greatest importance can be learned within the school period.

Before this can be done, however, consideration has to be given to certain units which are of importance for children but do not rank high among adult activities and ideals. For instance, dramatization, games, and fairy stories are clearly not major activities of the adult, yet for children they are of primary importance, according to the criteria of interest, use, and difficulty, because they fill very important functions in child life. So also among the ideals, obedience requires greater attention in child life, probably, than it does in adult society.

Thus the activities and ideals of children must also be ranked in order of importance; and when this is done those that rank high in child life and low in adult life should be raised to a point of such importance in the final list that they will be included in the portions which are to be taught within the school period.

When these two steps have been taken, when the ideals and activities of both children and adults are ranked and the proper selection of units for instruction is made, the material so retained should be graded according to the principles of interest, use, and difficulty.

In conclusion, the rules for curriculum construction may be stated as follows:

First, determine the major objectives of education by a study of the life of man in its social setting.

Second, analyze these objectives into ideals and activities and continue the analysis to the level of working units.

Third, arrange these in the order of importance.

Fourth, raise to positions of higher order in this list those ideals and activities which are high in value for children but low in value for adults.

Fifth, determine the number of the most important items of the resulting list which can be handled in the time allotted to school education, after deducting those which are better learned outside of school.

Sixth, collect the best practices of the race in handling these ideals and activities.

Seventh, arrange the material so obtained in proper instructional order, according to the psychological nature of children.

CHAPTER XI

THE SUBJECTS OF THE CURRICULUM

§1—PRIMARY AND DERIVED SUBJECTS

Subjects. — The reader who has been following the discussion has undoubtedly wondered where, among all the materials concerning ideals, activities, objectives, methods of control, etc., the subjects of the curriculum are to be found. Is there a place for organized information in the fields of chemistry, history, physics, mathematics, or geography?

This question we shall now proceed to answer. In the first place, it must be noted that the foregoing discussion has nothing to do with the independent elective studies which are studied from the specialists' point of view by those who are interested in specialists' problems. It is not concerned with the problems of the specialists or with the solutions that he finds for them. Neither is it concerned with the organization of his material for purposes of instruction. Rather, the discussion is concerned with the service portions of the subjects that are to be taught from the layman's point of view, or required as a basis or introduction to the acquisition of other fields of knowledge. With this distinction in mind the question then changes to this form: Does the proper performance of life activities under the control of appropriate ideals involve the use of the conventional subjects, and if so, can this material be organized into systematic form?

Primary subjects. — The first step in the answer can best be illustrated by the case of the job analysis made by Strong (p.292) in connection with the commercial engineering curriculum. Making the job analyses for the forty executives, and listing their duties, proved to reveal the material for several of the subjects. For instance, in the building construction occupations, the executives had, as some of their duties, to send daily reports to the main office; to make out weekly reports, including statements concerning weather conditions, etc.; to make out monthly statements from the time-keeper's reports; to prepare periodic cost reports; to write letters of many kinds, dealing with acknowledgments, inquiries, claims, complaints; to hold interviews in which oral conversation was carried on with the workmen, officers, customers, and the general public; to preside over meetings and conferences at which it would be necessary to discuss problems from the floor or in the capacity of presiding officer; to write up technical specifications according to established standards so that they are brief but fully cover the subject and are easily understood; and to read proof. These belong to the course in English.

When the material of the subject is in this way found within the items of the job analysis itself, the subject may be called a primary subject, to indicate that it is not derived from other subjects. The amount of material so obtained in the primary subjects in any occupation or in any group of activities other than occupations is very considerable and is usually easily classified. In the study just mentioned, for instance, there was a mass of material, as complete as that for English, in the subjects of pattern making, forging, carpentry, machinery, building sanitation, electrical engineering, accounting, cost accounting, handling men, and estimating. The answer to our question then is this: that with an analyzing of objectives the material which ordinarily is classified under the great divisions of subjects begins to emerge and can be gathered together without serious difficulty.

Derived subjects. — This is not the whole story, however. It was found, for instance, that the job analysis revealed very little physics or mathematics and comparatively little chemistry. But while only a small number of items were obtained from the job analysis itself, a very much larger number were found to be necessary as a background or basis for the proper understanding of the material contained within the job analysis. Specifically, mechanical engineering had a number of items listed in the job analysis, and in order to understand many of these items physics was essential.

This introduces derived subjects. These are service subjects which are important not because they are directly useful in the performance of activities, but because they are derived from material which has practical service value. They are necessary to a complete understanding of the primary material.

There are two kinds of derived subjects: items needed in order to understand primary subjects, and others which explain why certain processes in the primary groups are carried on. The Federal Board for Vocational Education calls the first kind "related subjects." In the machinists' curriculum worked out under the direction of Allen (p. 274), the related material in English, science, mathematics, and drawing is directly derived from the machine operations.

It is difficult to draw a sharp line between those items of derived subjects which are "necessary to understand" and those which "explain the reason why." Viewed without qualification the two uses are quite distinct. For instance, in order to understand how to construct a machine one must know how to read; the material read does not necessarily explain why certain processes are carried on. But, the distinctions shade off and become indefinite when we seek to define what is meant by "necessary to understand," because some people would hold that in order really to understand certain things properly one would need to know the reason for their operation.

The distinction is of interest because it calls attention to the so-called fundamental subjects. Psychology explains why certain methods are used in handling men. Physics performs a similar service in mechanical engineering. In foods, chemistry provides principles of explanation. And in house decoration the theory of design serves the same end.

The primary elements of the subject and the derived elements together constitute a very considerable body of information. When in mathematics we unite what is revealed in the job analysis with what is necessary to understand the operations listed in the job analysis, we have in many cases a quite respectable amount of mathematics. It is apparent, however, that the material included in the subject which is of service in particular groups of activities varies with the activities. There is a very small amount of mathematics used in sewing, while there is a very large amount of it used in engineering; the content of agricultural chemistry will be considerably different from the chemistry of sanitation. But the important theoretical point is that there is a place for the conventional subjects in a curriculum which is derived from an analysis of objectives.

For the derivation of material a definite technique has been worked out. In the current studies, Williams (p. 238) has laid down rules for the derivation of mathematics used in freshman chemistry. As reported later, he read the text, solved the examples, and listed under definite rules of procedure all the items of mathematics which he found. Mrs. Callaway (p. 238) made a companion study for clothing. Greene (p. 287) similarly determined what chemistry, botany, and zoölogy are fundamental to the understanding of the practices of sheep husbandry. The items in this case happened to be few in number, but taken together they might well be included in a general science course in the high school. Similarly, Mrs. Dodd (p. 255) determined the items of history to which specific reference was made in the poetry utilized for admission to the University of Illinois.

§2—Systematic Organization of Content

Systematic organization. — A very important question follows the one already answered. It has to do with the possibility of the systematic organization of the material so derived. Specifically, it is quite important to answer the question "Is the material that we obtain in this way a mass of unorganized material which lacks the closely knit coherence of the field as organized by the specialist?" Here again the objector can be reassured. It has been demonstrated that the service subjects are capable of being organized quite as systematically as the specialist can organize them when he is preparing his material for the solution of his own problems. This is made possible by introducing the idea of "connective tissue."

In the ordinary course of curriculum analysis we come in time to the point where, the material of a subject necessary for fulfilling a function having been provided, it becomes necessary to add information within the subject which is not directly useful but which is essential to the understanding of the useful material. In the mental field, this added material corresponds to connective tissue in the physiological field, whose function is merely that of supporting the organs which carry on the physiological functions. When the muscles of the body are in motion in an effort to catch a car the connective tissue cannot be of direct assistance, but without its help in supporting muscles they could not function. In a similar manner we find that when we have derived certain items of the subject which are necessary for the performance of activities, we must add additional items within the subject, needed for the understanding of the useful elements. We are able to illustrate this in two different types of studies.

Connective tissue. — When in the Kansas City grammar study (p. 194) the grammar rules which had been broken were collected, it was found that before the pupils could understand any rule, they had to grasp certain definitions. For instance, Rule I states that "The subject of the verb is in the nominative case." This involves knowledge of the definitions of subject and predicate and of the sentence. *Subject* involves a knowledge of noun and pronoun. *Nominative case* includes case and nominative case. *Predicate* involves a knowledge of the verb. Rule II states that "A substantive standing in the predicate but defining the subject agrees with the subject in case and is called the predicate nominative." This rule, to be understood, requires a knowledge of the copula, the expletive, and the predicate nominative, in addition to any definitions necessary to the understanding of Rule I. Rule III reads "The object of a verb is in the objective case," and this adds new elements of *objective, objective case,* and *transitive verb.*

When to the rules are added these definitions, and the material is arranged with definitions first and rules following them, we find that the material is just as coherent and just as systematic as is the conventional grammar of the eighth grade. There are fewer topics included, but what there are are capable of quite logical arrangement.

As a matter of fact, the constructor of the curriculum would be quite justified in adding the items which are introduced solely for the purpose of providing a system, if he felt that he could demonstrate an understanding of the whole organization as necessary to the proper control of the useful operations; but such a practice would be rather dangerous to adopt because of the ease with which the subject material tends to drop back into conventional grooves.

China information. — Another illustration is given by Miss Ringo.* In collecting her material she set up as control elements the following qualities which customers seek: durability, serviceability, sanitary quality, beauty, and trade-mark or guarantee.

We may quote from her statement as follows:

"When this point had been reached the selection and elimination of material assumed great importance. In addition to those facts stated in the explanation of any of the five control elements, another class of material was included, the so-called connective tissue. This was made up of facts which helped to bind together what would otherwise have been isolated processes and descriptions. In using this type of material, particular attention was paid to making accounts as vivid as possible. The method used may be shown by considering two paragraphs from Chapter III. The italicized parts are put in because they help to explain how the desirable qualities in china are secured. The parts which are not italicized are included because they help to weld the whole discussion together and to make it more vivid. Each fact suggested for the manual was subjected to the test of proving whether or not it served one of these two purposes. If it did not, it was rejected.

*Merchandise Manual for Salespeople in the China Department, Jane Ringo, Carnegie Institute of Technology; unpublished Master's thesis.

"(1) *Materials are often exposed to rain and sun in order that they may be thoroughly weathered and may be worked up most successfully.* When this process is completed, they are carried into the mill, where they are ground and mixed with water. The thick, creamy liquid which is produced in this way is called slip. (2) *Before it can be used it must be purified. It must be filtered through a thin gauze sieve which catches all bits of sand. This helps to furnish a smooth body and one which will fuse evenly.* Still another thing is necessary. (3) *If any particles of iron or other metals are left in the slip the firing will cause them to spread and stain the ware. Therefore they are carefully drawn out by powerful electric magnets. Because all of these bits cannot be removed, cobalt blue is put in to help whiten the product* just as bluing is used in laundering clothes to give them a good color. Sometimes even after all this care, specks of metal remain. (4) *They may be ground off, but this leaves a slight blemish on the surface of the china.*

"The liquid is next pumped into suspended canvas bags. High pressure is applied and the water is forced through the canvas, leaving the moist clay in the presses. *It now has a good deal of air in it.* (5) *This is removed in order to prevent bubbles or blisters.* The clay is passed through a pug mill, which also mixes the material very thoroughly by beating and cutting it with knives. (6) *When it comes from the mill it looks and feels much like putty. It is now so smooth that all parts of it should be acted on in the same way during the firing process and the ware should be free from flaws due to lumps in the clay.*

"An examination of the italicized parts will show that (1) and (2) state facts which affect the durability of wares. They stress the need for ingredients to be in the best possible physical condition before being mixed and for them to be purified in order that they may fuse evenly and produce ware that is free from weakness. The parts numbered (3), (4), (5), and (6) deal with means of obtaining good workmanship, which in the manual is considered as one essential of beauty. The sentences which are not italicized form the necessary connective tissue for points relating to the control elements."

These two illustrations present slightly different cases. The connective tissue of grammar is very logically derived; the investigator can study the rules one by one and decide with great exactness what definitions are necessary in order to understand the rule. In the china manual it is not so easy to determine this, because, as has just been said, an effort is made to make it vivid and interesting, and just what means will accomplish that result is subject to the individual opinion of the one who does the work. But here again the greatest care must be taken to see that irrelevant material is not introduced and that the connective tissues, as far as possible, obey the same laws of logic as do the main portions of the subject.

§3—Systematic and Incidental Teaching

Incidental teaching. — Still another question is frequently raised concerning the method of presenting service material. Some investigators are of the opinion that the material in the fundamental subjects should be presented as needed in connection with the primary subject. For instance, as the methods used in the handling of men or in retail selling are taken up, the psychological principles underlying each method may be discussed on the spot. Such a procedure does not require or facilitate a systematic organization of the fundamental subject.

Systematic teaching. — If this process were attempted in connection with the applications of mathematics, the problem would not be quite so simple as it seems to be in the case of psychology. In mathematics it frequently happens that one of the first things to be applied is the algebraic equation, and this might have to be used before the student could understand the fundamental operations of algebra. So, also, a rule in grammar may be needed before a student can understand the underlying definitions.

Those subjects which are closely knit, in which one operation is dependent upon preceding operations, cannot be successfully taught by the incidental method. There is no recourse from the systematic curriculum. The simplest parts have to be taught first and the superstructure has to be built upon them.

While some subjects must be taught systematically, and others may be, the question arises as to whether all subjects ought to be taught systematically. In that connection there is very definitely a difference of opinion which the author cannot hope to settle. It is apparent that there are certain advantages in giving systematic treatment before the applications occur, with the conscious purpose in the minds of the students of getting ready for the applications. A student may know just why he is studying, and may be easily convinced that all the material taken up will be used at a later time. On the other hand, if the material is presented point by point, as needed in its applications, there is a fineness of spirit in the contact which it is difficult to surpass. This, however, may be obtained when the applications are made after a preliminary systematic treatment has been provided. The only point that must be safeguarded is that when subjects are derived from activities it is not necessary that they be taught incidentally.

General service subjects. — A misunderstanding may easily arise to the effect that when subjects are derived in the foregoing way they must all be small and piecemeal in content. Specifically, it is claimed that there must be a carpenter's arithmetic, a grocer's arithmetic, a machinist's arithmetic, and a housewife's arithmetic; and that this will tend to duplicate courses and provide material in such slight quantities as to be trivial. While it is true that such organizations as the Federal Board for Vocational Education provide special arithmetic (and other subjects) for each of the trades which are taught, it is easily possible and quite justifiable to have a vocational arithmetic which will include the arithmetic needed in many occupations. For all that must be done is to throw together the different divisions of service arithmetic and teach them all as one course. It might be possible in college, for instance, to have a course in agricultural chemistry which would include the fundamentals for all the divisions of agriculture. Indeed, it would be theoretically possible to have a course in applied chemistry which would be applicable to the subjects in the colleges of engineering, agriculture, and home economics. Specifically all the service science to be used in a required high school course of study might be thrown into a single general science course. The question as to whether we should have special divisions or general divisions is purely a pedagogic one, settled upon the basis of the needs of the situation and the efficiency with which instruction can be given in one type or the other; but intrinsically there is no reason why there cannot be a combination of the similar units of each service subject into units as large as the instructor finds satisfactory.

Chapter XII

CURRENT STUDIES IN SCHOOL SUBJECTS

§1—The Selection

Most of the current studies which have been made have followed the line of least resistance and have dealt with subjects whose content is definite. Spelling, the most mechanical, has been carried farther than any other subject. Grammar has been more fully investigated than rhetoric, and arithmetic has proved more inviting than history.

While these definite subjects have been attacked, studies have not been confined to them alone. An examination of Table I, (p.195), shows that in addition to those mentioned, investigations have been made in banking, history, geography, civics, psychology, the machine operations, sheep husbandry, manual arts, physical education, and salesmanship.

Many of these studies are fragmentary, and the technique of investigation is much cruder now than it will be later. They represent the conscientious striving for methods of attack upon the most important educational problem with which this generation is faced.

§2—Assumed Functions

In Table I is shown a list of subjects in which studies have been made. This list omits a number of important studies now under way but not in form for reporting. It may not include all published studies because it is always likely that careful search through the literature and extensive written inquiry will not reveal everything of worth. It does represent all with which the writer is acquainted.

TABLE 1

TABULAR LIST OF INVESTIGATIONS

Investigator	Serial No.	Investigation	Assumed Function of Subject	W	d. e. s. a.	i. e. s. a.	ch. ac.	ad. ac.
Ayres, L. P.	1	Spelling — personal and business correspondence	Writing of social and business letters	X				X
Ayres, L. P.	2	Spelling	Writing by children	X				X
Cook, W. A. & O'Shea, M. V.	3	Spelling — personal correspondence	Writing of personal correspondence	X		X		X
Jones, W. F.	4	Spelling — children's themes	Writing of themes by children	X			X	
Smith, H. J.	5	do	do	X			X	
Anderson, W. N.	6	Spelling — parents' letters	Writing of letters by adults	X		X		X
Pryor, H. C.	7	Spelling — graded list	Writing by children	X		X	X	
Capps, A. G.	8	Spelling — high school	do	X			X	
Wilson, G. M.	9	Language — children's errors	To correct children's oral speech			X	X	
Charters, W. W. & Miller, E.	10	Grammar	To correct oral and written speech of children	X		X	X	
Thompson, O. S.	11	Language and Grammar	do	X		X	X	
Meek, C. S.	12	do	To correct oral speech of children			X	X	
Sears, I. & Diebel, A.	13	do	do			X	X	
Randolph, E. D.	14	do	To correct oral and written speech of children	X		X	X	

TABLE I — Continued

TABULAR LIST OF INVESTIGATIONS

Investigator	Serial No.	Investigation	Assumed Function of Subject	Classification				
				W	d. e. s. a.	i. e. s. a.	ch. ac.	ad. ac.
Barnes, W.	15	Grammar	To correct oral and written speech of children	X			X	
Betz, Annette & Marshall, Esther	16	Language and Grammar	To correct children's written speech	X			X	
Fillers, H. D.	17	Grammar	To correct oral and written speech of children	X		X	X	
Jones, J. K.	18	do	do	X		X	X	
Richardson, W. J.	19	do	To correct children's oral speech			X	X	
Charters, W. W.	20	do	do			X	X	
Charters, W. W.	21	Language and Grammar	do			X	X	
Johnson, R. I.	22	do	To correct the written speech of children	X		X	X	
Wilson, G. M.	23	Arithmetic — opinions of business men	To aid in solving business problems			X		X
Coffman, L. D. & Jessup, W. A.	24	Arithmetic — opinions of superintendents	To aid in solving "modern" problems			X		X
Monroe, W. S.	25	Arithmetic — four texts	To aid in handling "human activities"	X		X		X
Wilson, G. M.	26	Arithmetic — parents' problems	To aid in solving problems of everyday life			X		X
Charters, W. W.	27	Arithmetic — salespeople	To aid in solving business problems	X		X		X
Mitchell, H. E.	28	Arithmetic — cookbook, etc.	To aid in understanding certain printed material	X	X			X

TABLE I — Continued

TABULAR LIST OF INVESTIGATIONS

Investigator	Serial No.	Investigation	Assumed Function of Subject	Classification				
				W	d. e. s. a.	i. e. s. a.	ch. ac.	ad. ac.
Williams, L. W.	29	Arithmetic — chemistry text	To aid in understanding freshmen chemistry	X			X	
Callaway, Theodosia T.	30	Arithmetic — sewing text	To aid in understanding sewing	X			X	X
Wooters, J. E.	31	History — dates	To aid in learning history			X	X	
Bagley, W. C. & Rugg, H. O.	32	History — history texts	do	X			X	
Horn, Ernest	33	History — certain books	To aid in understanding "certain crucial life activities"	X		X		X
Bassett, B. B.	34	do	To aid in understanding civic problems	X		X		X
Dodd, S. H.	35	History — poetry	To aid in understanding poetry	X			X	
Whitbeck, R. H.	36	Geography—consensus	To aid in evaluating geographical facts				X	
Bagley, W. C.	37	Geography and History	To aid in understanding present-day problems	X		X		X
Branom, M. E. & Reavis, W. C.	38	Geography — standards	To aid in evaluating geographical facts			X		X
Charters, W. W.	39	Geography	Technical study					
Allen, C. R.	40	Vocations — Machinists' trade	To aid in mastering machinists' trade		X			X
Noel, B. W.	41	do	do		X			X
Dyer, Elizabeth	42	Vocations — Merchandise information	To aid in mastering salesmanship		X			X

TABLE I — Continued

TABULAR LIST OF INVESTIGATIONS

Investigator	Serial No.	Investigation	Assumed Function of Subject	Classification				
				W	d. e. s. a.	i. e. s. a.	ch. ac.	ad. ac.
Greene, J. H.	43	Vocations — sheep husbandry	To aid in mastering sheep husbandry		X			
Strong, E. K.	44	Vocations — commercial engineering	To aid in executive training					X
Struck, F. T.	45	Vocations — farm shop construction	To aid in constructing farm equipment			X		X
Fuller, L. D.	46	Manual Arts — home repair	To aid in making home repairs			X		X
Bassett, B. B.	47	Civics — political platforms	To aid in solving political problems			X		X
Rugg, H. O. & Schweppe, Emma	48	Social Studies — Lincoln School	To aid in solving modern social problems			X		X
Thorndike, E. L.	49	Vocabulary study	To aid in mastering vocabulary	X				X
Uhl, W. L.	50	Reading — child interest	A grading study	X			X	
Todd, E. M.	51	Physical Education — correctives	To aid in correcting physical defects				X	
Camerer, Alice	52	Banking — for depositors	To aid depositors to understand banking			X		X
Charters, W. W.	53	Women's Education — Stephens College	To aid in educating women			X	X	X
Charters, W. W.	54	Interviewing	A technical study					
Jones, A. J.	55	Education — job analysis of teaching	To aid in mastering the art of teaching			X		X
Secondary Association	56	Central Collecting Agency	A technical study					

The statements of the assumed functions found in Table I are, where possible, phrased in the investigator's own terms, but they are sometimes derived by the writer from the investigator's description in the absence of any specific statement. For purposes of exposition they are approximately correct.

The studies are classified in Table I to show whether they are based upon written material, as in the derivation of the spelling curriculum by the tabulation of the words found in written letters and in print, or whether they are based upon definite extra-school activities such as the operations in the machinist's trade, or upon indefinite extra-school activities such as the arithmetic used by the parents of children. A classification is also made to show whether the function of the subject is that of assisting children in their home problems, as in the writing of themes, or of assisting adults, as in the writing of business and social letters. These facts are shown by checks in the columns headed W (written and printed material); d. e. s. a. (definite extra-school activities); i. e. s. a. (indefinite extra-school activities); ch. ac. (children's activities); and ad. ac. (adult activities).

Varieties of functions. — The functions which any subject ought to serve in the curriculum must, in the last analysis, be determined by major objectives and relative importance; consequently the studies are not concerned with the relative value of the assumed function. The investigator must be allowed the privilege of assuming what functions he desires, while readers will judge of his results by the intelligence with which he carries out his investigation.

It is at once apparent in the perusal of Table I that a wide variety of functions for some of the subjects is assumed. All the studies in spelling assume that its function is to aid in writing, with but three variations. Jones (p. 177) and Smith (p. 177) tabulate the words in written school themes and thereby assume that the function is to assist children in their school work. Capps (p. 188) modifies this by collecting, not the words most frequently used, but those most frequently misspelled by students. Ayres (p. 171) and Cook and O'Shea (p. 173) are, on the other hand, concerned with the words used by adults rather than by children.

In arithmetic a similar wide variety of assumed functions is displayed. All but two assume the function to be that of solving numerical problems arising in human activities, but each introduces a variation. Wilson (p. 223) collects problems actually met by parents of school children and determines the arithmetic involved, his assumed function being that it assists in the problems of everyday life. Coffman and Jessup (p. 216) ask superintendents to make an informal analysis of human activities by stating whether or not an itemized list of topics shall be eliminated, or continued as at present, or given more attention. Monroe (p. 219) assumes the same function, classifies human activities following the Federal Census of Occupations, and examines arithmetic textbooks to see how their problems classify themselves on this basis. Wilson (p. 213) in another study assumes the solution of business problems as the function of arithmetic and obtains the opinions of business men as to what operations are most important. Charters (p. 231) finds the arithmetic used in business by salespeople. Mitchell (p. 236) makes a narrower assumption and investigates the arithmetic involved in reading certain printed matter intelligently. Williams (p. 238) and Callaway (p. 238) assume that mathematics is used in freshman chemistry and sewing, and Allen (p. 274) that it is necessary in the machinist's trade.

In grammar five assumptions are possible, but only one of these has been used. All the studies regard the function of grammar as being that of assisting in the correction of errors in oral and written language.

This variety of function applied to any one subject is of value in arriving at a composite curriculum. Particularly is this shown in spelling, where it has been possible to combine lists obtained from many of these studies into a common list. This has been done by Ayres, Pryor, Buckingham, Horn and Ashbaugh, Starch and Mirick, and others, and the procedure has resulted in a reasonable list of minimum essentials for a course in spelling.

§3—The Activities Studied

Written material. — It is interesting to note that when subjects and functions of subjects have been selected for study those in which the material is found in written or printed form are preferred. Twenty-eight studies listed in Table I are of such character. The reason for this lies in the ease of studying the material, since the gathering of written words is easier to perform than the compiling of oral errors. Reading a chemistry textbook to derive the mathematics gives less difficulty than getting the range of practical arithmetic problems encountered by the layman. Analyzing the processes in the operation of a machine presents fewer difficulties than the cataloguing of home repairs.

But, besides being easier, the use of written material produces a greater certainty of results. It provides all the data, while unwritten material requires unusual care in order to give assurance of completeness. The chemistry textbook obviously provides all the data within its covers, while a complete list of the arithmetic problems of the layman requires a vast amount of detailed collection and repetitive checking before the investigator can be satisfied that all types are presented.

Definite extra-school activities. — While definite written material has proved to be a favorite field for investigation, five analyses of definite extra-school operations, found notably in the trades, industries, and agriculture, have also been made. In some cases training courses based upon job analyses have been constructed, and the policy of the Federal Board for Vocational Education is definitely to construct all other curricula upon such analyses as that of Allen (p. 274), their chief investigator in the field. In agriculture, Stimson has, for several years, been making analyses of projects, written in syllabus form, with references. The studies of Greene (p. 287), who analyzed the sheep project, and the studies of Miss Dyer (p. 285), who collected merchandise information for salespeople, are of this more definite sort.

Indefinite extra-school activities. — Notwithstanding the fact that extra-school activities, such as geographical problems of timely moment, children's language errors, modern numerical problems, and adult correspondence, are admittedly more difficult to analyze than are definite vocational projects, thirty-five studies have been made in these fields. This is probably due in part to the fact that many of these indefinite activities are presented in written form, such as social letters, but particularly to the fact that since most of the investigations of the curriculum have been conducted by students of elementary education, attention has naturally been paid to the more familiar common branches. Among the indefinite extra-school activities listed are the language errors of children, geography problems of "timely moment," "numerical problems of human activity," "crucial life activities," and "home repairs." The mere mention of these terms indicates the difficulty of the operations of analysis.

The child *versus* the adult. — In spite of the very great insistence laid by many writers upon the necessity of constructing the curriculum so as to help the child to live his child life rather than to prepare him for adult life, twenty-nine of the studies adopt the adult point of view. Adult business and social letters, newspapers, cookbooks, and political and social problems found in advanced textbooks, are some of the material chosen from adult life; but, on the other hand, a number of studies dealing with the activities of children are included. Twenty-eight studies, including the errors of children's language, the spelling vocabulary found in their themes, the historical characters and events found in children's textbooks, the high school mathematics involving sewing, and the mathematics in college freshmen chemistry have been made with children's or with students' material.

§4—The Delimitation of Fields

The delimitation of fields. — In the analysis of material the problem of the delimitation of the different subjects enters at a number of points in the studies. This appears in connection with the query: What is an historical fact, a mathematical fact, or a fact in grammar? Sometimes the investigator makes no attempt to answer this question, but usually some limits are determined where it is necessary to have them. In the Kansas City study of grammar (p. 194) the teachers are told to collect grammatical errors without being informed as to what the limits of grammar are. This is done partly because the teachers are supposed to know what grammatical errors are, and partly because all non-grammatical errors could be eliminated from the tabulation later. When the tabulations were made it became necessary to define grammar. This was done by ruling that an error which could be explained by reference to a grammatical fact was a grammatical error. For instance, a confusion of *two, to,* and *too* is a grammatical error because the confusion can be clarified by saying that *to* is a preposition, *two* is an adjective, and *too* an adverb. On the other hand, a confusion of *learn* and *teach* is not directly grammatical because no rule of grammar will show when to use one and when the other.

In another case Williams (p. 238) defines what he means by mathematics by laying down seven rules. Mrs. Dodd (p. 255) defines historical characters as opposed to legendary and fictitious characters by reference to standard lists of several kinds.

In general, the more definite the field the less necessity there is for formal delimitation; and, *vice versa*, the less definite, the greater the need. Particularly any study which is used to determine the content of such a subject as sociology must be very carefully delimited because of the haziness of its boundaries; but in any case it is necessary that delimitation be performed before an attempt is made to divide the material of the curriculum into subjects.

Chapter XIII

CERTAIN TECHNICAL PROBLEMS

§1—Typical Material

In many fields of investigation it is impossible to study all the material. The derivation of a spelling vocabulary from the written work of children involves, theoretically, the tabulation of all the words in all their compositions, exercises, and letters; but since there are twenty million children who probably write an average of over one hundred words a day for every school day, there would be at least four hundred billion words for one year. Obviously the treatment of such a mass of material is so nearly impossible that some short cuts need to be found. Therefore, the selection of samples which will approximate what would be found in any total mass is of primary importance.

Complete data. — In certain studies the problem of sampling does not arise because the whole field is covered. When Williams (p. 238) found the mathematics used in a specific textbook on freshman chemistry he did not need to sample, although if he had claimed that his results would hold for all freshman chemistry texts, rather than for that examined, he would have had to show that the book he examined was typical of the whole list. Granting that Horn (p. 251) and Bassett (p. 251) had typical books, they did not need to sample the material in the texts; they examined it all. Mrs. Dodd (p. 255) had no problem of sampling because she studied all the poetry required for entrance to the University of Illinois; nor did Capps (p. 188), since he examined all the written material of all his high school students.

Sampling. — But these are relatively simple cases, and others of greater difficulty are much more frequent. For instance, to mention a few problems, Jones' 15,000,000 words (p. 177), written by

1050 children of five states, may or may not be typical of the national spelling vocabulary of children. Are Anderson's 3723 letters (p. 179) typical, or would more letters from other persons have yielded different results? Would Monroe's lists of problems (p. 219) have been different if he had examined another quartet of texts? Would Wilson's 14,583 problems (p. 223), collected from 4068 parents of sixth, seventh, and eighth grade children in the country and small towns of Iowa and in three larger cities, have been different if he had collected more problems from other parents of children in different localities? Are 6000 grammatical errors collected by teachers in one city (p. 194) enough to determine the central tendencies of the errors of a city system and of the nation? Were Bassett's political platforms (p. 308) typical of the nation? Were his twelve books typical books of the field? These queries set the problem of sampling before us.

Random sampling. — Statistical formulæ are devised by which one can determine the probability of error in any random sample. But these have been computed for very simple situations such as tossing coins or throwing dice and, therefore, are far removed from a random sampling of the compositions of the school children of the nation, or the replies to a written questionnaire. It is one thing to toss coins a thousand times and, counting the heads and tails, to determine the trueness of the sample; but it is quite another thing to say that 6000 errors represent the true facts concerning the errors of a whole city of children. Perhaps, for example, the children are more careful before teachers than when by themselves, or perhaps the teachers are blind to some errors. Material, therefore, which seems to be selected at random needs to be carefully scrutinized before claims about its trueness to type are made. Such a scrutiny is aided by a few rules and methods of examination.

Generality. — In the first place, trueness to type in material gathered from a small field should not be claimed for a larger field without careful investigation. A course of study based upon the spelling vocabulary of one city, or the opinion of business men of a single community, cannot represent with accuracy a national spelling vocabulary or the opinions of the business men of the nation. National material is obtained by a wider sampling.

This rule is given as a precaution to investigators because the most ridiculous claims are made about the universality of results obtained from the most meagre amount of data. A teacher gets results from the study of his school and blossoms forth with a national course of study. Even parents have been known to generalize in matters of handling children by reference to a highly fanciful idea of the nature of a single child. But while we can expect no more of parents, we must demand of schoolmen that they make no claims of universality unless they have studied enough data to be sure that they are typical of the field about which they make the assertion.

Partitioning data. — In the second place, the amount of material which it is necessary to examine may be approximately gauged by partitioning it into small units and treating each unit separately until no new variations emerge. For instance, if we wish to determine the number of cases which must be examined for errors in grammar before we can be reasonably certain of typical results, the cases may be divided into lots of one thousand each and treated as units. That is, the first thousand will be tabulated as if it were all the cases. The classes of errors and the percentage of frequency will then be determined. A second lot is treated in a similar manner. If new classes or a quite different frequency is determined, one can be sure that neither lot is typical. The two may then be combined and the total of classes and frequency be obtained. A third lot may then be examined and added to the first and second. If this obtained result differs materially from the total of the first two, the data are not yet typical; if it does not materially differ the probabilities are that it is approaching trueness. Finally, if a fourth lot when added still makes no material modification, it is reasonably certain that the four thousand cases are typical. If greater accuracy is desired, a fifth or sixth thousand may be added to see if the results are steady.

An excellent example of inability to find a typical sample is described by Cook and O'Shea (p. 173). For, after dividing the letters of each of their correspondents into units of one thousand words, they found that in each thousand up to their limit of forty thousand words, new words were appearing without diminution in number per thousand. It is quite clear, therefore, that if they had been interested in getting the total writing vocabulary of one person, they could not stop at any point below forty thousand running words nor could they cease at that point. Their examination would have to continue until no significant additions were made.

Variants. — In the third place, analysis of the field to find the variants represented in the total sample is a necessary prerequisite of good sampling. Large totals of samples will not guarantee trueness to type unless all the variants are represented. A very large list of 50,000 grammatical errors selected in one city would not necessarily be typical of a national error list because there might be other errors found in other language areas. To obtain a national grammar-error list it would be necessary to analyze the language variants in America. This would lead us to the fact that we have Anglo-Saxon areas such as New England and the South, German and Scandinavian areas, areas affected by French and Spanish influences, other areas influenced by Italian and Polish immigration, and so on. Or, cities might be selected which obtain all these variants. Whether samplings are made from cosmopolitan cities or from national language areas, it is essential that all the variants be recognized and represented.

Similarly, in obtaining a national spelling list, an analysis of the spelling variants will show that since spel ing is dependent upon what people write about and that what they write about varies with the environment, an examination of environments would need to be made. This would result in several classes of variants, one of which is the large city, the small town, and the country, and another, the coast and the inland, and so forth. From these, samples should be drawn. In sampling practical arithmetic problems if the variants are occupational, as Wilson (p. 223) and Monroe (p. 219) have assumed, a good sample will have many occupations represented. The twelve books selected by experts for Horn (p. 251) and for Bassett (p. 251), to be typical would have to be selected after an analysis by experts of the fields the books represent so that each subdivision is included. In selecting history textbooks, Bagley and Rugg (p. 246) analyzed their problem by dividing the fifty-year period from which books were selected to be examined into four periods and chose books from each period. Bassett (p. 308), in sampling political platforms, analyzed the political situation into political parties and into progressive, conservative, and pivotal states and had representation from all.

Tabulation by units. — When the selections have been made, the method of partitioning by variants can be used to advantage. For instance, if errors in language are to be tabulated by units, these units may be language areas, and the cumulative results may be compared with the returns from single areas until important differences cease to be observed. This differs from mere partitioning into units in that the units selected are those which contain variants.

Extreme variations. — In such cases, the extremes in variable units should all be examined so that if the tabulation cease the results may have a theoretically higher degree of accuracy. For, obviously, if the less extreme variations are tabulated the totals may not be true. For example, it would be better to tabulate the errors in Polish centers and Anglo-Saxon New England than in Anglo-Saxon New England and the Anglo-Saxon South, since the latter two do not present extremes in variation.

By way of summary, it may be said that to select typical material by sampling, care must be taken to analyze the situation in order to detect all classes of variants so that representation of each may be secured; and also that the totals subjected to examination be broken into units, so that by cumulative totalings a point may be reached at which important differences in items and percentages cease to appear. A necessary check in every attempt to obtain typical material is provided by the query: Are all the variants included and is the number of cases sufficient?

§2—DESCRIPTION OF METHODS

In many of the studies abstracted in the second section of the text, the investigators are primarily interested in the results and to a less degree in the methods used. The omission or the sketchy treatment of descriptions of the methods by which the results were obtained is thus explained. But several cases are found of a very full description of methods of collection and tabulation of material. Outstanding examples are those of Capps (p. 188) and Anderson (p. 179).

In the older sciences, it is bad scientific form to omit mention of previous descriptions of methods. But in the studies which we are analyzing, the investigators have, with a few exceptions, preferred to pioneer in new fields because there are so many problems to be studied that no one wishes to cultivate ground already broken when he can have the fun of striking out a new furrow. But this does not excuse the pioneer from recording his methods with his results.

Criticism. — There are four reasons for providing a detailed statement of method by the investigator. In the first place, the one who reads his results may wish to criticize his method, and such criticism is made possible only by a detailed description of methods. Criticism of the methods of Cook and O'Shea (p. 173) could not have been made if they had not given a statement that all derived forms of verbs were omitted from the list, although ability to spell the root form does not correlate with ability to spell the derived forms, as, for instance, in the words *write* and *writing*. Horn's method (p. 251) of determining crucial life activities by reference to experts who selected twelve books may or may not be correct; but there would be no basis for criticism if he had not described his method of determination. Criticism of the methods of selecting oral grammatical errors is possible when it is stated that they were selected by teachers in odd moments; but no criticism would have been possible without this statement.

Verification. — In the second place, verification of results is not possible unless the procedure is so detailed that an independent investigator can follow it step by step. The failure of Horn (033) to state the rules by which he settled questions of doubt as to "movements, influences, etc.," makes it impossible to verify his results. Williams's seven rules (p. 238) for inclusion of mathematical material make easier the task of checking his results, although their adequacy can be settled only by actual checking and not by his own use. He knew what he meant by the rules, but another might not. It is entirely possible to send out the questionnaire of Coffman and Jessup (p. 216) to the superintendents of the same cities and counties because the authors report the questionnaire and the method of selecting the cities. While Miss Camerer (p. 326) does not state specifically the banks to which she sent her questionnaire, it would be possible to check her results by a random sampling of banks in the same states. The absence of a report of Allen's method of derivation of material from the job analysis of the machinist's trade (p. 274) (which, it must be recognized, is a course of study and not a statement of method), precludes a careful attempt at verification.

Improvement. — In the third place, the methods should be given to enable other investigators to use them as a starting point. If they are not given they are lost to the craft. Every investigator has worked out devices which, if known, would save the time of his colleagues. The devices used by Horn (p. 251), Capps (p. 188), Anderson (p. 179), and others for scoring are all of great benefit to others. The rules given by Wilson (p. 223) for collecting problems, the form of the report and many other items, including the questionnaires, are all valuable.

Standardization. — In the fourth place, a full description tends to standardize the method. The investigator who follows a method can save his own time and make his method just as clear by stating that he has "followed Smith" or has followed him with stated modifications, as by restating the method. Particularly will this tend to destroy the present tendency of teachers all over the country to report upon their results without seeming to be aware that others have worked in the same field and thus to make comparison of results impossible.

The reporting of methods in full is laborious and space-consuming, but is it absolutely essential for the growth of the technique and should be recognized as such by all who are sufficiently interested in the field to work in it.

§3—IMPLICIT USE AND EXPLICIT REFERENCE

When an investigator attempts to determine what items of a subject are "necessary to understand" some situation, he has undertaken a difficult task. This is revealed in its most striking form in history.

If we seek to find what history is necessary to fully appreciate the line "Some village Hampden here may rest," we at once recognize the explicit reference to the historical character Hampden. An intimate knowledge of his life and his fight for his convictions would undoubtedly add to the appreciation of the line. But when we inquire into the historical contexts of *village*, which might make its meaning richer, we have no specific reference to tie to and we are without a clue to start us on a search; or, perhaps, it is more accurate to say that we have so many clues that we are lost among them. The etymology of the term will enrich the meaning; so will our knowledge of the Anglo-Saxon village and of the country villages of to-day. Again, what flavor is added to the word *rest?* Will the history of the word enrich it? What are the fragments of information and experiences which have cohered to the word throughout the life of the reader? Is there a common, standard, contextual meaning for the word, or does each individual have an individual context? And whether the latter or the former, how can these be determined? The answer to these questions and others of like difficulty will provide a technique for determining the history "necessary to fully understand."

This difficulty has led all the investigators in history to collect explicit references and to omit its implicit uses. Indeed Bagley (p. 262) frankly recognized the difficulty and substituted the claim that the history we need is the history that is taught in school in textbooks. But this is clearly not an answer to the question, which still deserves investigation.

In the same situation are other "background" subjects, such as sociology, economics, chemistry, physics, and mathematics. Of some of these it is easier to determine the "service" contributions. An examination of Williams' work (p. 238), for instance, shows that he has obtained all or most of the mathematics explicitly and implicitly integrated with freshman chemistry. But, in the main, all studies have confined themselves to explicit references.

§4—THE SPECIALIST *versus* THE LAYMAN

Attention should be called to the fact mentioned by Monroe (p. 219) that in analyzing material to determine the curriculum a clear distinction must be kept in view constantly between expert operations and lay operations. In connection with the arithmetic of the grocery store it is apparent that the consumer needs one level of arithmetical skill and the salesman a much higher level, since the former merely checks up simple purchases while the latter must know mark-ups, discounts, bookkeeping, and so forth. Again, the things which a consumer needs to know about electrical appliances are not so highly specialized as those which an electrician must know. The shoe manufacturer needs to know much more about shoes and leathers than does the salesperson or the customer.

This fact has profound significance in the derivation of arithmetic and other subjects from the occupations. For, since children are to be consumers of the products of these occupations, it would be quite unnecessary and, indeed, quite impossible for them to master a curriculum based upon the needs of those who follow the occupation. An arithmetic curriculum made up of the common elements found in a wide range of occupations might or might not be sufficiently near to what is needed; but what is needed is determined by an analysis of the operations in arithmetic by

consumers and not by production specialists. The highly specialized information needed to follow the occupation is given in
elective vocational courses, and does not belong to the general
course given to children who later will be experts in only one line
and laymen in many.

An interesting example of this difference is found in the distinction which is made in engineering information needed by
executives and by experts, between what a civil engineer needs
to know about civil engineering and what an executive in an
engineering concern needs to know. Obviously the former needs
to know how to perform the task, while the latter needs to know
only enough about it to understand and pass upon it. What
this amount is may be difficult to determine, but it is clearly not
equal to that needed by the expert.

The content of all subjects of the elementary school should
be based upon the layman's needs.

§5—Short Cuts

When masses of material of great proportions or methods
of analysis of great laboriousness are involved, it is important
to seek for methods which will shorten labor without incurring
serious danger of error.

Such methods have not been developed in great number,
but two cases are of interest. It was discovered by application
of correlation formulæ in tabulating the frequency of occurrence
of geographical references, that the most tedious part of the labor
could be safely omitted. As described in Study 39 (p. 270), an effort
was made to determine all the geographical references to places
in thirteen issues of *The Literary Digest*. These included names
of countries, and localities, names of people, nicknames, pronouns, and distributed terms. But it was found that names of
countries and of peoples, and the distributed terms, had a correlation of .96 with the totals. Therefore, for the approximate
results necessary for a determination of relative emphasis, the
three items were sufficient. It would have been interesting in

this study to determine the correlation between these items and the items found by ignoring more than one mention of countries, peoples, and distributed terms per paragraph and per article. If the correlation were found to be high, additional labor would have been saved.

A second method is used by Cook and O'Shea (Study 3, described on p. 173). The material to be examined can be sampled by being divided into small portions and each portion worked up until no new classes of items are added and the percentages do not materially change.

Undoubtedly many other devices, unknown to the writer, have been demonstrated. That there is a need for them is apparent to any one who has done much work of this sort.

§6—THE QUESTIONNAIRE

The questionnaire is widely used as a means of collecting information; Wooters (p. 245), Wilson (p. 213), Coffman and Jessup (p. 216), and Miss Camerer (p. 326) all use the usual forms. If we consider directions to be a form of questionnaire we find other examples in all the language studies, in Horn (p. 251), Anderson (p. 179), Capps (p. 188), and others. Its use is so frequent and of such importance that its limitations and the safeguards necessary for reliable use should be pointed out.

Limitations. — There are five limitations. In the *first* place the written questionnaire is intrinsically difficult to fill out. Reports show that frequently an office force will spend one or two days on a single questionnaire. In any case, whether the amount of time is long or short, the questionnaire requires unusual labor because it frequently cuts across the order of thinking of the one who answers, and asks for information which is not easily at hand in the files, the records, or the memory. In the *second* place, the questions may not be clearly understood by the one who answers. The sender has one idea of what his terms mean; the receiver may get a quite different idea and, therefore, in his answers will fail to reply satisfactorily. In the *third* place, the same misunderstanding may occur when the sender interprets the answers: he may give the terms a content which the writer did not intend. In the *fourth* place, the sampling may be poor. Even when the original list has been carefully sampled, the replies will not be a true sample if all do not reply, because only certain types of people answer questionnaires. Recently a questionnaire on store service was sent out to one thousand customers selected at random, and one hundred and fifty replied. The sender does not now know the extent to which the replies were representative, for they came only from people who write with facility and who are interested in the questions asked. In the *fifth* place, questionnaires are often answered by people who do not give the exact facts. This may be due to lack of knowledge or to haste. Wilson's questionnaire (p. 213) to business men on the uses of arithmetic is probably subject to both sources of error. If the business men received the questionnaire in the mail or answered it in the office, it was filled out, in all probability, at the same rapid rate at which letters are dictated and proportionally little thought would be given to it. Or, even if more attention than this is put upon it, it is a question whether even with much thought a business man not trained in such matters actually knows how much use he makes of operations in arithmetic.

Remedies. — Several devices are of use in making the questionnaire more reliable. In the first place, before one is sent out, it should be tried out on a few people. This preliminary test has several advantages. The answers show whether or not the questions are understood and are properly framed. In the second place, a questionnaire should, as far as possible, be so constructed as to be answered by "yes" or "no" or checks. The one used by Coffman and Jessup (p. 216) is of this sort. However, it is frequently impossible so to arrange material that this can be done; the sender may not have the data at hand to enable him to make the analysis prerequisite to framing analytical questions.

Interviews. — This leads us to the third device. In all cases the oral questionnaire is preferable to the written form. This means that when the sender becomes an interviewer and asks the questions orally he will obtain more reliable answers. He can clear up misconceptions of his meaning, and can supplement his questions by others which will elicit more definite answers. The chief objection to the oral questionnaire is the labor required of the interviewer; but this is amply compensated for by the greater trustworthiness of the information, the comparative ease with which the answerer is able to provide it, and the greater amount of time he will spend upon it. Answerers who dislike to write, and would spend very little time on written answers, are glad to devote considerably more time to an oral interview.

Recently, the superiority of the interview over the written answer was shown in a study of fifty cases. Seven questions were asked of fifty executives, among them being the following: How do you show your subordinates that you are interested in them? One answer to this question was "By being interested in them."

Clearly this reply is useless because it does not tell how he *shows* them that he is interested in them. Now in the written questionnaire there would be no recourse from this, because the answer could not be easily followed up. But — equally obviously — the person conducting an oral interview could at once follow it up with a more searching question to bring out the missing information. This is what actually occurred in this instance; the executive stated, upon further questioning, that he helped them to get better positions, even outside his department, and fought for increases in salary for them.

Further, in this same study, when the written answers had all been turned in, the same people were interviewed orally. The interviewers wrote up their reports upon the same questions asked of the same people, and it was found that the returns on the oral were 350 per cent fuller than those on the written. Specifically, fifty executives gave in *writing* forty-two suggestions (counting duplicates), and gave *orally* 184 suggestions (counting duplicates).

Needless to say, senders of questionnaires who are wise will cultivate an apologetic attitude toward those upon whom they wish to thrust the labor of writing answers, and will imply appreciation of the effort to be expended. This usually includes a promise to send the findings to anyone interested; and when such a promise is made it should be scrupulously observed. The writer, who always sends such replies to his correspondents, felt the thrill of a good deed done when recently one of them wrote to say that she was startled to receive a reply because in all her experience it was the first time that she had ever heard again from the material she had furnished.

So far as graduate schools and schools of education are concerned, no questionnaire should be issued by a student which has not been passed upon by some officer. If this is not done, too many may be sent out to a small clientele, some foolish ones may be issued, and some may be poorly phrased. Since there is a technique of the questionnaire, someone who knows it should supervise the issuance.

CHAPTER XIV

THE PROJECT AND THE CURRICULUM

§1—INTRODUCTION

The project and interest. — The term *project* is used to cover a narrower field than that sponsored by Kilpatrick,* who characterizes the essential quality of the project as purposeful. By Kilpatrick's definition any act which is "whole-heartedly purposeful" becomes a project. This is true of making a dress, running a newspaper, listening to a story, or working an original in geometry. In short, it is fair, I think, to say that upon this basis any school problem, example, topic, drill exercise, test, review, application, illustration, demonstration, or practicum becomes a project as soon as it has been whole-heartedly motivated. Therefore, every school activity may be a project, providing the learner prosecutes it with a "dominant purpose."

As soon as we attempt to use this definition as a method of classifying activities, we are completely at sea. Is making a dress a project? This we cannot tell until we have watched the individual engaged in the operation. When we find that the activity is "whole-heartedly purposeful" it becomes a project by the definition, but it is not a project until that point is reached. The twelve-year-old girl who has been sewing on an apron for the past six months in school, but who is not whole-heartedly interested in the activity, is not working on a project. But her companion, who loves the work and joyfully sews upon an identical apron, has a project.

Moreover, an activity might, by this definition, be a project to-day and cease to be one to-morrow. Our girl who has spent six

---

The Project Method, Bureau of Publications, Teachers College, 1919; Teachers College Record, September, 1921.

months upon an apron may have selected it with great enthusiasm
and worked on it with vigor for two months. Then her interest
may have disappeared for one reason or another. So, for two
months making the apron was a project and for the other four
months it was not.

The truth is that in this case no definition is adequate which
seeks to classify subject matter upon the basis of interest alone.
Interest is *subjective*, dependent upon a series of factors other
than the content of the subject matter itself; whereas to make an
adequate classification, the factors according to which the classifying is done must be *objective*.

The project and the problem. — It happens, curiously enough,
that those who claim to be satisfied with the limited definition
based on "whole-hearted interest," and to follow it, when they
come to actual projects tend to select activities which are all
characterized by still another element: the problematic — they
involve relatively complicated and extensive thinking. This is all
unconsciously a nearer approach to an adequate definition, because
the project is, in addition to being "whole-heartedly purposeful,"
undoubtedly of the problem variety. The student starts with a
purpose whose realization is reached by thought and planning
rather than by mere habit. But, even so, we have not yet embraced in our definition the whole of the essence of the project.

The natural setting. — As we know, the project came into
general education through agriculture. Prior to the entrance of
the "home-project idea" into agriculture, corn was studied out
of a textbook, with a few experiments in the laboratory. But
with the introduction of this idea, the boundaries of the schoolroom were enlarged, so that the student, as part of his process of
learning about corn, had to grow corn in a cornfield, under the
concrete conditions of the farm. All home projects sought to do
the same thing, that is to say, sought to provide conditions for
school work which should not be different from conditions outside of school work.

This is essentially what is meant by the "natural setting."
If the project is to be used as a vehicle for the study of arith-

metic, or composition, or physiology, in its "natural setting," the problems studied must be carried on under conditions as nearly as possible identical with those outside the school.

It is quite evident that under these circumstances a student may or may not be interested in the project. If he is interested at all, he is likely to be very much interested, but presumably he will not always be interested, since outside the school not every person is interested in everything that he does.

In conclusion, we may say that for curriculum purposes an adequate statement is found in the definition elaborated by Stevenson,* that "The project is a problematic act carried to completion in its natural setting."

§2—The Project as Curriculum Content

Life activities. — The whole trend of our treatment of the curriculum leads us to the position that it is based upon life projects. The activities whose analysis we have insisted upon are essentially life projects. The individual is dominated by systems of interest, for the fulfillment of which he carries on mental and physical activity. We analyze these, and by complicated processes teach him how to carry them on effectively.

As we have seen, our first task is to determine which of these projects are of most importance and to collect the various methods of performance. Our second duty is to teach such of these in school as are not learned better outside the school.

In teaching this material we may use subject organizations or we may use the project. If we use the latter, then the school projects must parallel life projects. We may transfer the project from life to the schoolroom, or we may enlarge the schoolroom to include life.

This would be a simple task if the period of schooling were long enough to include all the life projects, but actually it becomes so complicated that several modifications must be made.

*The Project Method of Teaching, Macmillan, 1921.

The selection of projects. — Because only a few of many life projects can be taught in school, it is necessary to set up selective machinery. The analyses of life activities and their control give us a great mass of information, skills, and duties to master, and in teaching we have to determine which are the most important and which the most difficult. We can then determine with considerable definiteness what items of subject matter must be learned in obtaining efficient control of certain life activities. Not being a question of opinion, it can be objectively determined.

We face, however, three or four possibilities. We might teach all the life activities with concurrent training in the subject matter which gives control. But, since this is not possible, we have to make a selection from life activities. When we decide which to select, we have to take into account the subject matter which has been derived from the totality of life activities. In other words, it is not enough that our school projects shall parallel life activity. We must be sure that in the selection of the school projects we are giving the proper amount of training in subject matter in order that the pupils may be prepared to meet the larger range of life projects.

Stating the matter in another way, we may say that when subject matter has been determined from an analysis of a large number of life activities we may upon the basis of this analysis know which subject matter is of most importance. When we come to select projects we must, if we are to use the project method successfully, see that the selected projects will give the proper amount of training in the important elements of the subject. We have to see, for instance, that our projects give the proper amount of drill in arithmetic or in spelling. If we do not do this, but merely pick out some projects which parallel some of the life projects, we may conceivably fail to give the student the training he needs for carrying on other important life projects; but if we see that our school projects both parallel life activities and include sufficient emphasis of certain important parts of the subject matter, we shall then be upon safe ground.

This brief statement will be made clear by reference to Fuller's study (p. 300). Assuming that he found the most important projects in home repair to be the fifty-seven shown in his first table, his next step required him to determine what tool processes were involved in carrying out these projects. As a result, we find in his fourth table that screwing occurs fifteen times; nailing, fourteen times; filing, twelve times; sawing, eleven; etc. If it is not possible (as it is not) to teach the fifty-seven projects analyzed, then a selection of projects has to be made. Now, my point is that the selection cannot be made at random, or based merely upon the interests of children. They must be so chosen that the graduates of the course obtain skill in those processes which are most useful. It is absolutely essential that the teacher shall know the amount of skill that is needed in screwing, nailing, filing, and sawing, and shall select home-repair projects to be performed which will provide a sufficient amount of these and other processes. As a practical measure it is, therefore, wise for projects to be supplemented by such amounts of drill as are necessary to give an adequate degree of skill.

This naturally involves the introduction of difficulty of learning as a principle of selection. In some cases those principles most frequently found are learned so easily that little attention needs to be given to them. Others, occurring less frequently, may need to be emphasized because of their difficulty.

These situations show clearly that the selection of school projects cannot be lightly undertaken if they are to form the sole basis of curriculum content. It is not sufficient that they be merely projects occurring outside the school or that they be of maximum interest to children: they must parallel home projects, but at the same time the projects as selected must provide the proper amount of skill and training in the processes and activities. What the "proper amount" shall be depends partly upon importance and partly upon difficulty.

Miss Wells, in her admirable book,* attempts to show what skills, information, and attitudes were contained in a series of

*A Project Curriculum, Lippincott, 1921.

projects. The arithmetic for the first three grades, for instance, looks very impressive. But as one examines it he raises the query, "How closely does this arithmetic provide the skill upon given topics which will best meet all natural, out-of-school conditions?" This the author does not answer — nor can anyone until a very comprehensive study of life activities shall have been made.

The alternative to the use of the project as a curriculum unit is the school subject. In the latter case the pupils study arithmetic, geography, and spelling. In the former case they study, following Miss Wells, for instance, playing fair, animals, flowers, peanut stands, side shows, playing city, playing house, playing store, police department, etc.

The Revolution. — Nothing can show more vividly than the two foregoing sentences the revolution which would be made in school procedure if projects were substituted for subjects. Arithmetic, geography, and spelling would disappear and in their places we would have such projects as personal cleanliness, the decoration of the home, the writing of letters, the growing of flowers, city sanitation, city beautification, purchasing, etc. Conceivably these might be listed as *projects under subjects*, but if the project idea be logically carried out, subjects must disappear except where, for pedagogical reasons, those service subjects which are difficult to learn incidentally are taught by themselves.

But it must be insistently emphasized that, whether we teach by subject or by project, subject material is derived from life projects. We may discard the school project as a unit of instruction, but we cannot discard life projects as a basis for deriving the material of the curriculum. To discover what shall be included in the subject of grammar we begin, let us say, with the life project of correct speech, and derive the broken rules and the necessary grammar as shown in Study 10. To determine what tool processes to teach in manual arts we analyze home repairs, or some other activities, and derive the processes. Keeping fit leads to hygiene. From hygiene we go to physiology, and from that we derive biology to understand the physiological facts.

There is a constant procession of derivatives from the primary activities.

That the material so derived differs from the conventional subject material is clear, but that the amount of change is great is sometimes evident and sometimes not. For instance, in spelling, undoubtedly the lists based upon the recent studies are very materially different from those found in the textbooks. In grammar, the studies indicate that when correction of errors of speech is made the basis, the content of the grammar is lessened only by the omission of the more difficult and detailed parts of the subject. The mathematics necessary for chemistry is found to be very much less than the amount which chemists have usually thought to be necessary. In the study in commercial engineering made by Strong (p. 292) it was found that the addition of a very large field of information concerning the handling of men was necessary, and that a considerable decrease could be made in the fundamental subjects such as mathematics and chemistry.

The content of the subjects — arithmetic, geography, and history — is very difficult to determine. The great mass of activities common to all people irrespective of vocation must be determined and then analyzed. Methods of control must be collected. Some of the subject content will be found in these methods, and the rest of it will be found as a derivative from other primary subjects. From these two sources, by direct inclusion and indirect derivation, the material of each school subject is drawn.

§3—INFORMATION *versus* CONDUCT

The curriculum which is so organized that life projects become school projects necessarily involves two types of change.

Increase in range of subject matter. — In the first place it adds an enormous mass of method from which selection must be made. For instance, if, instead of making information about rules and definitions the function of grammar study, the correction of error becomes the purpose of that study, there is needed not only a mass of information about rules and definitions, but also an assemblage of methods by which the children may learn to set up the correct habit. In a very real sense the project of correct speech involves both grammar and psychology. Without question the methods of developing good speech are as essentially a part of the subject of language and grammar as are the rules and definitions of grammar. Not only are they an essential part, but they are if anything more important than are the rules and definitions.

Similarly, when we consider hygiene as a subject which involves conduct rather than as one which adds to information, we find that the psychology of health and happiness becomes a part of the school training. The student must certainly know the rules of hygiene — but he must also practice them. The teacher's task becomes not merely that of giving important information, but equally of seeing that he puts the information into practice. When conduct displaces information as the aim of education, the methods of setting up right action after the necessary information has been learned become an integral part of the curriculum.

In the second place, since conduct is made an element in the educative process the natural setting is included in the curriculum. As a school exercise, the making of a waist consists of three factors: the material, the design, and the sewing; but if it becomes a project (*i.e.*, is carried on as an act in its natural setting) several new factors enter. The student has to consider the matter of the preference of the family, the amount of money at her disposal so as to decide whether to make a general-purpose waist or one for special occasions, the amount of time she can spend making it and, therefore, the elaborateness of the design, the likelihood that the fashion may change before the article is worn out, and so on.

The same thing is shown in the case of the boy who is lacking in ambition. As a school exercise the method of handling this is to provide him with reading material showing the advantages of ambition, with stories of the ambition of great men, and with talks upon the value of the virtue. As a project, in which he is not descrted until he has become ambitious, it is

necessary for him to diagnose his failure to show ambition and
to seek to remove these causes one by one. He must be watched
for specific situations in which ambition functions, and he must
be provided with devices which will enable him to show ambition in these situations.

All of these illustrations indicate that when conduct becomes
an aim in education the situation becomes much more complicated and the subject material more diversified. Moreover, since
conduct is specific rather than general and grows by small working
units rather than by general principles, it is necessary that a great
mass of detail be added. Character is built step by step under
situations in which great principles affect character only by
specific application to specific situations, so that the amount of
material studied will need to be doubled.

Change of boundary. — In the third place, if the project
method is used as a medium of instruction the school plan will
be revolutionized, as has been done in the case of vocational
agriculture. Here, where the home project is used, many startling
changes are found. The school year is twelve months long and
the teacher takes his month's vacation in February. The reference
library becomes more important than textbooks. The school
day is changed from the 9-to-4 period to irregular hours, during
which the boys may be at home or in school or even trading work
with each other. Automobiles become a necessary part of school
equipment to enable the teacher to visit his classes. The training
and equipment of the teacher must be more practical and wider
in range than is necessary in the school-subject plan. Nor is
this peculiar to agricultural projects. Health projects necessitate
the development of procedure for carrying the school influence
into the life outside the school. It is very apparent that the
movement for the use of the school nurse and for health clubs,
for propagating the work among parents, will all have their
definite place in the school work when health has been placed
upon the project basis.

Further illustration is not necessary to show what revolutionary results would follow the whole-hearted use of the project

method of teaching, results so expensive and difficult of achieving that the matter cannot be settled without mature deliberations and fundamental changes. We shall undoubtedly find that some material can best be taught by projects and that other material will not lend itself easily to project instruction. If consideration is given to the economical use of the physical plant it will be found that certain projects may be taught in one school and not in another and that some projects cannot be taught in any schools.

Summary. — The deciding facts in the relation of the project to the curriculum are these: *First*, a project curriculum may or may not be taught as a collection of project units, but *second*, even when taught as a collection of subject units, the subject material is derived from life projects. Curriculum content is derived from an analysis of life activities and ideals even though it be not taught by the school project method. In the third place, the change from the ideal of information to the ideal of conduct will necessitate a wider use of the project method and many fundamental changes in the organization of school work.

Chapter XV

THE ELEMENTARY SCHOOL CURRICULUM

§1—Introduction

The climax of all thought about curriculum construction is reached in the curriculum of the elementary. schools of the nation in which some twenty million are educated each year. Here will be found the testing ground of effort and the verification and evaluation of methods and curriculum content.

Unfortunately for ease of treatment, the field is so filled with complexities and problems that the determination of the exact content of the curriculum is beyond the possibility of immediate settlement. In order to determine the curriculum it is necessary, on the one hand, to apply the principles laid down in the foregoing pages and, on the other, to consider a number of specific problems which have emerged in the discussions of the last few years.

The principles. — The principles to be applied are simply stated. The activities and ideals of society must be determined, evaluated, and selected; the best methods of performing the activities under the domination of appropriate ideals must be collected; and the material so determined must be presented at the psychological moment in the life of a child. These principles need no further elaboration at this point since they are the topics of the text, but attention can profitably be given to a few of the specific forms in which they have appeared in the expository statements and controversial discussions of the past few years. Specifically, it is important to consider, first, subjects *versus* activities; second, normal child activity *versus* normal adult activity as the basis for the curriculum; and third, ease of learning as a curriculum factor.

147

§2—SUBJECTS *versus* ACTIVITIES

Activities precede subjects. — In order of time, activities precede subjects. When, in the course of events, barter and exchange had progressed to a point where quantity became important, a system of numbering was invented. Geographies were first written after generations of men had traveled in pursuit of adventure and riches. Chemistry grew out of the effort to obtain a limitless amount of gold by the simple transmutation of the baser metals.

Subjects are abstracted from activities. — When concepts such as "number" or "place" have been discovered it has been customary to abstract them from their concrete settings and to study them in isolation. Number, in the guise of mathematics, is an outstanding example of the isolation of a factor from activities and of a later magnificent exploration of what is implied in the product so abstracted. It likewise provides brilliant examples of the later use of certain portions of such abstractions in the handling of concrete activities.

We have here the age-old distinction between the organized fields of knowledge and their use in human conduct. From all the activities we abstract the concept of number, and study it as a whole in the form of arithmetic. We add, subtract, multiply, and divide by means of symbols without immediate regard to their influence upon human relations. Skill is secured and technical information is mastered in isolation from concrete situations.

Social value of subjects. — But always behind the operation there lies in the minds of all (except the specialists) the significant hope that the technique may be used in the control of life activities. The concept is drawn out of activity for *study* and is then returned to activity to *improve* the performance of activity. We begin by bartering and use number, then we abstract number and study it, and finally we return with the results of this study of number to the activity of bartering with the hope of making improvements. Such is the *social* justification of the specialized study of any subject.

This simple procedure becomes the topic of heated controversy according as partisans lay emphasis on one or the other of these two points of view. Subjects in more or less abstract form have for the most part, until recently, formed the material of the school, and teachers have not held their applications to be of significant importance. Arithmetic has been studied, while its applications, buying and selling, have been partially neglected. Spelling has been learned without sufficient regard to the writing of themes and letters. Grammar has been taught without attention to its use in the improvement of the errors of speech. Physiology has been memorized without relation to the laws of hygiene. And tool processes have been learned without application to construction and home repair.

Keenly conscious of the failure to apply the mastered subjects to practical subjects, educators have instituted a new movement for the emphasis of application. This has resulted in what we have described as the project.

The neglect of subjects. — Owing to the notorious tendency of the voluble part of our pedagogical constituency to drop the old and familiar when in full pursuit of the new, the subjects are at the present time feeling the neglect (at least on paper) from which the staid portions of the profession have in the past protected them. Already curricula are now being constructed as projects in which theoretically the subjects as such do not appear. In Meriam's significant experiment in Missouri, for instance, the subject titles of arithmetic and writing, spelling and grammar do not occur in the program of study. The children are supposed to learn what they may need of these subjects as they need it for carrying on their activities, and it is found that when pupils of this school enter the conventional elementary or high school it is possible for them to keep abreast with those who have learned the conventional curriculum.

It is perfectly clear to me after a number of years of fairly close study of the Missouri situation, that the failure to teach portions of these subjects as independent material is answerable for definite losses of time. For instance, occasions arose when, if the teacher had not surreptitiously introduced grammar or arithmetic, the students would not have gained enough of the necessary skill to enable them to save their own time. When children began the study of grammar in the high school without having had any in the grades a very heavy strain was placed upon mothers and fathers in helping the children to catch up. In the lower grades there were cases when instructions in the phonic construction of the word would have materially aided children with weak memories to learn to read with desirable speed.

It is philosophically impossible to adhere to one extreme or the other. There are advantages in subject study which arise from the absence of concrete items to interfere with the learning of bonds and relations. There are advantages in project study which arise from the intensifying of motivation and the improvement of conduct. On theoretical grounds, therefore, any efficient system of instruction would include both methods of attack, until on scientific grounds it should be demonstrated that one is superior to the other.

As has been pointed out elsewhere, some subjects need less independence of operation than do others. Handwriting and spelling may be learned incidentally to a much more complete degree than can arithmetic. This subject, and all others with a closely knit logical connection, are less amenable to incidental treatment than such loosely organized subjects as handwriting and spelling.

Primary and derived subjects. — The derivation of the subjects from the activities is made still more complicated by the existence of two classes of subjects. As has been seen elsewhere, we have *primary* subjects which are found in the job analysis of life activities, and *derived* subjects which are obtained by the processes of derivation from the primary subjects. Hygiene is a primary subject since the rules of hygiene operate directly in the control of health. Service physiology is derived from hygiene because it explains why the rules of hygiene operate as they do. Civics is another primary subject and from it parts of service history are derived. Language is likewise a primary subject and from it grammar, handwriting, and spelling are derived. As a matter of fact, most of the subjects in the elementary course of study are derived subjects, and before the content can be determined it is necessary to determine the primary subjects by analysis of the activities.

This fact shows clearly the magnitude of the task of reorganizing the elementary curriculum. We find it possible to eliminate the obviously useless from the subjects by a partial reorganization and thereby to perform a useful service, but to secure an objective basis for a complete reorganization we must carry through an analysis of life activities. The absence of such an analysis undermines the validity of any comparisons between what the curriculum is and what it ought to be.

As a matter of fact, and as has been said above, we must determine the subject material from an analysis of life projects, and determine it in sufficient detail so that we may know which elements of the subjects are of most importance and require the most attention, either because of importance or because of difficulty of learning. Then, school projects must be so selected that they will give drill and instruction on each of the items so as properly to prepare the student to use them in the broader range of life activities. School projects cannot be selected haphazard. They are controlled by two factors: on the one hand they must parallel life activities, and on the other hand they must include the items of the subjects in their proper proportions.

§3—Normal Child Activities *versus* Normal Adult Activities

The adult. — The traditional method of arriving at the curriculum has been to select adult subjects organized for mature people. In early days the schools taught the quadrivium, the trivium, and the classics in essentially the same form as these were used by experts. Within the memory of those now teaching, the textbooks in grammar, arithmetic, history, and morals differed from the treatises of the scholarly only in their smaller number of pages.

The child. — Such treatment of subject matter obviously takes no account of the laws of learning or of interest, and the inevitable has happened — the champion of the child has arisen to demand that the form in which the material is taught shall be determined by the needs, interests, and ability of children rather than of adults. Such a requirement looks very simple on its face, but as soon as it is subjected to analysis a number of tangles appear. Meriam* cuts one Gordian knot by asserting that the curriculum should be based upon the "normal activity of children." But we find difficulty in determining what is "normal activity" for children. It is not easy to say even what is normal activity for adults, yet the task is not impossible. The housekeeper's activities, both mental and physical, are ninety per cent standardized; the degree of variation in them is small, because physical circumstances determine them to a considerable extent.

It is a more difficult problem, however, to determine, with anything like the same degree of certainty, a list of normal child activities. The little daughter of the housekeeper may in part have duties prescribed as practical activities, as when she helps her mother, but for the most part practical conditions do not enter. The range of play activity is limitless, and so is the range of reading. Anything can be played and any book can be read. Yet in a very real sense normal child activity is determined by normal adult activity. The normal life of a Chinese child differs from the normal activities of an American child because, and necessarily because, adult Chinese civilization differs from adult American civilization. As a matter of fact, those who lay down a curriculum which is said to follow normal child life either copy a child life which is already a copy of adult life or they make their own guess about important adult activities and prescribe them for children. From *Emile* to *Schools of Tomorrow*, the educators who base their curricula upon normal child activities either consciously or unconsciously use adult activities as a guide.

The balance. — Here, as always in educational problems, we have two forces which act together to determine the order of the

*Child Life and the Curriculum, The World Book Company, 1921.

curriculum; neither alone will produce a well balanced product. The adult curriculum must be adapted to child needs and abilities, and children's interests must be molded by a consideration of the problems which they will face as adults. When Meriam, for instance, claims that "efficiency now is the best preparation for efficiency later," the assertion will hold in direct proportion to the parallel maintained between the skills, ideals, and activities used "now" and "later." Much remains to be proved before it can be claimed with certainty that "efficiency now" in Russian childhood is the best preparation for "efficiency later" in American adult activities.

This Meriam recognizes when he says that "adult activities in simpler form make up the lives of little people." But I should prefer to turn the statement around: instead of saying that in improving their normal activities* we bring them in touch with a great range of adult activities, I should say that in touching a great range of adult activities we improve the normal activity of children. For, whether we do it directly or indirectly, the patterns of education are adult activities.

Child activities are modifications of adult activities that are produced by differences in ability, interests, and character; but the core of the activities is the same. The social recreations, æsthetic interests, and courtesies are of the same sort among children and adults, but because children are less able, they handle simpler forms than the adults use. Because their character, judgment, and wisdom differ in degree, the subject matter of the curriculum must be modified; the psychological moment in the program of studies for dealing with activities is moved forward or back as the children's interests change.

On the other hand, if we approach the problem of directing and training child interests and instincts from the child's point of view, it is apparent that there must be considerable symboliza-

*Bonser, *The Elementary School Curriculum*, The Macmillan Company, Chapter I; Coursault, *Principles of Education*, Silver, Burdett & Company, Chapter XII; Dewey, *The Child and the Curriculum*, University of Chicago Press.

tion of adult activities and ideals. The form that the adult needs may not suit the child, though any modification of the adult form for the child must reach the adult solution. The adult may be induced by *argument* to tell the truth, while the child, who would be unmoved by argument, may be deeply impressed by a *narrative* conveying the same idea; but the end in view for both must be truth-telling — the solution of the situation is essentially the same for both. Modifications must necessarily be made because of the differences in ability, ideals, and activities; but the point to be remembered and emphasized is that these are modifications of adult activities and not independent entities depending upon some concept called "normal child life."

The same idea appears in another guise when an attempt is made to build a curriculum upon the basis of instincts. Here again the program of instinct development or control is determined ultimately by adult instincts and activities. Whatever may be the material used in manipulation of the instincts, those who train either consciously or unconsciously keep the perfect adult in mind. The learner is trained to-day so that while living his life at this moment he will not be lacking to-morrow. If this is not done then the training is chaotic and ineffective.

§4—Ease of Learning

The amount of time devoted in a curriculum to items of a subject is determined by the importance of the material and its difficulty. That is to say, when we have decided that an item is of enough importance to be learned, the amount of time given to it is determined by how long it takes to learn it. Consequently, while the inclusion of an item in the curriculum may be largely, though not completely, determined by frequency of use, the emphasis upon the included items is largely determined by frequency and persistency of error.

The case is not handled so simply as the foregoing statement would suggest, because something depends upon the standard of satisfactory learning. Some items have to be learned until they are automatic. For others, the mere gaining of a general idea is sufficient. And for still other material, a learning sufficient for temporary use but not for permanent retention is adequate. But speaking generally and without qualifications, it is approximately correct to say what when an item has been considered of enough importance to be included in the curriculum, the amount of time spent upon it will be determined by the difficulty of learning it.

Ease of learning affects the sequence of the material in the curriculum. Obviously, other things being equal, the easier items are taught first; and, other things not being equal (as for instance, when items of somewhat greater difficulty possess very much greater interest), interest rather than ease will be the deciding factor in placing the item.

The enormous importance of the evaluation of difficulties is pointed out by Allen in *The Instructor, The Man, and The Job*, by Trilling and others in *Home Economics in American Schools*, and by many other writers. Part of the technique worked out in vocational education requires the instructor to list the tasks to be performed in a job according to the ease of instruction with the expectation that the simple material should be taught first.

§5—PARTIAL REORGANIZATION

When school faculties are confronted with a periodical modification of the course of study, the query naturally arises, How can all these methods help us, since we cannot radically reorganize our curriculum? Such a question is fair and the answer can be given rather concisely. While a radical reorganization may not be practicable, it is possible to work over the current curriculum and eliminate and add according to selected functions. Particularly is it possible to add project and multi-problem material to supplement the subject material. When certain life activities are important but are not included within the subjects it is possible then to add them in the form of projects or of problems.

A plan. — A plan for the reorganization of the course of study by a faculty which has worked under practical conditions, runs as follows:

Place the study in the hands of a steering committee with a representative from each subject and one or more from the administration. The function of this committee will be (1) to lay down the rules of procedure, (2) to determine by conference the desires of the faculty as a whole and the ideals to be developed in the system, and (3) to pass upon the general adequacy of the subject material after it has been worked over by committees. On this steering committee should be one person for whom the whole project is the major duty. He should be, *ex officio*, a member of all committees. He should, if possible, have the major assistance of the bureau of research, if there be one in the system. In any case, he should have by him all the studies in curriculum material, the course of study used in systems of size about equal to that of his own, findings of expert commissions, and a collection of practical projects.

The membership of the steering committee should include a chairman of each of the subject committees. Each subject committee should be composed of teachers of the subject and particularly, in addition, of teachers of other subjects. This latter group is included because those who teach a subject are inclined to magnify it at the expense of the education of the child, while those who do not teach it are likely to be better able to view it in an objective way and give it its proper emphasis. Consequently, in a committee composed of both types, the teachers of each subject are usually its advocates, and the remainder of the committee are more likely to sit in a judicial capacity upon the argument used for it.

The function of the subject committee is to determine the objectives of the subject in relation to the major objectives of the whole school system as determined by the steering committee. When the objectives of the subject have been determined, the revision of the subject is necessarily left in the hands of those who teach it. They are responsible for the details of the subject committee's findings, and they report to it for review as to the adequacy of the material in fulfilling the objectives already agreed upon.

There may be twelve of these committees: arithmetic, geography, history, reading and literature, language and grammar, writing and spelling, art, music, physical education, home economics, civics, and the handicrafts. To these, others may be added as needed, or combinations may be made.

Particularly, there should be a committee on coördination whose duty it is to collect a comprehensive group of projects and multi-problems. They could place their material at the command of the various subject committees and could add to the curriculum large and comprehensive projects which do not belong particularly in one subject or another.

Administratively, the chairman of all committees upon whom the major portion falls should at the proper moment be relieved of other duties, since it is impossible to accomplish any adequate amount of revision if this is added to the other regular work of the individual. Unless the school provides for such plan in its budget, it is extremely doubtful whether the work should be undertaken. The course of study cannot be revised as a side issue. Even if undivided attention be given to it, the task is still difficult.

§6—Some Curriculum Studies

Much work of a valuable sort remains to be done in the investigation of individual subjects without waiting for the radical reorganization of the whole field. A few problems in several of the subjects are suggested in the following pages and to them numerous other studies can be added by anyone interested in the matter. Such investigation should be made by taking small problems rather than large and by doing a thorough job with insistence upon both care in devising technique and conscientiousness in reporting new methods or modifications of reported methods. The making of hundreds of technical studies is the outstanding need of curriculum construction at the present time.

Handwriting. — Superficially the curriculum in handwriting seems a settled matter. Twenty-six small letters, twenty-six capitals, a few figures, and some characters comprise the list. But, when we consider vertical *versus* Spencerian forms, and arm *versus* finger movement, as questions of content, we see that there are a few problems of selection in even this simple subject. In attacking the problem, the first step is to assume some objectives, which in this case we may state as the inscribing of ideas in script so that they may be preserved or be imparted from one to another.

In analyzing this function we discover three sub-problems: the inscribing, or movement; the script, or form of the letters; and legibility. To this may be added by some the elements of beauty as part of the function. And since the imparting of ideas is an essential part of the function, speed becomes an item of importance.

There are, then, several problems, such as the following, which may be studied:

(a) What movement will produce the greatest speed in sustained effort?

(b) What forms of letters are the speediest?

(c) What are the standards of speed for each of the grades expressed in maximum performance and percentiles for large groups?

(d) What are the elements of legibility?

(e) What movement produces greatest legibility?

(f) What forms produce greatest legibility under normal writing conditions?

(g) Assuming that handwriting has been learned with some degree of efficiency, what are the defects in the handwriting of each individual which produce illegibility or slowness?

(h) What are the most frequent class errors?

(i) What rules for writing will tend to overcome these defects?

(j) What is the place of beauty in handwriting? Does it need to be considered apart from legibility? If so, is it highly correlated with it?

(k) What ideals should dominate in handwriting?

(l) How are these obtained?

It will be noted that in problems g, h, and i, frequency of error is utilized, and this is important because of the probability that in the upper grades instruction in handwriting will produce the best results when movement and form are directed toward curing specific defects in legibility and speed.

It should be noted that deficiencies in any subject are dependent upon standards. Frequency of error cannot be utilized as a method in any subject in which standards are not available; it is one which, to be applied generally (outside such subjects as spelling and arithmetic, where absolute accuracy is the standard), has had to wait until the past few years, when standards have been formulated.

Spelling. — The investigation of the spelling curriculum content has been carried farther than that of any other subject, as the descriptions in preceding chapters have already made clear.

The assumed objectives may be several: adult writing, children's writing, reading, and the correction of the errors of children. The problem of deciding the value of these assumed objectives is one worthy of attention. The standards of speed and accuracy should be formulated for classes and grades. Frequency of use has been the common method of investigation; but frequency of error is of primary importance for both individuals and classes in the upper grades. There the problems correspond to similar problems in handwriting as outlined above.

An important question to study is the value of the individual curriculum in spelling for each class-member based upon his own errors, of which record is kept by the pupil or the teacher. It involves additional labor and it is important to know definitely whether or not it is worth while.

Language. — The studies of language have all been based upon frequency of error. Several questions remain to be studied:

(a) What is the best objective to assume?

(b) How should the common errors be apportioned among the grades?

(c) Collect materials which will give the most thorough hold upon the correct forms (such as language games).

(d) What materials will produce the artistic use of language?

(e) What are the most common errors in individual school systems?

(f) What is the correlation between the most common and the worst-sounding errors?

(g) Are language lessons an aid to correct speech?

(h) List voice defects.

(i) Collect corrective exercises.

(j) Collect language games.

(k) What ideals should dominate in the use of language?

(l) How are these attained?

Grammar. — The studies in grammar are, like those in language, based upon the frequency of error. Here, again, several studies will be of value:

(a) What is the best objective to assume?

(b) Does the study of grammar in the grades affect correction of errors?

(c) Should false syntax be included in grammar material, as determined by ability to speak correctly?

(d) What sorts of sentences are the best material for parsing and analysis?

(e) What is the relative importance of oral and written parsing?

(f) What should constitute the content of a grammar curriculum?

(g) What influence does formal grammar have upon artistic expression?

(h) What ideals dominate in the use of grammar?

(i) How are these attained?

Hygiene, physical education, and physiology. — Assuming that the functions of this group of subjects are to keep the body at a high level of efficiency and to provide recreation, the analysis proceeds as follows:

For efficiency two factors are involved—the conditions under which each adult individual lives, such as occupation, opportunities for exercise, and so forth; and an establishment of standards of a high degree of efficiency. The first is important because health is an individual matter in so far as exercise is concerned, though it is a group matter in infectious diseases. The second provides a basis for the detection of defects. The following problems may be listed:

(a) A study of "normal" conditions of adult life with regard to possibilities for exercise
(b) The definition of standards of good health
(c) A defect analysis—functional and structural
(d) Frequency of diseases
(e) Remedies for functional and structural defects (c) and diseases (d)
(f) Derivation of service physiology to explain c, d, and e
(g) Collection of devices for putting facts and exercises to use

For the assumed function of recreation, two problems are suggested:

(a) Analysis of forms of recreation
(b) Selection on basis of interest and of usefulness for a to f above
(c) Selection of dominating ideals and collection of methods of attainment

Civics. — The function of civics is to help people to realize the objectives of citizenship in relation to the machinery of government. Several problems present themselves:

(a) What are the defects of citizens?
(b) What are the duties of citizens — local, state, national?
(c) What are the defects of government in the local community?
(d) What information will help to solve these (a, b, and c)?
(e) What procedure will help to solve them?
(f) What concrete substitutes for adult problems can be found for the use of children?
(g) What ideals dominate and how are they attained?

History. — One assumed function of history is to utilize past information and practices to explain modern problems and offer solutions. History is used informally in all subjects, and formally in history classes. The procedure in both cases is the same: list the modern problems and select the historical material that will explain them.

The following problems are important:

(a) List by frequency of occurrence all problems — moral, political, economic — upon which history can throw light.

(b) Collect material (biography, etc.) which will help to solve these.

(c) Decide what can be handled (1) informally and incidentally, and (2) systematically in a history class.

(d) Arrange the material in a and c in proper teaching order.

(e) In formal history, decide upon dates and events to memorize.

(f) Evaluate chronological and topical methods of handling history.

(g) Decide upon the grades in which formal history should be taught.

(h) Decide what ideals should dominate, and collect methods of attaining them.

Arithmetic. — Assume the function of arithmetic to be the handling of numbers with speed and accuracy by laymen. The following problems suggest themselves:

(a) What are the arithmetical problems solved by laymen (frequency of occurrence)? List the types of situation which should be examined in order to get a basis broad enough for a course in elementary arithmetic.

(b) Determine the arithmetical processes used in these.

(c) Establish standards for speed and accuracy in fundamental processes and reasoning.

(d) Collect errors in arithmetical operations in upper grades.

(e) Collect methods of remedying the defects.

(f) Place the fundamental processes in the proper grades.

(g) Evaluate systematic and incidental arithmetic.

(h) Make a difficulty analysis of arithmetical operations.

(i) Derive "service arithmetic" from other subjects.

(j) Select dominating ideals and collect methods of attaining.

Handicrafts. — These involve handwork, manual arts, cooking, and sewing. If we assume the functions to be (1) illustrations of other school work, (2) expression of ideas, and (3) the performance of practical tasks, the following problems may be listed for each:

(a) What material can be illustrated?

(b) What media can be used?

(c) What are the degrees of difficulty of handling these media?

(d) Arrange illustrative material and topics by grades.

(e) What repairs and articles of use or adornment can schoolboys make with tools?

(f) What processes are necessary to perform these?

(g) What procedure is necessary in them?

(h) What objectives are of greatest value in (1) sewing, (2) cooking?

(i) What (1) sewing and (2) cooking processes are needed to teach them?

(j) What is the order of difficulty in instruction of the (1) sewing and (2) cooking processes?

(k) How should they be arranged by grades?

(l) What are the dominating ideals and how attained?

Geography. — Assume the function of geography to be the location of valuable objects and the ability to explain them when possible in terms of geographical data. Some problems are:

(a) Study place references in a series of issues of selected papers and magazines.

(b) Derive the place geography of a textbook in history, economics, etc.

(c) Derive the rational geography of the same subjects.

(d) Which of these are of greatest importance? Set up standards.

(e) Determine the place geography of the United States which should be taught in the grades.

(f) Determine objective basis for the selection of a content for nature study.

(g) Determine dominating ideals and collect methods of attaining them.

Reading. — The assumed function of reading is to provide means for getting, and for giving to an audience, ideas which are expressed in writing. Some problems worthy of investigation are:

(a) What should be the vocabulary content for the primary grades?

(b) What should be the content of phonics?

(c) Where should phonics be placed?

(d) What is the amount of vocabulary repetition which is most efficient?

(e) What are the standards for speed in silent reading by percentiles for grades?

(f) What are similar standards for reproduction?

(g) What are the defects of silent reading by individuals and classes?

(h) What are the methods of correction?

(i) What are the defects in oral reading?

(j) What are the methods of correction?

(k) What should be the content of and the time allotment for lessons by grades?

(l) What ideals dominate and how are they attained?

Literature. — Assume the function of literature to be the verbal expression of the solution of problems in beautiful form. Some problems are the following:

(a) Analyze elements of beauty for children of different ages.

(b) Get expert opinion to provide lists of good literature for children of different ages.

(c) Classify good literature by intellectual content.

(d) Classify good literature by simplicity of vocabulary.

(e) Apportion literature to grades upon basis of the results of a, b, c, and d.

(f) Determine the dominating ideals and collect methods of attaining them.

Music. — Assume the functions of music to be the appreciation of good music and the ability to sing or play some musical instrument. Some problems are:

(a) Analyze elements of beauty for children of different ages.

(b) Evaluate good music by expert opinion.

(c) Classify good music in regard to ease in singing.

(d) Classify music by grades on basis of the results of a, b, c, and d.

(e) Determine in what grades note singing should be taught.

(f) Classify children on basis of ability to sing.

(g) Collect defects in ability to sing.

(h) Collect remedies.

(i) Determine the relative value of rote and note singing.

(j) Determine the relative value of singing or playing, and listening.

(k) Determine the dominating ideals and collect methods of attaining them.

Art. — Assume the function to be the appreciation of works of art, the development of taste in dress, the artistic furnishing of homes, and the representation of ideas in artistic form. Some problems are the following:

(a) In what practical adult situations is art of use as a service subject?   What are the house-furnishing problems? The problems in dress?

(b) Evaluate art by expert opinion.

(c) Classify art according to content.

(d) Classify art in regard to ease in drawing.

(e) Analyze the elements of beauty for children of different ages.

(f) Classify art by grades on the basis of a, b, c, and d.

(g) Determine the uses made of drawing by the layman.

(h) Determine the content of drawing technique.

(i) Determine the relative emphasis to be placed upon drawing and appreciation.

(j) List community artistic defects.

(k) Collect remedies.

(l) Evaluate different assumed functions of an art course.

(m) Make an analysis of extra-school activities to which art contributes.

(n) Determine the ideals and collect methods of attainment.

Ideals. — To the foregoing list of problems in the content of subject matter may be added a list which deals directly with the ideals which parallel and cross the content of the subjects in the course of study. A few of these are appended as illustrations of numerous significant problems that lie within the field. The methods of controlling ideals directly are as much a part of the curriculum as are geography, history, and mathematics. This is true whether they are included in a formal course or are taught incidentally in connection with other subjects.

(a) Have the faculty objectively determine the ideals which they wish to develop in children.

(b) Select a list of activities through which the ideals will be taught: (1) school activities and (2) extra-school activities.

(c) Collect the form of each activity which best embodies the ideal.

(d) Collect games through which to develop certain ideals.

(e) Collect examples of personification of ideals.

(f) Collect reasons for the observance of ideals.

PART II

STUDIES IN CURRICULUM CONSTRUCTION

CHAPTER XVI

SPELLING
(Studies 1-8)

§1—INTRODUCTION

The second part of this book is made up of a number of studies found in print and in manuscript. No claims are made that this list is complete, although care has been taken to correspond extensively during the last two years with those likely to know of unpublished studies. But with no central magazine existing devoted to curriculum construction, or other central agency, it is impossible to be certain that all significant studies have been secured. Some of the studies have been found quite by accident.

In deciding which among known studies to include, the choice has been made of those which present in some detail the methods used in their investigations, since we are primarily concerned with that phase of the studies. Because this book represents the first attempt to formulate the objective methods used by curriculum builders, historical considerations have influenced the compiler to select all the commonly known studies made up to this time, although in some cases they may not be of first rank nor described in sufficient detail to be verified.

Critics who are accustomed to the exact procedure of the older sciences will find much to criticize in the gropings of the investigators after a new technique; but such criticism is to be expected, and indeed is to be desired, because only through criticism is improvement made. So, even when the methods are crude, they must be compiled and analyzed in order to be conveniently at hand for both criticism and improvement.

In the summaries which follow, citations are made to the original sources where the printed materials may be found fully described. Our object has been to describe the methods completely and to make briefer summaries of any conclusions which are of technical or popular interest.

Apology may not be necessary but is, nevertheless, offered to a number of investigators who have been working in the field of curriculum construction, but whose methods are not in form for definite description. If the appearance of this fairly complete body of studies stimulates them to publish as soon as definite results are obtained, so that others may have the benefit of their experience, definite good will result from the publication of this book.

The studies in spelling are particularly interesting for the following reasons:

(a) The assumed functions and the material studied are varied. The members of one group assume that the function of spelling is to assist pupils to write themes; these collect themes from several states, from a large city, and from the high school children of a small town. One investigator collects all the errors made by all the children in a high school in all their written work. Another group assumes that the function of spelling is to assist adults to write letters, and collects social and business letters from many sources by going to the files of organizations, by obtaining access to the preserved letters of families, and by using current letters of the families of school children.

(b) All the investigators use frequency of use or frequency of error as a basis for determining importance. Usually the lists presented in the studies are composed of words used or misspelled more than an arbitrarily determined number of times; but two investigators limit their lists to words used by more than a certain specified number of people.

(c) Several investigators make secondary composite lists of words found in primary studies, and these are being widely adopted by the schools.

(d) The instructional order of teaching the words is studied by two investigators. One bases his order by grades on the time of first emergence of the word into the vocabulary of the grades, and the other tries out composite lists in the grades of several cities.

(e) We are particularly fortunate in having two very detailed descriptions of methods used in collection and tabulation. In one of these the technique of delegating the task of collection to children and, in the other, to teachers, is described.

§2—VOCABULARY OF PERSONAL AND BUSINESS LETTERS

(Study 1)

Ayres* endeavored "to find out whether or not there exists a fairly definite body of words so generally used in ordinary correspondence that they should form the core or basis of the spelling vocabulary taught in the lower grades of our elementary schools. The investigation was limited to the analysis of simple business and personal letters because the ordinary person requires a knowledge of spelling only when he writes and he writes only personal memoranda and letters, but does not write books or articles."

The material consisted of 2000 letters obtained from adults who wrote to twelve sources as follows: a mail order business, a physician, the query department of a city newspaper, a lawyer, school teachers (from parents of pupils), a publishing firm, secretaries of the Y. M. C. A., a playground association, a philanthropic organization, family letters, and a few love letters.

The letters contained 110,160 words. A random sample was obtained by tabulating the first words of each line of every letter and making separate tabulations of the different salutations and endings. By this means 23,629 words were obtained. Of these the total number of individual words was 2001—that is, there was a total vocabulary of 2001 separate words obtained as a result of tabulating nearly 24,000 words taken at random from 2000 letters written by 2000 different people.

*The Spelling Vocabularies of Personal and Business Letters, L. P. Ayres, Division of Education, Russell Sage Foundation. Pamphlet No. E 126, 1913. (Out of print.)

Of the 2001 words, 751 appeared only once and one of them was repeated 1080 times. The records show that 43 words furnished one-half of the aggregate number. The first nine of these, consisting of one quarter of the occurrences, are as follows: *I, the, and, you, too, your, of, for,* and *in.* One-eighth of the occurrences were furnished by the three words *I, the,* and *and.*

Special attention was paid to the salutations and endings. The 542 words which constitute seven-eighths of the words, tabulated with the figures showing the number of times each word appears, are given in the monograph. The writer calls attention to the fact that this is a very small group of words and that additional study should be made to discover which those words are that constitute the foundation of the vocabulary used in ordinary letter-writing, with the recommendation that these words should then be taught first and taught so thoroughly that through applying them to everyday use the children will permanently master them.

§3—THE SPELLING SCALE

(Study 2)

Ayres* carried his investigation further and sought to determine a curriculum of 1000 words which could be arranged in order of difficulty with standards for the different grades. In doing this he combined the lists of Knowles, Eldridge, his own 1913 list, and the Cook and O'Shea lists. The 1000 words were selected by "finding the frequency with which each word appeared in the tabulations of each study, weighting that frequency according to the size of the base of which it was a part, adding the four frequencies thus obtained, and finding their average. The resulting figure shows how many times the word was repeated in each 100,000 words of written English. The aggregate of written material analyzed in securing these results was approximately

Measuring Scale for Ability in Spelling, Division of Education, Russell Sage Foundation, Pamphlet No. E 139, 1915.

368,000 words written by some 2500 different persons. More than two-thirds of the material consisted of personal and business letters."

When the 1000 words were collected they were divided into fifty lists of 20 each and these lists were given as dictated spelling lists of 70,000 children in 84 cities. By statistical computation the words were scaled and combined for the particular grades, so that eventually a spelling scale was obtained in which words were arranged in 26 columns each of which contained words of approximately equal difficulty, and the median standards for each grade from two to eight were determined.

Many other scales and studies of relative difficulty have been made in this field. Buckingham* determined the difficulty of a small, selected list of words in terms of distances from a zero of spelling ability. He has also added recently an extension to the Ayres Spelling Scale**. Ashbaugh took the three thousand words derived by Anderson and found the difficulty of each word for each grade * * *

§4—Intensive Study of Family Letters
(Study 3)

Cook and O'Shea * * * * studied over 200,000 words in the personal correspondence of thirteen persons, of whom five were men, eight were women; six of this group were related. Their academic training ranged from third grade to college graduation. The letters bore forty postmarks from many sections of the country and from abroad. Six contributed 5,000 words each; three, 40,000; one, 24,000; one, 6,000; one 8,000 and one, 12,000. The investigators claim that the written vocabulary of letters between mem-

*Spelling Ability: Its Determination and Distribution, Teachers College, 1913.

**Public School Publishing Co., Bloomington, Ill.

***Iowa Spelling Scale, University of Iowa Extension Bulletin, 1919.

****The Child and His Spelling, W. A. Cook and M. V. O'Shea, The Bobbs-Merrill Co., 1914.

bers of a family is more nearly typical of a standard vocabulary than are business letters or themes, since the personal letters between members of a family constitute the bulk of correspondence not performed by stenographers.

In arranging the vocabulary a number of rules were kept in mind. The dictionary basis was adhered to, resulting in the listing of nouns in the singular nominative only, except where the plural is habitually used, and then the singular form does not appear. All forms of the personal pronouns were used except *ours, yours,* and *theirs.* Only the positive degree of adjectives occurs, except that the comparative or superlative occurs for those few that have no positive form. In verbs the present infinitive is considered the root form, with the result that *is, are, was,* etc., are always checked as *be.* Words of identical spelling and like pronunciation are not differentiated in any way; for instance, *pin* is not differentiated as a noun and as a verb when so used. Words of identical spelling but dissimilar pronunciation are included only once. *I, a,* and *O* are not included. All syncopations are entered as though written in full, except *o'clock.* All abbreviations are written in full, *Mr., Mrs. etc.,* and *O.K.;* except the initials of persons, which are disregarded. Baby talk is excluded, but colloquial expressions if found in the *Standard Dictionary* are included. All dates, street numbers, all quantities of money expressed in figures, all hours of the day expressed in numerals, as 5.45, and all numbers over one hundred, except round numbers like a thousand, are excluded. Compounds are counted as two words. Foreign words and proper names are segregated in a special list. Their totals are noted but their occurrence in the vocabularies of individuals is not determined.

The vocabularies of the thirteen individuals are kept separate so that the individual range and the common occurrence can be noted. The latter is significant because the relative frequency of totals needs to be supplemented by indications of the common use by all as against high frequency by a few. A word with high frequency and common use should be given greater importance than one of similar frequency but used by a smaller number.

Then, too, the excessive use of an unusual word by one person might give it undue importance in the totals if the individual lists were not used as a check.

The words so obtained are classified in four lists. List I consists of 186 words used by all the correspondents; List II is made up of 577 words used by a majority of the correspondents; List III, composed of 2207 words, is used by less than a majority; and List IV comprises 2230 words used by one writer only, and of these 1804 occur only once. In these lists (only the first three of which are published) the frequency of total occurrence of each word is shown as well as the occurrence of each in three spellers which were used as checks. Their occurrence in the Ayres and Chancellor lists is also noted. Distinctions are noted to show whether the words are common to all women and all men, to a majority of men and of women, to less than a majority, and to only one correspondent among men and among women.

Twelve hundred and nine different proper names occurred in the 200,000 running words, with a total of 9,740 occurrences. Words identical in spelling except for the final s (as William and Williams) were counted as a single word, all nicknames, pet diminutives, and spellings based on personal predilections were reduced to standard orthography; and the envelope addresses were included when present. All towns of less than 10,000 population, all strictly local publications, organizations, and streets, all family names except those of historical characters or of men in the public eye, are omitted from the lists presented. These lists are composed upon the same basis as the lists described in the preceding paragraph. List I consists of the one word *Saturday*, used by all correspondents. List II is composed of 30 words used by a majority. List III of 137 words used by less than a majority. And list IV of 862 names used by only one correspondent, of which 544 occur but once.

Comparison is made between these lists and the words found in 3 spellers, one of which is probably the most widely used speller in the schools of the nation. It is found that only 35 per cent of the words in the three spellers occur in the letters, but seventy per cent of the words common to the spellers occur in the letters. In spite of the fact that the common words should appear more heavily in List I and less heavily in Lists II and III, it appears that twenty-seven per cent of List I, thirty-three per cent of List II, twenty-eight per cent of List III and twelve per cent of List IV occur in the spellers. No proper name is common to all spellers. The chances of any proper name occurring in two spellers range from sixteen in one hundred to forty-two in one hundred. Of the 110 different proper nouns in the spellers only six appear in the letters.

Furthermore, one word, *in*, in General List I does not appear in the spellers; eleven in List II, 202 in List III, and 625 in List IV.

Tabulations of the number of new words added per thousand words of each correspondent are made. This shows that even as many as 40,000 running words do not exhaust the vocabulary. Interesting analyses of individual writers' vocabularies are made. Six comparisons are also made showing the wide variation between the vocabularies of men and of women. Among women, the dominant words are connected with articles of food, terms relating to consumption and preparation thereof; articles of wearing apparel, textiles, terms related closely thereto; parts of the body, care of them, personal appearance; animals; esthetics, color; diseases, their treatment, concrete sensitivity for good or ill, terms closely related thereto; parts of house, furniture and furnishings, measures; correspondence, other domestic activities and relationships, and an unclassified list of 180 words. The words dominant in the letters of men are classified as follows: terms of aggression, contest and domination, physical and mental; institutional life and social organization; and an unclassified list of 91 words.

Dominance is determined by the occurrence of a word in a higher list in one sex than in the other. For instance, *blister* is considered a dominant word among women because it belongs to List III for women correspondents and to List IV among male correspondents. In general there are 404 of these words found in women's letters and 128 found in those of men.

§5—The Vocabulary of Children's Themes

(Studies 4 and 5)

Jones* (4) investigated the problem: "What words, grade for grade, do children use in their own free written speech, and what words, therefore, do they need to know how to spell?"

Themes were collected from 1050 students in grades two to eight in Illinois, Maryland, Iowa, and South Dakota. One-third were collected from Illinois, one-third from Maryland, and one-third from the other two States. Approximately 150 children from each grade above the first were included. Themes were set by the teachers as part of the regular class work, not on book topics (to avoid a reading vocabulary). They wrote not more than thirty minutes. Over-age students' themes were not included. (A second-grade pupil whose age at the beginning of the year was over eight years and no months was considered over-age.) The theme-writing was continued until the tabulations showed the addition of no new words. By the time most of the students had handed in forty themes the flow of new words had almost ended, and when for eight or ten themes no new words were added the student's "word-well was counted approximately dry."

The number of themes ranged from 56 to 105 per student; the total number examined being "a little over 75,000" and the themes averaged a little less than 190 words. Thus the total number of words recorded was approximately 15,000,000. In this large array there were only 4,532 different words used by two per cent or over of the children in the grades in which the word first appeared. About 200 words in all were ruled out as being used by only one or two students. For spelling purposes derived forms, such as *have* and *having*, were counted as different words, but where there was little chance of misspelling, as in the addition of *s* or *ed* to another word, the word was not counted as different, as in *shoe* and *shoes*.

*Concrete Investigation of the Material of English Spelling, J. F. Jones, The University of South Dakota, 1915.

The words are classified according to the grade in which they first appear and are used by two per cent of the students in that grade. Consequently, the second grade has the largest number. The numbers run as follows from grades two to eight: 1927, 469, 442, 432, 425, 419, and 418. The average vocabulary by grades from two to eight is as follows: 521, 908, 1235, 1489, 1710, 1926, and 2135.

Practically every word in the list of 4532 was misspelled by one or more students; the highest number misspelled by any one student was 87, and the smallest, 18. The average for the 1050 students was 48.

The most frequently misspelled were *which*, 321 times; *their* and *there*, 612 times; and *separate*, 283 times. This investigator compiled the well-known list of "One Hundred Spelling Demons" as follows (the order is not significant after the first four):

ONE HUNDRED SPELLING DEMONS

which	used	would	wear
their	always	can't	answer
there	where	sure	two
separate	women	loose	too
don't	done	lose	ready
meant	hear	Wednesday	forty
business	here	country	hour
many	write	February	trouble
friend	writing	know	among
some	heard	could	busy
been	does	seems	built
since	once	Tuesday	color
making	tired	every	piece
dear	grammar	they	raise
guess	minute	half	straight
says	any	break	sugar
having	much	buy	shoes
just	beginning	again	enough
doctor	blue	very	truly

whether	though	none	ache
believe	coming	week	tonight
knew	early	often	hoarse
laid	instead	whole	said
tear	easy	won't	wrote
choose	through	cough	read

Cook and O'Shea append lists of 1158 words collected by Homer J. Smith (5) from the examination of 75,000 running words taken from the spontaneous composition of children from grades three to eight inclusive, in equal quantities from each grade, in the Madison, Wisconsin, schools. He omits personal, possessive, and demonstrative pronouns; the numerals, ordinals, and articles; about thirty of the most common prepositions, conjunctions, verbs, and adverbs; and local proper names.

Following the classification of Cook and O'Shea he finds 272 words used by all grades; 542 words used by at least three of the six grades; and 344 words used by only two different grades.

§6—An Extensive Study of Letters to Parents
(Study 6)

William N. Anderson, in his dissertation* on *The Determination of a Spelling Vocabulary, Based upon Written Correspondence,* studied 3723 letters to supplement and expand the work done in previous studies, to show, comparatively, the number of words that are common in the writing vocabularies among persons of various callings, to show the extent and range of vocabularies used by persons in certain different callings, and to point out the educational significance of these findings.

The letters were written by adults engaged in over 35 different occupations and callings in the State of Iowa and, with a few exceptions, were collected by the public school children of the seventh, eighth, and ninth grades of 23 towns and cities.

The directions are as follows:

*University of Iowa, unpublished.

"To the Superintendent and Teacher:

"We are asking your kind assistance and coöperation in this study on spelling, to be made according to the 'Directions for Pupils' sent you. Our purpose is to make a careful and extensive study of the words collected in this manner. We prefer to have the work done by any two grades above the fifth, including high school. Other things being equal, the seventh and eighth grades would probably be the most suitable.

"In order to simplify the work we have endeavored to make the directions as complete as possible. These directions have been worked out while the work was carried on in different grades of the Experimental School of the University and in the public schools of Iowa City. We found most of the pupils very much interested and glad to do the work. The enthusiasm of the pupils, however, will depend largely on the attitude and spirit of the one in charge of the class. It is desirable that pupils use paper of uniform size.

"In order to assure greater accuracy in the recording of the misspelled words, we ask that the pupils be drilled on the following list of words before they begin the work:

to	new	hole	loose
too	knew	whole	lose
two	seem	brake	principle
there	seam	break	principal
their	meet	ate	whether
where	meat	eight	weather
wear	mail	seen	separate
here	male	scene	been
hear	which	piece	meant
deer	witch	peace	choose
dear	need	accept	coming
	knead	except	received

"Nearly all these words have been taken, because of their frequency, from the list of 'One Thousand Most Common Words' as found by L. P. Ayres, and from the list of 'One Hundred Spelling Demons' as found by W. F. Jones. Many of the words occur in both lists. Hence, according to the findings of these studies, they are both commonly used and frequently misspelled.

"After beginning the work it should be carried through without delay. We should greatly desire to have your returns in by December first as the work here cannot be started before all returns are in.

"The data may be returned by Express C. O. D."

"Directions for Pupils

"*Purpose*

"The purpose of this study is to find out what words are used in letter-writing so that we may be better able to tell what words we should first know how to spell.

"*Collecting of Letters*

"Each pupil is asked to collect from three to five letters, written in the State of Iowa by people over eighteen years of age. The letters collected by any one pupil should all be from people in the same occupation or profession, such as domestic or housekeeper, farmer, dry-goods merchant, druggist or drug clerk, teacher, minister, doctor, real estate man, milliner, etc. The letters should, as far as possible, be from different individuals in the same occupation or profession; that is, not all from the same person. If you have difficulty in getting letters from your parents ask some other relative or friend to help you. No doubt some classmate can get more letters than he needs and help you out. Letters that you are not allowed to mark up or spoil can be copied word for word and the copy used for this purpose.

"*Misspelled Words*

"For misspelled words proceed as follows: Go over the letters and place a checkmark immediately over each word that is misspelled. If in doubt about the spelling consult a dictionary or write the doubtful words on a piece of paper and ask your teacher about their spelling. Homonyms misused should be marked as misspelled. To illustrate: If the word *pear* or *pare* is used in speaking of a pair of shoes it is misspelled.   If the word *to* or *too* is used in speaking of two men it is misspelled. Capitalization can be disregarded.

"When you have checked the misspelled words (if there are any) arrange them on a separate piece of paper in alphabetical order, in a vertical column. See any dictionary for alphabetical order. First write the word correctly and immediately following, on the same line, write the word as it was misspelled in the letter. Example:

> cabbage — cabage
> degrade — degrad
> enlarge — inlarge
> fought — faught

"*Recording All Words*

"On a large sheet of paper (about 8 x 10 inches) record all the words in columns. Use the long side of the paper for the top and write the words in vertical columns. By doing this you will be able to get more columns on one page and if you write small and distinctly you will be able to get all words beginning with the same letter in one column. There will be few words commencing with the letters j, k, q, v, x, y, z, and some others. Proceed as follows: First go through all the letters and draw a firm line through each word commencing with the letter *a*. Immediately after each line is drawn write the word on the large sheet of paper. Begin in the upper left hand corner and form the first column down the left side of the paper (the end or short side of the sheet). In this way go through all the letters and record all words commencing with the letter *a*, then all words commencing with *b*, and so on through the alphabet. Keep your pencil well sharpened and write small and distinctly so that you may be able to get all the words on one or two sheets of paper. Both sides can be used. The names of the parties need not be recorded, but all other words in the headings and closings of the letters should be included.

The single letters *a, I, O,* and all figures (numbers not written out) need not be recorded. Write all abbreviations as they occur in the letters. Any different spelling is to be considered as a different word. For example: Such words as *have* and *having, plan, plans* and *planning,* and *refer, referred,* and *referring,* should be recorded as different words. When the same word occurs two or more times do not rewrite it but indicate its frequency by making a mark each time it occurs. If, for example, the word *very* occurs fourteen times, record it as follows: very ⫽⫽⫽⫽ ⫽⫽⫽⫽ 111-14.

"In counting these words remember that the first mark was made when the word occurred the second time and that the word and marks must therefore be added together. Keep these marks close together so that they will not be in the way for the next column of words. The marks can also be written immediately above the word.

"When all words beginning with *a* have been recorded start a new column with the words commencing with *b.* In this way start a new column for each letter. By doing this instead of continuing the first column you can add any word that may have been overlooked the first time. It is well to draw a line between the columns. You will find that you can pick out each succeeding list of words more easily and more rapidly because two or more successive words and even entire lines will soon be marked out.

"*Arranging Words in Alphabetical Order*

"You are now ready to rearrange and copy the words in ink as follows: On a new sheet of paper arrange the words in the same manner as before but in alphabetical order according to the first three letters of each word. You already have them arranged according to the first letter. After the first three letters the order can be disregarded.

abate	back
accede	bail
acid	bear
added	**bite**

"Note carefully the following: Before you begin to copy the words write (in ink) at the top of the first page the number of letters collected and the occupation or profession and sex of the persons who wrote and received the letters. Write this in the following manner:

"Five letters written by three doctors (two men and one woman). Three were written to a housekeeper (women) and two written to a druggist (man). It may be, of course, that your letters are from a farmer or dentist written to a grocer and tailor. Then your heading would probably appear as follows: Four letters written by two farmers (men). One was written to a grocer (man) and three to a tailor (man). You may have different occupations but they can always be recorded in the same manner. You will need to write this heading only once (on the first page) and your columns of words can be started immediately under it. You can tell from your first page whether any of the columns of words will be too long for your paper. If so, use the short side up; that is, write the heading at the top the short way and form the columns of words under it the long way. If none of the columns of words are too long, always use the long side of the paper for the top.

"When these lines have been written on the first page proceed as follows: Number your first list of words 1, 2, 3, 4, etc., with a lead pencil in the order that they are to be placed (alphabetically). Then copy them (in ink) on the new sheet according to the order that they are numbered, drawing a line through each word before you copy it. In this list the number of times a word occurs can be indicated by the figures after the word. The word *very* would then be recorded as follows: very 14. This list of words and the list of misspelled words will be sent by your teacher or superintendent to the University of Iowa and will be published with your names later. It is necessary therefore that you do the work neatly. Write your name, grade, and town at the bottom on one side of each sheet of paper and fasten all your papers together.

"*Grouping*

"If you have less than five letters analyzed in your list combine your work with that of some other pupil who has analyzed letters from people in the same calling or profession: that is, add the words of your two lists together and make a single list (in ink). It will not take long to do this after the words are alphabetically arranged. Each pupil can do half of this work or you can work together. This places a premium on getting five letters. If you can get as many as five letters in your own list you need not do this. If, however, one pupil has only three letters and another has four (from people in the same calling) combine the two into a list of seven. Where two lists are added together you need not write the letter again on this third combined list, but be sure to fasten the three lists together so that they will not come apart. Write both your names on this third list. The average pupil can do all the work in a few hours after the letters have been collected.

"Always reread carefully that part of the directions which has to do only with the work which you are doing at the time. By doing this you will not become confused.

"*Summary*

"All papers sent in to the University should be neatly written in ink and should show the following:

"(1) All misspelled words and how they were misspelled.

"(2) The number of letters analyzed in the list of words.

"(3) Occupation and sex of the persons who wrote the letters.

"(4) Occupation and sex of the persons who received the letters.

"(5) All words should be alphabetically arranged.

"(6) Where pupils have less than five letters two sets of papers should be combined into a single list.

"(7) Your name, grade, and town should be on each separate sheet.

"(8) All papers of each pupil should be fastened together."

The lists were classified as professional; business; domestic, including homemakers and housekeepers, domestic servants and employees; untrained nurses; personal; doctors; bankers; farmers; automobile dealers; and miscellaneous.

A total of 361,184 running words were compiled. The investigator reports that, on the whole, the work done by the pupils was very satisfactory. The lists so obtained were then compared with those made by other investigators. A total of 3105 words used five or more times was tabulated.

In addition the misspelled words were also tabulated and these were found to include 238 words misspelled from 2 to 21 times each. Only about a dozen words showed any marked frequency of misspelling. These were: all right, coming, didn't, don't, for, haven't, mamma, niece, thought, and until. These were missed ten times or over. The investigator draws the conclusion that relatively few of the words tabulated in the total lists show any special spelling difficulty.

§7—Graded Lists
(Study 7)

Pryor* made comparisons of the lists obtained by Eldridge; W. F. Jones; Studley and Ware (a secondary source study); Woolfolk; in the Johnstown, Pa., course of study (also a secondary source study); Ayres; Cook and O'Shea; and in the spellers of Chancellor and Hicks. As explained in the quotation just following, he obtained the common words, arranged them by grades, and gave them a trial in several schools.

"After the lists had been selected, each one was numbered and all the words were checked off in a dictionary. The figure 'one' was placed before every word in the dictionary which occurred in the Eldridge list. 'Two' was placed before each word that was found in the Jones list. The other ten lists were checked against the dictionary after the same fashion. Altogether, about

*Part I, *Sixteenth Yearbook*, pp. 73-84, H. C. Pryor. Where reference is made to *Yearbook* the National Society for the Study of Education is understood. These may be obtained from the Public School Publishing Company, Bloomington, Ill.

30,000 words were checked. By far the greater number occurred in only one list, a somewhat smaller number in two lists, and so on down to 121 that were common to 10 lists, 54 common to 11 lists, and only 9, viz., *again, any, believe, look, many, money, remember, there,* and *through,* that were found in all of the lists.

"It was arbitrarily decided to include in the final list all words which occurred in at least six of the twelve lists examined; there were 1309 such words. To this number were added 169 words from the Ayres scale which were not among these 1309 words, making a total of 1478 words.

"Arranging the words by grades presented a much greater difficulty than their selection. An examination of eight different graded lists, viz., the California and Johnstown spellers, Hicks' *Champion Spelling Book,* and the Boston, New Orleans, Richmond, Smith, and Woolfolk lists revealed much difference of opinion as to where some of the words should be placed. Thus, *accept* was put in the 3d grade list by one author, in the 4th by a second, in the 5th by a third, in the 6th by three, and in the 7th by two. It appears among the 6th grade words in the appended list. *Address,* which appeared in three 5th, one 6th, and one 8th grade list, has been placed in the 5th grade of the appended list. *Am,* which was found in 1st, 2d, and 5th grade lists (most frequently in the last), was placed in the 5th grade. Each word in the entire list was assigned to the grade agreed upon by the majority of authors investigated, although in some cases the placing appeared to be pedagogically unsound. Some words, about whose location there was an exact division of opinion, were placed in the lowest grade mentioned; others could be classified very readily because of the close agreement as to where they belonged. As was expected, most of the words fell in the primary grade lists, a considerably smaller number in the intermediate grade lists, and comparatively few in the grammar grade lists. The distribution was as follows: 343 words in the second grade, 408 in the third, 216 in the fourth, 187 in the fifth, 157 in the sixth, 131 in the seventh, and 38 in the eighth.

"Obviously many of the words, such as *am,* are not properly placed and therefore the list is not the best for school purposes. Lists are now being tried in the public schools of Antonito, Boulder, Carbondale, Central City, Cripple Creek, Del Norte, Fowler, Goldfield, Loveland, Manzanola, Matheson (rural school), Pueblo, and Victor, Colorado; Douglas, Wyoming; Hershey, Nebraska; and in one building in St. Louis, Missouri. Reports so far seem to indicate that there will be little alteration in the assignment of words to the several grades. It is hoped that a year's use of the words in the actual school situation by capable, conscientious teachers will result in a highly satisfactory rearrangement. The writer invites the coöperation of superintendents, principals, and teachers who would like to use the list and to assist in its revision."

Several other compilations of primary studies have been made and used as bases for grading spelling books by Starch and Mirick, Horne and Ashbaugh, and others. The method used by Horne and Ashbaugh is as follows:

Words in the first grade had to show a *frequency* within the first 1,000, a *spelling difficulty* as evidenced by the accuracy with which children spelled these words without special instruction not greater than a certain degree, and *occurrence* in at least five of ten widely used first readers. Words to be placed in second or third grade were checked on the same three bases with a shift in the frequency and difficulty of the words and the use of second and third reader occurrence. Words in other grades were placed on bases of frequency of usage and difficulty of spelling, following the general principle that words of highest frequency should be taught first unless they were too difficult.

§8—SPELLING ERRORS IN THE HIGH SCHOOL

(Study 8)

A. G. Capps collected errors made by all the students in a small high school in all written school work for eight months (the school year). In this time 956,000 words were written by 88 pupils and in these 3,388 errors in spelling occurred. Ten pupils made less than one error in ten pages of 150 words each, and one pupil made approximately three errors per page. The median pupil made one error per two pages, one-quarter of the pupils made less than one error in five pages, and one-fourth made more than eight errors in ten pages.

The material was collected and tabulated as follows:

"(a) *Directions to Teachers*

"I. Each pupil writing any school work either in school or at home should put in the upper left-hand corner of the first page of the composition his name, the date, and the number of words in the composition, as follows:

> Name......................................
> Date......................................
> No. of words..............................

"II. The teacher should underline with red ink or red pencil the incorrect words in all the written work of the students. (Formal spelling lessons are not included in these studies.)

"III. After such use has been made of the papers as the teacher desires, they are to be finally returned unfolded, to the desk, and kept.

"IV. Each set (or assignment) shall be kept separate from others. The papers in each set shall be arranged in strictly alphabetical order. On the top of each set shall be placed a sheet of paper on which is written the name of the course; the year, I, II, III, etc.; the section (if any), *e. g.*, Eng. I, Sec. 1; the date on which the assignment was written, and the name of the teacher. Each assignment should be tied in a flat bundle with cord. Papers are not to be folded when bound in a bundle.

"V. These papers should be sent to the office on Monday mornings.

"VI. In the case of loose-leaf note-books the teacher shall collect them once a week, and shall handle as other written work, except that a paper clip shall bind together the papers of any one student, and the material shall be returned to the teacher and the students as soon as the office is through with it.

"When note-books are not loose-leaf they are to be collected on the first and fifteenth of each month. The mistakes are to be marked and the books are to be sent to the office. They should be returned without delay.

"VII. In spelling, abbreviations are supposed to have a period at the end; contractions have apostrophes. Disregard hyphens, syllabication and capital letters, except that if proper nouns are not capitalized they shall be counted as errors.

"In written work of foreign languages the student in counting the number of words used shall count only English words. Teachers shall mark errors only in these.

"Simplified spellings should be accepted as correct only when a pupil uses them deliberately.

"In mathematical work the student shall not count mathematical symbols; he shall count only full words and abbreviated words:

"For instance, in the statement, 'Let $x = $ No. of ac.,' x and $=$ are disregarded.

"When you have examined your first set of papers please see the person making the study immediately concerning difficulties, if there are any. Do not mark a second set till you have seen him. If a new ruling is necessary he should write to Mr. Charters. Always refer cases of doubt to the person making the study.

"VIII. At the beginning of the school year, but only then, the students may be told about the study being made, and should be warned about always putting a period after abbreviations, and capital letters for proper nouns. If a student enters late he may be told these things privately.

"Note: We are attempting to get at the normal spelling errors and teachers must, therefore, handle the spelling question just as they always have, giving no more attention to spelling with the class than usual.

"(b) *Directions for the Distribution of Error Slips*

"I. For preliminary distribution there should be kept five boxes, one for regular Freshmen, one for regular Sophomores, one for regular Juniors, one for regular Seniors, and one for irregular pupils.

"II. When the errors for each student have been written on the slips and the information tabulated upon the class record then the error slips shall be at once thrown into the appropriate box. *Note:* This means that an irregular in a Freshman class will have his errors thrown into the box of irregulars.

"III. For further distribution take the slips in one box and distribute these into 26 boxes, according to the first letter of the correct spelling — A, B, C, etc. Then take one of these boxes, for example A, and arrange all slips in strictly alphabetical order under A, etc. Each of these may then be tied into a bundle with a cord and preserved for future use. Each bundle should be put in a separate envelope appropriately marked.

"(c) *Directions for Keeping a Class Record*

Date		6–29	6–30	7–2	7–3
Name	No.	Errors/Voc.	Errors/Voc.	Errors/Voc.	Errors/Voc.
A	101	6/127	6/180	3/250	4/160
B	502	2/150	1/240	2/125	5/350

"A class record should be kept according to the plan above. Eng. I, Sec. I refers to Section I of Freshman English course.

"Date (horizontal column) is that upon which the set of papers to be tabulated was written.

"In the name column the students are to be arranged in strictly alphabetical order.

"In the number column is to be set down the student's number as described in later paragraphs.

"In the columns marked thus, | Errors Voc. |, the number of errors made in a paper is given in the numerator, and the number of words in the paper is given in the denominator.

"This record should be kept on loose-leaf ruled note paper, uniform in size for all the records.

"At the end of the year there should be given by the teacher of this section a statement of how the spelling errors are handled with the class.

"(d) *Directions for Copying Errors*

"Errors shall be copied upon slips of paper of uniform size about 4 inches by 1 inch and shall contain the following information:

awful	6/24 Eng.	I 24
	aweful	

"Explanation: the error is in the center; the correct spelling is in the upper left-hand corner; 6/24 refers to the date; Eng. refers to subject; I refers to Freshman course.

"24 refers to number of the pupil, in a strictly alphabetical list according to classes — Freshman, Sophomore, Junior, Senior, with irregular students as a fifth group.

"Regular Freshmen means students in the Freshman class who are spending their first year in this high school. They shall be numbered from 100 to 199.

"Regular Sophomores means those who have credit for a full year's work, are carrying a second full year's work and are spending their second year in this school. They shall be numbered from 200 to 299.

"Juniors similarly described shall be numbered from 300 to 399.

"Seniors similarly described shall be numbered from 400 to 499.

"All other students shall be called irregulars and shall be numbered from 500 on.

"In case there are more than 100 students in any of these groups except the last, the same definition of groups should be used, but other markings should be devised."

The errors were classified by years and subjects and by fre-

quency of occurrence. The list of errors occurring more than
twice during the year was compared with the Ayres list, and it
was found that 62 persisted into the high school and they were
misspelled 497 times. These 62 words constitute 38 per cent of
the words misspelled more than twice and 42 per cent of the
total errors. The words misspelled more than nine times are
the following: parliament (92), too (47), until (31), quantity
(25), etc.

"*Misspelled 10 or more times.*— Parliament (92), *too (47),
*until (31), quantity (25), *their (23), vassal (22), *there (21),
*government (21), *separate (19), *finally (19), *they (18),
straight (16), didn't (16), *water (15), Bibles (15), council (14),
growth (13), iodine (13), *coming (13), *lose (13), isosceles (12),
*disappointed (11), perpendicular (11), quantities (11), Delaware
(11), *to (11), *and (10), Christians (10)."

*Words found in the Ayres list.

Chapter XVII

LANGUAGE AND GRAMMAR
(Studies 9-22)

§1—Introduction

Several studies in language and grammar have been made as tabulated in the following lists. In so far as these have been published, references are found in Part I of the Sixteenth Yearbook of the National Society for the Study of Education with the exception of W. Barnes's study (15) which constitutes Vol. 3, No. 1, of the Bulletin of the Fairmont (W. Va.) State Normal School, and R. I. Johnson's study (21). Mimeograph copies of the Hibbing study may be obtained by writing to W. J. Richardson, Public School, Hibbing, Minn.

These studies all agree in the aim of discovering the errors of school children in language or grammar or both. The distinction between language and grammar lies in the fact that a grammatical error is one which can be referred to a rule in grammar for correction. The use of "ketch" for "catch" is not strictly a grammatical error because it violates no rule of grammar, but rather one of pronunciation; while *He don't see me* is a grammatical error since it breaks the rule of agreement of subject and predicate.

The objectives of the studies are variously stated. Charters and Miller say, "The purpose of this investigation was to find (1) what errors in the use of oral and written language forms violating rules of grammar were made by the children of the Kansas City elementary schools, (2) what rules in grammar were necessary in order to include and understand these items, (3) what items in the present course of study in Kansas City were included but unnecessary, and (4) what items should be included but were omitted."

TABLE I

LANGUAGE AND GRAMMAR STUDIES

Serial No.	Investigator	School	Oral or Written	Language or Grammar	Oral Errors	Written Errors		Method of Collection
						Pages	Errors	
(9)	Wilson	Connersville, Ind.	Oral	Grammar	226			By teachers
(10)	Charters and Miller	Kansas City, Mo.	Both	Grammar	5883	4819	10554	By teachers and from written work
(11)	Thompson	Northern Illinois	Both					By teachers and from written work
(12)	Meek	Boise, Idaho	Oral	Both				By teachers with preliminary study
(13)	Sears and Diebel	Cincinnati, O.	Oral	Both	2268			By teachers
(14)	Randolph	Speyer School, N.Y.	Oral	Both	2954			Stenographic report
(15)	Barnes	Several	Both	Grammar	Not given			By himself
(16)	Betz and Marshall	Kansas City, Mo.	Written	Both		112		From written work of third grade
(17)	Fillers	Bonham, Texas	Both	Grammar	500			By teachers and from written work
(18)	Jones	Columbia, Mo.	Oral	Grammar	500			By teachers and from written work
(19)	Richardson	Hibbing, Minn.	Oral	Grammar	10191			By teachers
(20)	Charters	Detroit, Mich.	Oral	Grammar	11207			By teachers
(21)	Charters	Pittsburgh, Pa.	Oral	Both	25376			By teachers
(22)	Johnson	Kansas City, Mo.	Written	Both		5538	2947	From written work

This, it will be noted, is a study concerned only with grammatical errors, but in both oral and written speech. All other studies listed collect only oral errors, except those of O. S. Thompson, W. Barnes, and H. D. Fillers, while seven collect grammatical errors only, and five collect errors in both language and grammar.

Some of the investigators contend that the only objective which justifies the study of grammar is that of correction of errors; but for purposes of investigation it is necessary merely to assume this objective, not to defend it. This is discussed by the writer in the following quotation.*

"There are at least five points of view from which the problem of determining the minimal elements in a course of study in grammar for the elementary grades may be attacked. Each has its own technique and all produce curriculums which have grammatical elements in common, but in which there are different elements.

"The five points of view referred to are the following: (1) discipline of mental activities, (2) a knowledge of the structure of thought as exhibited in the sentence, (3) the understanding of literature, (4) the improvement of speech through the artistic use of grammatical information, and (5) the improvement of speech through the elimination of errors. Five differs from four in this respect. Four seeks to raise speech which is grammatically correct to the plane of rhetorical effectiveness through a knowledge of grammatical elements which may become tools with which to manipulate the expression of ideas. Five aims to study the errors of speech and present a body of information which may be used to make the language as spoken, grammatically accurate.

"The methods of investigation utilized in each case have elements in common. The first essential is to analyze the terms in order to tabulate the elements and arrange these in the order of their importance. The arrangement in order of importance is necessary because in practical use it is usually found that the element of time for study makes it impossible to teach all the

*Part I, *Sixteenth Yearbook*, pp. 85-6.

items in any such list. In the case of the discipline of mental activities, a psychological analysis of mental activities must be made in order to obtain a list and in the list the function of each item and its bearings must be determined in order to evaluate the elements and designate their relative importance. In the case of the use of grammar as a means of studying the structure of thought, a logical or psychological study of thought processes and a philological study of the sentence must be made and the elements evaluated. In the study of grammar as an aid to the appreciation of written thought it is necessary to make an exhaustive examination of the use of grammatical forms, to evaluate these forms, and to arrange them in order of importance. A study of the elevating of speech from grammatical accuracy to rhetorical effectiveness necessitates a study of the technique of rhetorically effective writers and speakers in the manipulation of grammatical forms and rules. The forms and rules so manipulated must, as in the case of the others, be evaluated and arranged in order of importance. In the study of grammar for the elimination of errors, it is apparent that the first step is to ascertain the rules which are broken and to determine their relative importance.

"The second step in the procedure is the designation and evaluation of those grammatical elements which will give assistance in reaching the objectives discerned from each point of view. Such lists of elements or curriculums will in all probability have many common items; but on the other hand, some will have elements not found in others, and probably in no two curriculums will the items be arranged in the same relative order of importance. For instance, if training in delicacy of discrimination is one element in the list of mental activities, we should find the stress laid upon those fine points of grammar which would give practice in discrimination of shades of meaning; or among those elements which are used in attaining rhetorical effectiveness, participial constructions and infinitives would have a position of high honor, while in the use of correction of errors as a basis of selection, we should find the participles and infinitives lightly regarded and the simpler tense form of verbs and cases of pronouns evaluated highly."

§2—Methods of Collecting and Classifying

In all the studies except that of E. D. Randolph, who obtained stenographic reports, and of Barnes, who collected at leisure in person, the oral material was collected by teachers. The detailed form used in Kansas City, Bonham, Columbia, Hibbing, Detroit, and Pittsburgh, is as follows except that where oral errors, only, were collected, the portion referring to written work was omitted, and when both language and grammar were studied the term "errors in grammar" was changed to "errors in language."

"The following directions for collecting both oral and written work were given to the teachers:

"Written Language

"Aim of Investigation: To find what errors in grammar children naturally make in writing when not corrected by the teacher.

"1. Who shall collect written work. All teachers of grades III to VII inclusive shall hand in to the principal the written work of their pupils.

"2. What written work shall not be handed in. No dictated work or work copied from books or blackboards shall be handed in to the principal. No work which is rewritten after corrections have been made by teacher or the class shall be handed in to the principal by the teacher.

"3. Subjects of written work. Written work ordinarily done in the regular order of school work should be included. No special effort to get written work should be made, except that if possible the pupils should select or be assigned once a week some topic upon which they will write with great freedom and at some length. If they write freely and at some length, they will reveal their errors, which is the desired end.

"4. Form. (a) Any kind of paper may be used. (b) Ink or pencil may be used. That which will give greatest freedom in expression should be used. (c) No unusual mention should be made of neatness or legibility. (d) At the top of each page each pupil should write the name, the school, the grade, the room, and the date.

"5. How to bundle the papers. When the teacher has finished with a set of papers, the set should be bound together securely with a cord, and in a conspicuous place on the bundle should be given the name of the school, the grade, the room, and the date. Each set should be bound by itself in one bundle, and on November 21 all the bundles should be bound securely into one large bundle, conspicuously marked as to school, grade, and room, and sent to the principal's office. Along with this bundle should be sent, in an envelope, the names of all pupils in the room, arranged alphabetically by sex together with age in years and months on November 21. The principal will then forward all the bundles to the superintendent's office upon the first visit of the trucks after November 21. The principal should, if convenient, fasten the room bundles together, marking each large bundle with the name of the school.

"6. Length of period for collection. Papers written between October 27 and November 21, inclusive, should be handed in.

"Note.—Children must not be told that their papers are being collected for grammatical errors, nor should anything be done to make them unusually careful or to make them unnatural or stilted. If papers are corrected or recopied, the rewritten work must not be handed in, but the original work must be. No corrections should be made on the original paper.

"Oral Language

"Aim of Investigation: To find what errors in grammar children naturally make in talking when not corrected by the teacher.

"1. Who shall collect the oral errors. All teachers of grades II to VII, inclusive, and principals shall collect all oral errors in grammar made in the schoolroom and around the school building by children of any age.

"2. Time to be spent in collecting errors. From eight o'clock Monday morning, November 17, to four o'clock Friday evening, November 21.

"3. Details of tabulation. (a) Carry a notebook constantly for these five days and jot down every grammatical error made orally in your presence. If the same error occurs more than once, either with or without the use of the same words, note it each time it occurs. (b) Copy each error as nearly as possible with the exact words used. (c) In copying the errors from the notebooks to hand in to the principal, each error should be written in ink on a separate piece of school paper 1 inch by 4 inches in size. This will save the office much copying work. (d) Seal all these in one or more large envelopes, writing on the outside of each envelope 'Oral errors reported by .... of the ....school, grade ....' (Name of teacher.) (e) The principal will bind all these envelopes into one package and conspicuously mark 'Oral errors from .... school,' and send as soon as possible to the superintendent's office."

Meek (12) modified this method by having his teachers make a preliminary collection of errors for a short period. These were then classified and the classification re-submitted to the teachers to note errors when they occurred and record the frequency of occurrence of each class.

After the oral errors were collected, the classification was, in the W. W. Charters and E. Miller study (10), allowed to grow of its own accord. The method of listing all syntactical rules found in grammar and checking against these might have been used as is necessary in some obscurely delimited subjects like sociology or economics; but it seemed objectively better to let the classes grow, although it is quite apparent that one who has studied grammar is likely to follow unconsciously the grammatical rules which he knows. Those studies which followed this study (Bonham, Columbia, Detroit, Hibbing, and Pittsburgh) used the Kansas City classification as a basis. The method of classification used by the rest of the investigators is not stated in their reports.

When the written material in the Charters and Miller study was examined, the oral list was used as a basis and additional classes grew as the material was read. Difficulties were met with here because some items which the tabulators later used were omitted from the early reading — the capitalization of proper nouns, in particular — and a separate study of this had to be made. The later study of Betz and Marshall is much more completely classified.

§3—METHODS OF DERIVING GRAMMAR

When the classes of errors had been determined in the Charters and Miller study the problem shifted to that of determining upon the basis of these errors the grammatical rules which should be taught. It was necessary first to change the form from the statement of the error to the statement of the rule broken. For instance, the simple statement of error, *"Subject of the verb not in the nominative,"* had to be changed to a statement of the rule broken, namely, *"The subject of a verb is in the nominative case."* In a more difficult example where the error read *"Wrong forms of noun and pronoun,"* fifteen rules had to be listed. This procedure was carried out for all the errors and resulted in a list of about sixty rules which were found to have been broken by the children.

At this point it was discovered that the children, if they were to understand and use the rules, must be taught certain grammatical definitions. For instance, to undrestand the rule *The subje.t of a verb is in the nominative case,* a knowledge of *subject* and *predicate* and, therefore, of the *sentence* was necessary. In addition, a knowledge of *subject* involves acquaintance with *noun* and *pronoun*. *Nominative case* includes *case* and the *nominative case* in *pronouns*, and *predicate* involves the *verb*.

Each of the 29 classes of error was treated in this way, and finally a point was reached at which there lay before the investigators a complete list of the grammatical rules and definitions necessary to correct the errors of the children of Kansas City. This material was then classified under parts of speech as found in §4 of this chapter, Result No. 5.

§4—RESULTS

1. All the investigators agree in the finding that errors in verbs are most frequent, constituting, as they do, around sixty

per cent of the grammatical errors, except Randolph, whose stenographic reports show the verbs to be about ten.

2. Because it is a well-known fact that when errors become very common they cease to be thought serious and in course of time are accepted as good form, the query naturally arises as to whether or not the most common are considered to be the most serious. Obviously, the most common are serious from the point of view of frequency, but they may not attach so deep a stigma to the user as do some much less common errors.

With this in mind the teachers of Pittsburgh were asked to list the ten errors which each considered to be the worst. These were compiled. The relative frequency with which each was mentioned by teachers and the proportional percentage which each was of the total "worst list" was compiled. This percentage was compared with similar percentages of frequency of occurrence of the error. It was found in the case of 41 specific items that the correlation between the frequency of mention by teachers as being one of ten worst errors, with frequency of occurrence was .63 by the Spearman Foot rule. This is fairly high and suggests that, in general, the gravity follows the frequency when measured in this rough way.

The twelve errors in which there was the widest divergence between frequency of occurrence and frequency of mention by the teachers may be d vided into two classes. Five errors were, in the opinion of the teachers, much *worse* than they were *frequent*. The use of *was* for *were* was ranked 30.5 in the frequency of error list, but in the teachers' opinion was second to worst; *learn* for *teach* (18) frequency, (36.5) gravity; *that there* (4), (15.5); double comparatives (26), (34.5), and *them there* (20), (27). In seven extreme cases the reverse was true. The teachers did not think the errors so bad as they were frequent. *Ain't got* ranked twenty-eighth in seriousness in teachers' opinions, but ninth in frequency of occurrence; *give* for *gave* (31.5), (15.5); *is* for *are* (16), (6); misuse of *me* as in *It is me* (22.5), (14); wrong sequence of pronouns as in *Everyone must do their work* (36), (28); *come* for *came* (18), (11); and *will* for *shall* (31.5), (24.5).

3. In Pittsburgh twenty-three specific errors with a frequency of over 200 constitute 56 per cent of the total. These, with their frequencies in a total of 25,676 errors, are as follows:

TABLE II

THE TWENTY-THREE MOST FREQUENT ERRORS

was for *were*	1555 errors
seen for *saw*	1513 "
ain't	1361 "
can for *may*	1150 "
done for *did*	895 "
is for *are*	777 "
don't for *doesn't*	721 "
this here	684 "
John, he went	671 "
didn't have no	531 "
them things	479 "
that there	472 "
ain't got	443 "
have got	439 "
ain't got no	435 "
come for *came*	350 "
it was (is, ain't) me	340 "
why, there was	330 "
didn't do nothing	302 "
lay for *lie*	280 "
off for *from*	276 "
went for *gone*	245 "
give for *gave*	202 "

4. Comparison between percentages of error in Kansas City, Detroit, Hibbing, and Pittsburgh is given in Table III. The two items which are listed in Pittsburgh alone are due to the fact that errors in language rather than errors in grammar were reported by the teachers. The three items mentioned in Hibbing alone present certain interesting facts. The use of adverbs instead of

TABLE III

COMPARISON OF PERCENTAGES IN ORAL ERRORS IN KANSAS CITY, DETROIT, HIBBING, AND PITTSBURGH

	Per Cent				
	K. C.	D.	H.	P.	
Subject of the verb not in the nominative case	4	4	3	3	
Predicate nominative not in the nominative case	2	1	1	2	
Object of the verb or preposition not in the objective case	1	1	1	1	
Wrong form of pronoun	2	2	3	2	
First personal pronoun standing first	2	1	2	2	
Failure of a pronoun to agree with its antecedent	0	1	1	1	
Confusion of demonstrative adjective and personal pronoun	3	3	2	2	
Failure of a verb to agree with its subject in number and person	14	12	9	13	
Confusion of past and present tenses	2	12	7	3	
Confusion of past tense and past participle	24	14	8	14	
Wrong tense form	5	3	5	5	
Wrong verb	12	18	20	18	
Incorrect use of the mood	0	0	0	0	
Confusion of comparative and superlative	1	1	1	1	
Confusion of adjectives and adverbs	4	2	2	2	
Misplaced modifiers	0	0	1	0	
Double negatives	11	9	8	10	
Confusion of preposition and conjunction	0	0	0	0	
Syntactical redundance	10	15	21	16	
Wrong part of speech due to similarity of sound	1	1	0	0	
Confusion of prepositions				2	
Pronunciation and enunciation				3	
Adv. instead of negative form of verb			2		
Words omitted			1		
Miscellaneous			2		
(Total number of errors)...............	5883	11207	10190	25676	

negative verbs is illustrated by *I never done it* for *I didn't do it.* Words omitted are found in such sentences as, *I go basement* and *Mother went Chisholm.*

This table should be read as follows: The error, *"The subject of the verb not in the nominative case,"* constitutes 4 per cent of the total of 5883 errors reported in Kansas City, 4 per cent of the 11,207 errors reported in Detroit, and so forth. Any type of error given 0 percentage appeared with a percentage of less than .5.

Randolph* (14), in his stenographic report of the speech of children, lists 1412 errors in sentence structure out of a total of 2954 errors. None of these are collected from teachers in the other studies. This is a significant difference and, while incomplete answers may have constituted a very large part of Randolph's list, other errors not belonging to this class were present. It is, therefore, quite certain that the stenographic report is superior to collection by teachers.

5. The grammatical rules and definitions included in the course of study based on the errors of Kansas City children may be summarized as follows:

A. Nouns.
    (a) Definition
    (b) Inflection (1) number (2) case [possessive] (3) gender [slight use]
    (c) Common and proper
    (d) Syntax—(1) subject of a verb (2) subjective complement (3) object of verb or preposition (4) the indirect object. (These are chiefly of use as an aid in the understanding of pronouns.)

B. Pronouns
    (a) Definition
    (b) Personal pronouns (case and person, gender, number)
    (c) Compound personal pronouns
    (d) Relative pronouns (gender, case)

*Part I, *Sixteenth Yearbook*, pp. 98-99.

C. Adjectives
  (a) Definition
  (b) Demonstrative adjectives
  (c) Cardinal and ordinal adjectives
  (d) The derivation of proper adjectives
  (e) Comparison of adjectives

D. Verbs
  (a) Definition
  (b) Transitive and intransitive verbs
  (c) Person
  (d) Number
  (e) Tense (particularly present, past, and past perfect)
  (f) *Shall* and *will*
  (g) *Can* and *may*
  (h) Mode (very slight)
  (i) Voice
  (j) Past participles
  (k) Infinitive (very slight)—split infinitive

E. Adverbs
  (a) Definition
  (b) Comparison

F. Prepositions
  (a) Definition
  (b) Government of case

G. Conjunctions
  (a) Definition
  (b) Classification

H. Misplaced modifiers

I. Double negatives

J. Syntactical redundance

K. Spelling—when explainable by reference to grammar:—*to*, a preposition; *two*, an adjective; and *too*, an adverb

L. Sentence structure
  (a) Definition

(b) How to write it

Begins with capital letter

Ends with a period, exclamation mark, or interrogation mark

M. Parsing and analysis

(a) Definition of both

(b) Division of sentence into parts

(c) In general, the parsing will follow the elements outlined in the foregoing outline

(d) The xtent to which the parsing will be carried should be determined by the errors of the children

Barnes (15), in general, agrees with the foregoing items. Differences are as follows: He adds collective nouns, although the one who listens to a speaker can only infrequently tell that he has made a mistake in number. He also adds appositives in nouns, none of which were noted in the Kansas City study. He also adds the plural of demonstrative adjectives, which was an oversight in the Kansas City study. He adds gerunds but omits negatives and syntactical redundance, which are possibly not strictly grammatical in nature.

6. An examination of these lists shows that grammar is greatly simplified as to both the complexity of the sentences used and the narrow range of facts to be learned. Much of the difficulty of grammar is eliminated. Unusual tenses, gerundives, infinitive constructions, and most of the mood forms are among those in which mistakes are infrequently made or not made at all.

In the Kansas City study it was found that the following could be omitted from the course of study which was in operation in the schools at the time of the investigation: the exclamatory sentence, the conjunction, the appositive, the nominative of address, the nominative by exclamation, the objective complement, the adverbial objective, the indefinite pronoun, the objective used as a substantive, the classification of adverbs, the noun clause, the conjunctive adverb, the retained objective, the moods (except, possibly, the subjunctive of *to be*), the infinitive (except the split infinitive), the objective subject, the participle (except the definition and the present and past forms), the nominative absolute, and the gerund.

It is evident that some of the items in this list could not have been revealed by this method. For instance, one cannot tell from reading whether or not the writer should have used an exclamation mark to convey the meaning he intended. Again, the material read did not happen to include any cases of the nominative of address where the comma was not used correctly; and, in fact, the use of the nominative of address was very slight. The oral sentences reported by the teachers did not include noun clauses; and the children's themes which were read seldom used the complex sentence, the preference seeming to be for the compound sentence.

It is quite clear that a much more simple set of sentences could be used for analysis and parsing than are presented to children when it is necessary for them to learn to analyze and parse sentences involving subtle rules in grammar which they do not naturally break.

7. W. J. Richardson (19) and Charters (Pittsburgh) (21) classified the errors by grades, to see what natural eliminations occurred during progress through the grades. Clearly, no absolute standard could be set up, because certain errors may be stressed more heavily and, therefore, noticed more sharply by teachers in the upper grades. But, if a type of error has completely disappeared, the fact is of some significance. None such, however, were noticed except the use of quite childish incorrect forms of the past and perfect tenses; and in many cases, due to the reason just mentioned, some errors increased in number or total per cent.

§5—HIGH SCHOOL AND COLLEGE FRESHMEN
(Study 22)

Johnson* tabulated the errors in written composition of 132 high school Freshmen and of sixty-six college Freshmen in Kansas

*"The Persistency of Errors in English Composition", R. I. Johnson, *School Review*, October, 1917.

City, Mo., in which the former wrote 50,371 words and the latter 32,693 words on elective themes written upon for fifteen minutes during three successive class exercises at the beginning of the year. On the first day of the three the following instructions were given to the pupils: "Tell about any incident suggested by (1) 'Missing the Train', (2) 'A Day's Journey', or (3) 'A Lucky Mistake'." On the second day the instructions were: "Describe (1) a person you know, (2) any scene that has impressed you, or (3) a department store during a busy hour." The instructions on the third and last day were: "Explain (1) how to use a dictionary, (2) how you would spend a vacation at home to the best advantage, or (3) your ideas of a Freshman's responsibilities."

Following is a statement of methods of scoring and tabulation:

"1. *The category of error.* — In tabulating the errors, it was necessary to decide upon some sort of classification. First, a temporary working list of errors was made. This was modified from time to time as new kinds of mistakes appeared in the papers, until, finally, when the tabulation was completed, it was found that forty-seven different headings had been utilized. These forty-seven kinds, however, grouped themselves by the laws of natural relationship into fourteen major classes, or types — if the inevitable miscellaneous group can be said to constitute a type.

"Only technical errors, of course, were included in the tabulation: errors that relate to the 'mechanics of writing,' such as errors in grammar, spelling, the use of the apostrophe, etc. The thought of the sentences and paragraphs was not criticized, unless by some violation of grammatical principle it was rendered ambiguous or otherwise confusing in meaning. Furthermore, no *doubtful* errors were tabulated. Anything about which there is a common difference of opinion, such as the observance of some of the mooted rules of punctuation or the use of simplified spelling, was omitted from the study.

"2. *Distribution of errors according to kinds.* — With the foregoing list as a basis, all the errors in the 83,064 words of manuscript were carefully classified."

The classes of error and frequencies were as follows:

TABLE IV

Showing (1) number of errors, (2) proportional ranking,
(3) errors per ten thousand words, in themes of
high school and college Freshmen.

Class No.	Mistakes	H. S. Errors			College Errors			
		1	2	3	1	2	3	
I	Case of Pronouns	11	14	2	2	14	1	
II	Others in Pronouns	102	7	20	40	6	13	
III	Verbs	93	8	18	32	7	11	
IV	Adjectives and Adverbs	52	10	10	28	9	9	
V	Prepositions and Conjunctions	50	11	10	24	10	8	
VI	Sentence Structure	220	4	44	32	8	11	
VII	Clearness of Meaning	46	12	9	17	12	6	
VIII	Punctuation	232	2	27	100	3	33	
IX	Apostrophe	150	6	30	75	5	25	
X	Capitalization	196	5	39	120	2	40	
XI	Careless Omission or Repetition	223	3	45	77	4	26	
XII	Spelling	675	1	135	208	1	69	
XIII	Quotation Marks	25	13	5	9	13	3	
XIV	Miscellaneous	85	9	17	23	11	8	
	Totals	2160		43	787		24	

Table IV, which is compiled from data given in the investigators' tabulations, should be read as follows: eleven mistakes in case in pronouns were found in the 2160 errors made by high school Freshmen. This class of error ranked fourteenth in frequency among the errors made by these students and occurred at the rate of two per ten thousand words. The college Freshmen made two mistakes of this kind out of a total of 787 errors. These two were fourteenth in order of frequency of error and occurred at the rate of one (approximately) per ten thousand words in the 32,693 words written.

The percentage ranking compares closely with those found in the study of grammar in the written work of the sixth and seventh grades in Kansas City (p. 194).

Johnson finds that the relative rankings of errors by frequency of occurrence do not vary greatly as between high school and college Freshmen. That is to say, the most frequent high school error was likely to be the most frequent in college. But the columns marked 3 in the table, which have been added by the writer, show that in errors per ten thousand words the frequency has materially decreased during the four years of the high school. The totals have decreased from 43 to 24 or nearly 45 per cent. Most noticeable improvement is found in ability to use good sentence structure, the decrease in errors being 75 per cent, and in ability to spell, with a decrease of about 50 per cent. The only marked increase is in punctuation, which is explained on specific accidental grounds.

Generally speaking, if 150 words are counted as a page, the total number of errors per page found in the high school Freshmen's themes is about 6.4, in the college Freshmen's themes about 3.6. The errors in spelling run about two and one per page respectively. Spelling and punctuation together constitute 42 per cent of the high school Freshmen errors and about 39 per cent of the errors of college Freshmen.

From the data, by an unstated method, Johnson derives the following order of teaching emphasis upon the different classes of error, the first being most important:

(1) Mistakes in capitalization. (2) Mistakes in the use of the apostrophe. (3) Mistakes in punctuation. (4) Mistakes in the use of adjectives and adverbs. (5) Mistakes in spelling. (6) Mistakes in pronouns, not including case. (7) Careless omissions and repetitions. (8) Mistakes in the use of verbs. (9) Mistakes in the use of prepositions and conjunctions. (10) Sentence meaning not clear. (11) Sentence structure not grammatical. (12) Mistakes in the use of quotation marks. (13) Mistakes in the cases of pronouns.

Chapter XVIII

MATHEMATICS

(Studies 23-30)

§1—Introduction

In examining the studies in the field of mathematics, the reader's attention is called particularly to the following points:

1. Except for the item of instructional order, four of the studies analyze the mathematical material in sufficient detail to permit of the construction of a limited course of study. Wilson gives the limits of complexity that need to be taught in connection with the operations which were found to be necessary in his material. The same is true of the studies of Williams, Callaway, and Charters. These studies show not only that an operation such as addition is used, but also that 90 or 95 per cent of the cases of addition involve the adding of four addends of three places. This detailed information is significant because it is quite one thing to show that business men believe that addition should be taught, or that superintendents are convinced that more attention must be paid to addition, and quite another to be able to limit the range of addition to operations of definite complexity, beyond which it is relatively immaterial to give practice.

2. A wide variety of classification of the material is illustrated. Mathematical operations constitute a convenient method of classifying the information for technical purposes, and this is used by all the investigators; but, in addition, the material is classified according to other criteria. Monroe and Wilson compare the frequency of the occurrence of problems dealing with occupations, with the lists of occupations used in the Federal Census. As has already been noted, classifications have been

made according to the magnitude of numbers and the range of complexity of the operations.

3. Methods of deriving service mathematics are illustrated. Textbooks dealing with the subjects of chemistry and clothing have been read and their exercises worked out. In doing this the investigators have described all the concepts and operations which are mathematical in nature. This enables them to determine with considerable exactness how much mathematics it is necessary for students to know in order successfully to understand the texts and work the exercises.

4. Descriptions of method are stated in detail in several studies. Monroe's study and Wilson's second study are particularly full. Williams's statement, while short, involves simple elements and is sufficiently exact to be followed and verified. As has been noted in Chapter XIII, §2, detailed descriptions of methods are particularly necessary at this stage of the science of curriculum construction. Only by recording methods is it possible to avoid duplication and secure refinement of the procedure.

§2—The Arithmetic of Business Men
(Study 23)

G. M. Wilson* addressed a questionnaire to the business men of Connersville to get their advice concerning the content of arithmetic. The questionnaire follows. Interspersed among the items are the conclusions drawn from the returns.

" 'Questionnaire to Business Men

" 'The teachers are working with me on the problem of making changes in our course of study in arithmetic, as suggested by advanced educational thought and the commercial progress of our community. I desire the assistance and support of the best thought of our business community. You are therefore

*Course of Study in Mathematics, Connersville, Ind.

asked to give your hearty coöperation and a few minutes of your time.

" 'Please fill out and return by March 22.

'Thanking you,

'G. M. Wilson.

" '1. At present the school time in the grades is divided approximately as follows:—Reading, 26 per cent, Arithmetic, 16 per cent, Language, 12 per cent, History 11 per cent, Geography, 8 per cent, Spelling, 7 per cent, Music, 6 per cent, Drawing, 6 per cent, Writing 4 per cent, Physiology, 4 per cent.

" 'Does this appeal to you as a proper division of school time in the grades?'

"The replies indicate a general agreement with the above division of school time in grades. The exceptions are, calling for less time in drawing and more time in spelling and writing. The arguments given are based upon the fact that our graduates do not write and spell as well as they should. This we do not deny, nor do we attempt to defend it. The fact remains, however, that pupils of to-day write better and spell better than formerly. This is proved by every actual test that has been made, the Springfield test being most conclusive. The studies of Corman and Rice on spelling show that extra time on spelling does not improve the results. Their studies are exhaustive and involve tests including thousands of pupils, and their conclusions are therefore more or less authoritative.

" '2. Stated differently, English receives 49.27 per cent of the school time in the grades; the three R's receive 65.24 per cent; the fundamentals (the three R's plus geography and history) receive 86.09 per cent; the special subjects (physiology, music, and drawing) receive 13.91 per cent.

" 'Does your experience suggest any changes of emphasis?'

"No points are mentioned here which are not included in one (1) above.

" '3. Following are some of the topics we, as boys, studied in arithmetic in the grades. Check ($\sqrt{}$) the topics for which you have had considerable use during the past six months. Cross (x) the topics for which you have had little or no use during the last six months:—

Troy weight	Compound fractions
Apothecaries' weight	Foreign exchange
Longitude and time	Compound proportion
The surveyor's table	True discount
The greatest common divisor	Cases 2 and 3 in percentage
The least common multiple	Compound interest
Complex fractions	Partial payments
Cube root	Partnership

" 'May some of these topics be omitted from our arithmetic work without material loss? What ones?'

"The sentiment of the replies is strongly in favor of the elimination of the subjects indicated above. The G. C. D., L. C. M., and complex fractions failed to get any support. Cube root, compound proportion, cases in percentage, and the surveyor's table received only the meagerest sort of support. All told there were thirty-four votes for and seventy-seven against these topics. The reasons given for eliminating these subjects are that they have no practical value to most people, and that the time is needed upon the fundamentals. These reasons appeal to me as getting at the truth of the matter.

" '4. Following are some of the topics we did not study in arithmetic as boys:—

Saving and loaning money
Mortgages
Modern banking methods
Building and loan associations
Keeping simple accounts
Investing money
Bonds as investments

Real estate as investment (cheap rentals, good residence
property, business blocks, or farm lands—as investments).
Marks of a good investment. (It is estimated that the get-
rich-quick concerns fleece the American people out of
$60,000,000 a year.)
Taxes, levies, public expenditures
Profits in different lines of business
Life insurance as protection and investment
" 'Check (√) any of the above that appeal to you as worthy
of a place in present-day arithmetic work.'

"Almost without exception every topic in the above was
checked by everyone replying. This was indeed a surprise, and
a pleasant one. Much of the work on these topics will necessarily
be handled as informational work. The figuring involved will
be simple and will center in the fundamental processes and percentage. We are certainly glad to have the approval of the business men of the community upon the work attempted along
these lines.

" '5. Connersville is developing important industrial and commercial interests. To what extent should those interests have
an influence in shaping a course of study for our schools, especially
the course in arithmetic?'

"The sentiment is almost unanimous that the schools and the
course of study should take into consideration the industrial and
commercial interests of our community.

" '6. Suggest some feasible plan of bringing the school into
closer relations with the industrial, commercial, and business
interests of our community. Give some figures or problems from
your own business.'

"Few of those replying attempted suggestions as to feasible
plans for accomplishing the purpose indicated above."

§3—OPINIONS OF SUPERINTENDENTS
(Study 24)

Coffman and Jessup sent a questionnaire to 1700 superintendents of cities of 4000 population or over, and to every sixth county

superintendent in the United States. Replies were received from 52 per cent of the superintendents of cities of all sizes and from all sections of the country. Replies were received from 24 per cent of the superintendents of counties, representative of all sections.

The questionnaire is as follows:

"Economy of Time as Related to Material Used in Arithmetic

"Underscore once the subjects which should receive slight attention; underscore twice the subjects which should be eliminated:

"Apothecaries' weight, Troy weight, furlong, rod in square measure, drachm, quarter in avoirdupois weight, surveyor's tables, foreign money, folding papers, reduction of more than two steps, long method of finding G. C. D., L. C. M., true discount, cube root, partnership, compound proportion, compound and complex fractions, cases in percentage, annual interest, longitude and time, unreal fractions, alligation, metric system, progression, and aliquot parts.

"Others...

"Underscore subjects which should receive more attention than is usually given:

"Addition, subtraction, multiplication, division, fractions, percentage, interest, saving and loaning money, banking, borrowing, building and loan associations, investments, stocks and bonds, taxes, levies, public expenditures, insurance as protection and investment, profits in business, and public utilities.

"Economy of Time as Related to the Method Used in Teaching

"Percentage of recitation time in arithmetic which should be given over to strictly drill work in each grade.

"Grades.......	1	2	3	4	5	6	7	8
"No. Minutes..	...	...	..	...	...	...	...	.."

This questionnaire would have yielded more valuable returns if the topics in arithmetic had not been divided and if a system of underscoring had been used to indicate increased attention, slight attention, and elimination. For instance, it would have been possible to double-underscore increased attention, single-underscore slight attention, and cross out eliminated topics. The difficulty with the present form is that there is no opportunity to indicate elimination or slight attention in the second group, or added attention to the items of the first group.

These returns were tabulated, showing the reaction of the superintendents (1) of cities, (2) of counties, and (3) of cities of 100,000 and over. The tables were thrown into percentage and graphic form. The material shows that the superintendents of the larger cities are inclined to favor more elimination than are the superintendents of the smaller cities. Tabulation by districts shows that there is a slight difference between the North and the South, but this difference is not greater than between the North Central and North Atlantic States.

Tables were made to show that the amount of time spent in minutes per week on arithmetic recitations varies from none to 450 in the first grade, and from none to 450 in the eighth grade. The percentage of time given all the way through the grades was shown to run in the city schools from a median of 43 per cent in the first grade to 53 per cent in the third grade, with a decreasing amount of time spent upon drill through the grades to the eighth.

The study shows that there is a normal tendency on the part of half of the superintendents in favor of either eliminating or lessening the attention to be given to certain subjects in arithmetic, such as alligation, cube root, unreal fractions, progression, and certain obsolete tables such as folding paper, surveyor's measure, etc. It reveals also an overwhelming total in favor of increased emphasis on the four fundamentals, and a strong disposition towards increased emphasis on social and economic applications in arithmetic. It is recommended in the study that the 50 per cent of the cities spending the most time on arithmetic reduce this to the amount being expended by the 50 per cent spending the least time. It is further suggested that the median percentage of recitation time given over to drill in each grade be adopted as a standard until scientific investigations have proved this to be an error.

§4—Problems in Four Textbooks
(Study 25)

Monroe* in a preliminary study of the economy of time in arithmetic utilizes four textbooks as material for study.

"The investigation described in this report is based upon the assumption that the primary purpose of teaching arithmetic in the elementary school is to equip the pupil (1) with that knowledge of facts, principles, and relationships existing between quantities, etc., which is needed to decide what arithmetical operations are to be performed in solving valuable practical problems; and (2) with the skills which are necessary to perform these operations. A practical problem is defined as a problem which occurs in the course of a human activity. Human activity is not restricted to vocations or occupations, but, as the following pages show, four major divisions of human activities have been recognized: (1) occupational activities, (2) activities of the home, (3) personal activities, and (4) activities of school children. This definition of a 'practical problem' has no reference to the economic or social importance of the problem. It simply means that in order to be classed as 'practical' a problem must be one that occurs in some human activity.

"One major purpose actuated this study, namely, to secure a list of the arithmetical problems which arise in human activities and which possess a sufficient degree of utilitarian or socializing value to justify their being designated as minimal essentials of purpose. At this time it is possible to give only the method of investigation and certain tentative observations on the data which have been collected.

*Part I, *Sixteenth Yearbook*, pp. 111-127, W. S. Monroe.

"In determining this list of problems the plan has been, first, to secure as complete a list as possible, and, second, to determine which problems possess sufficient value to be designated as minimal essentials of purpose. In accomplishing the first purpose problems have been collected from textbooks and other available sources. Since the final list is to consist only of problems which arise in human activities, problems which did not contain some clue to identify them with a human activity have been rejected. For example, the following problems probably do not occur in any human activity:

"880 times the area of Porto Rico is 2,800 sq. mi. less than that of the United States. Find the area of Porto Rico.

"One year Montana produced 30,820,000 pounds of wool. If this was 2.17 of the total production of the United States that year, how much did all other states produce?

"Problems such as the following do occur in several human activities, but the statements of the problems contain nothing to identify them with any particular activity. For this reason such problems have been rejected:

"The sides of a triangular field are respectively 236.7 ft., 257.9 ft., and 248.4 ft. What is the perimeter?

"The plan of this study involves the assumption that the problems possessing sufficient value to be included in the list of 'minimal essentials of purpose' *are to be found in our present arithmetic texts and in other accessible printed problem lists.* The validity of this assumption cannot be tested until the examination of texts and other printed lists of problems is completed, but the study has been carried far enough to show that the list which is obtained will be far more complete than is now found in any one textbook. It should also be noted that since our purpose is to obtain a list of minimal essentials of purpose, all problems that do not possess a sufficient degree of value will be excluded from this final list. Since this is the case, the fact that unimportant problems are found in the textbooks will not influence the final list.

"The writer recognizes that the ideal procedure would be to

make a complete survey of activities to ascertain what arithmetical problems exist and the frequency of their occurrence. However, the plan now being followed was chosen because it was felt to be far more feasible. It is not believed that the assumption which it involves will place serious limitations upon the results, but after the sources of problems now being used have been exhausted, the writer proposes to test the validity of the assumption and its influence upon the final list."

The problems were classified and sub-classified first on the basis of occupational activities, activities of the home, personal activities, and activities of school children. This classification into four groups is based on the investigator's own opinion and is adopted because it seems to him to suit his purposes. The sub-classification of occupational activities followed the Federal Census and took cognizance of the relative importance of each in terms of the number of people engaged in it.

The problems are further classified under arithmetical types or difficulties which are included in the solution of each. The two following problems present different difficulties: (1) A family buys a quart of milk a day at 8c. a quart. How much is its milk bill in a month of 30 days? (2) How much will be left of $1 after paying for 8 pounds of sugar at 6½ cents a pound? The first involves multiplication of integers while the second involves multiplication of fractions and subtraction. These are then listed as different types.

With these classes, social and arithmetical, in mind, the practical problems of the four books were listed. From the study it was possible to make two comparisons. First, the numerical importance of the occupations could be determined from the census and the number of types of problems could be determined for each with observance of absence or great frequency in each case. Second, the frequency of problems of each technical type could be ascertained. This frequency was quite interesting because it appeared that 511 type problems occurred only once, and 140 only twice, out of a total of 1023 types; while on the other hand, one type occurred 434 times and a second 256 times out of a total of 5936. And, indeed, 18 per cent, or approximately one out of five, of all the problems listed were from the following types:

"At $1.75 each, what will 17 books cost? (Multiplication.) A man borrowed $250 on January 15, at 6%. How much was the interest on October 15? (Simple interest.) If I borrow $50, at 6%, on February 8 of this year, how much will be due on May 2 on next year? (Amount.) What change should be received from a five-dollar bill in paying a monthly bill for 30 qts. of milk at 8c a quart, and 5 jars of cream at 15c a jar? (Multiplication.) What is the cost of 50 gals. of paint at $66\frac{2}{3}$ cts. a gallon, and $4\frac{1}{2}$ gals. of varnish at $1.25 a gallon? (Multiplication of fractions and addition.)

"Conclusions

"1. Out of a total of 1023 types of practical problems found in four textbooks, 720, or 71 per cent, occur in occupational activities.

"2. No problems have been found to assign to a large number of the specified occupations. These occupations make up 55 per cent of the total working population. If further research does not reveal a considerable number of occupational problems which come under these heads, a limitation of arithmetic as a vocational subject will be obvious.

"3. The authors of four textbooks are far from being in agreement on the type problems of arithmetic. Only one author out of four has recognized 511 out of 1023 type problems, and 140 type problems have received the recognition of only two authors out of four.

"4. If we take the judgment of authors of textbooks as a basis for determining the importance of the problems in arithmetic, we arrive at the conclusion that there are not more than 372 type problems which are judged important enough to be included in a text by three out of four authors."

§5.—SOCIAL AND BUSINESS ARITHMETIC

(Study 26)

A study was made by Wilson* "to determine the arithmetic actually used by adults in their social and business relations." The material was collected in the following manner:

A sheet containing the following instructions was sent to each superintendent and teacher assisting in the study:

"Arithmetic Survey

"The purpose of this study is to find out by a simple and direct method what mature people are figuring, and to get some idea of the amount of figuring which they actually do. The material should be collected by sixth, seventh, and eighth grade pupils and this should be done in such a way as to interest these pupils in gathering the data. The following details should be observed:

"Every father and mother of a sixth, seventh, or eighth grade pupil in your schools should be represented in the final returns. The effort should be made to get these data without particularly bothering or worrying the parents. In the evening, after the dishes are washed and the members of the family are together, the pupil should simply ask the mother (and father) whether or not she had any use for arithmetic during the day; if so, what? Then note the problems. They may relate to buying some eggs of a neighbor, or to figuring the bill from the grocer. In each case, the pupil should simply note the arithmetic involved and the statement should appear in simple problem form. No solutions are required. Where there is more than one child in the same family, the work should be divided. If the mother reports no use whatever and this continues for the two weeks, the report should be turned in just the same, giving the name of the person, the occupation and the dates covered.

*A Survey of the Social and Business Uses of Arithmetic, G. M. Wilson, Teachers College, Columbia University, 1919.

"It will doubtless be more satisfactory if the pupil will note on rough paper and then copy the problems the next day at school under the teacher's direction, using the regular sheets which give the necessary general data at the top.

"Please note that it is particularly desirable to get all of the data from every father and every mother, and not to get any extra data 'trumped up' for the occasion. These directions should be followed and the pupils should be so thoroughly instructed that they will get into the game and get things right. If they see the purpose of the study, they will quite surely be interested. They will want to solve problems that actually come up for solution by mature people and they will want, also, to omit problems which do not have any practical value. Both of these are purposes in which the school is very greatly interested."

The blanks on which the data were to be gathered, referred to in the above instructions, contained the following heading:

"Arithmetic used by Mature People

"Mr. or Mrs...

"Occupation...

"Problems figured during two weeks following date..........

"(List problems briefly; do not solve.)"

Many teachers had their pupils indicate the date of each day reported on. This had the additional value of checking more closely the work of the pupils. Many schools used uniform paper for making reports; while this is not essential, it added to the convenience in scoring. These added details are recommended in future applications of the study.

Some 14,583 problems were obtained from 4068 persons who were parents of the sixth, seventh and eighth grade children in the country, in small towns, and in large cities. Small schools in Iowa and the large school systems of Topeka, Sioux City, and Duluth are represented. The adults were listed by occupations; this list was compared with Ayres' list of wage-earning occupations and found to include all except six out of the total of 68 occupations. Comparison with the nine groups of occupations of the Thirteenth Census (1910) showed a smaller percentage in agriculture and domestic and personal service, and a greater percentage in trade and transportation.

The material was scored as follows:

"*Directions for Scoring*

"Each problem should be studied and scored on the following points:

"1. Cross out any problem that appears to be made up for the occasion. Only real problems should be scored.

"2. Buying or selling.

"3. United States money involved and the number of places involved in the factors of the problem.

'4. Topic or article bought or sold (or involved).

"5. Arithmetical processes, as addition, subtraction, etc.

"(a) In addition, subtraction, multiplication, and division, the degree of difficulty is to be noted as one place, two places, three places, etc. In addition and subtraction this means the addends or the terms involved and not the answers. In multiplication the multiplier is to be considered, in division the divisor.

"(b) In fractions, every fraction appearing is to be scored. The list will be sufficiently short.

"(c) Other processes are to be scored without noting the degree of difficulty."

The following is a sample of the scoring:

Paper No. 247—Marshalltown

The Paper   The Scoring

Name: Mr. and Mrs. J. M. C.
Occupation: Carpenter.
Problems figured during two weeks:
    Dec. 8 to Dec. 21. (List problems
    briefly; do not solve.)

1. What will be the cost of 5 yds. of crepe de chine at $1.75 a yard?

Buying
U. S. M.—3 place
Dry Goods
Mult.—1 place

H

2. In Christmas shopping today, I bought a razor at $1.50, a belt and belt buckle at $3.50, and a wrist watch at $25. What was the total?

Buying
U. S. M.—3 place, 4 place
Miscellaneous
Add.—4 place

H

3. Find the cost of meat at .35, bread .10, cookies .15, and a can of pork and beans at .15.

Buying
U. S. M.—2 place
Groceries
Add.—2 place

H

4. Find the cost of material $150 and men's labor $7.

Buying
U. S. M.—4 place, 5 place
Materials and labor
Add.—3 place

The following are difficulties encountered in scoring, which are illustrated in the sample papers above:

1. The problems of Father and Mother were seldom reported separately. It was necessary, in order to avoid confusion and misrepresentation, to indicate the problems belonging to each, and this was done by marking with an "H" (meaning housekeeper) all problems belonging to the mother. The problems so marked were collected and tabulated under housekeepers, leaving the others to be tabulated under the occupations of the fathers.

2. The difficulty of indicating the topic or articles involved in Christmas shopping first led to the use of the class, "Miscellaneous," for this purpose. This is illustrated in problem 2, paper 247—Marshalltown. Occasionally department store purchases are so listed. In spite of the instruction to list nothing under "Miscellaneous" that could be classified elsewhere, the total scores under this caption reached 630.

3. Problem 4 of paper 247—Marshalltown, shows dollars without any cents being involved. The scorings under "U. S. Money" are 4 place and 5 place, but under "Addition" only 3 place. Since it is unnecessary to express the cents, it is manifestly an addition problem of only 3 place—$150 + $75. The scoring for "U. S. Money" is therefore two places too high. This is a common error, as explained elsewhere.

These typical papers, as scored and commented upon, should make clear any ambiguities in the directions for gathering the data, or scoring and evaluating the returns.

The instructions required that only real problems be scored. In order to determine how fully the spirit of the work was understood, a careful study was made of the problems thrown out. One cannot help being impressed with the fact that the work was taken seriously and performed in the spirit of honest coöperation. There is an occasional problem (estimated at about 1 in 1,000) which is apparently a "made-up" problem; at any rate no motive was apparent to the scorer and it was thrown out. The following is an illustration: "If a stream flows at the rate of 10 yards in 1 minute, how long will it take it to go 5 miles?" One can conceive a situation where the above might be a real problem, but no such situation is apparent in the report.

The most common cause for throwing out problems was that the facts given were not sufficient to permit a solution, or were too simple to require a solution. The following are illustrations:

1. The cost of two flower boxes including the dirt and flowers.
2. My mother had to add up the grocery bill to see how much was required to pay it each week.
3. Mamma wanted to get me a dress. She knew how much a yard would cost and she had to figure out how much 4½ yards would cost.
4. If I pay ten dollars a month for board and room, five dollars for clothing and five for amusements, putting the rest in the bank, how much do I put in the bank?
5. My mother wants to buy a peck of potatoes. They are 28c. a peck. How much will she have to pay?

The "thrown-outs" from the Topeka returns may be taken as illustrative of the numbers thrown out. The following is the summary:

Papers thrown out............................... 82
Additional problems marked out of papers left in.... 113

The papers were thrown out chiefly because the occupations were not reported. The individual problems thrown out contained insufficient data and are well illustrated by the "thrown-out" problems given above. Throwing out papers and problems not usable was one of the important tasks of the scorer, and in the later scoring this and the separation of papers according to occupations were the first things done.

The material is classified both by "social topics" and by technical arithmetical processes involved. The "social topics" are as follows:

9804 problems involved buying, 1500 involved selling, and 1441 involved money where there was neither buying nor selling. Money was involved in 83 per cent of all the problems. One thousand unselected problems, involving money but neither buying nor selling, were analyzed and found to be concerned with (1) labor and wages, 45 per cent; (2) interest, 11 per cent; (3) rent, 6 per cent; (4) insurance, 4 per cent. One hundred other items are included in the remaining 34 per cent. Problems involving no money are equally widely distributed. Time or hours of labor constitute 20 per cent of these problems; measurement of capacity, 12 per cent; and estimates of building material, 10 per cent. Housekeepers turned in 7345 problems; farmers, 1077; mechanics, 330; and merchants, 550. Ninety-four kinds of material are represented. Those most frequently mentioned are groceries, 3398; dry goods, 1195; miscellaneous (Christmas), 834; labor and wages, 743; milk, 736; meat, 663; eggs, 462; clothing, 430; and butter, 394.

The arithmetical processes were determined for each problem as shown above and were then classified. Forty-three processes are listed and contained 21,898 cases in the 14,583 problems.

Multiplication is used 6974 times; addition, 4416 times; subtraction, 2833 times; division, 2437 times; fractions, 1974 times; accounts, 1212 times; and percentage, 417 times. These are the most frequent. Decimals, other than found in money, occurred only seven times. Ten problems, "possibly but not probably," in proportion are listed. Apothecaries' weight was reported four times — by physicians. Three problems involve square root and one involves partial payments. Single instances of Troy weight and partnership occur.

In the fundamental process of addition occurring 4416 times, 79 were one-place numbers; 2143, two-place; 1655, three-place; 467, four-place; 66, five-place; and 6, six-place numbers. Three-place or less constitute 90 per cent of the cases. The addends computed for two cities were 1737 cases. Of these 542 contained two addends; 508, three addends; 291, four addends; and 184, five addends. The greatest number reported was 28. Problems involving five addends or less constitute 90 per cent of the cases. The chances are, therefore, 9 in 10 that no problem in addition will occur more complicated than the addition of five quantities of three places.

In subtraction, 97 per cent of the problems have four places or less in the minuend and obviously no more than that number in the subtrahend.

In multiplication, 99 per cent of the 6974 cases have three places or less in the multiplier. Fifty-three per cent are one-place multipliers and 39 per cent two-place.

In 2347 division operations four places or less in the divisor constitute all the cases but one. The per cents run from one to four as follows: 40, 43, 13, and 5, neglecting decimals.

Ninety per cent of the 1974 fractions tabulated consist of $\frac{1}{2}$, $\frac{3}{4}$, $\frac{1}{4}$, and $\frac{1}{3}$. One-half is most frequent with 1289 cases (65 per cent), followed by $\frac{3}{4}$ with 189 cases, $\frac{1}{4}$ with 159 cases and $\frac{1}{3}$ with 119. Fifty separate fractions are met. The complete list occurring more than twice is: $\frac{1}{2}$, $\frac{1}{4}$ and $\frac{3}{4}$; $\frac{1}{3}$, and $\frac{2}{3}$; $\frac{1}{5}$, $\frac{2}{5}$, and $\frac{4}{5}$; $\frac{1}{6}$; $\frac{1}{7}$; $\frac{1}{8}$, $\frac{3}{8}$, $\frac{5}{8}$, and $\frac{7}{8}$; $\frac{4}{9}$; $\frac{1}{10}$, $\frac{9}{10}$, and $\frac{7}{10}$. Occasional appearances of fractions with the following denominators are tabulated: 11, 12, 15, 16, 17, 18, 24, 25, 32, and 100.

Conclusions

1. The omission of the following processes which appear in the study is suggested: Decimals, except United States money; apothecaries' weight; partial payments; partnership; square root; proportion; and Troy weight.

2. The following processes do not appear, from which fact "it would appear to be a safe and conservative procedure to recommend (them) for omission from the elementary work in arithmetic:"

(a) G. C. D. and L. C. M. beyond the power of inspection. (b) Long, confusing problems in common fractions. (c) Complex and compound fractions. (d) Reduction of denominate numbers. (e) Tables of folding paper, surveyor's tables, and tables of foreign money. (f) Compound numbers. (g) Longitude and time. (h) Cases 2 and 3 in percentage. (i) Compound interest. (j) Annual interest. (k) Exchange. (l) True discount. (m) Partnership with time. (n) Ratio beyond the ability of fractions to satisfy. (o) Most of mensuration. (p) Cube root. (q) The metric system.

3. The processes left are the four fundamental operations, fractions, accounts, percentage and its applications, simple denominate numbers, cancellation, mensuration, decimals, counting, and square root.

4. The study, as it stands, while having some sources of error, is believed to be the best single basis yet available for determining the content of arithmetic as it should appear in schoolroom practice and courses of study.

5. The situation revealed in these adult problems is a surprisingly simple one when compared with present school practice.

6. It is doubtful if arithmetic is entitled to the large time-expenditure which is now allotted to it in the elementary grades.

7. On the negative side, this study shows that adults do not figure through complete situations, such as budgeting the

family income, determining by careful estimate in advance the desirability of buying a carload of steers and finishing them for market, or determining the relative advantages of renting or buying city property. Work of this kind would not involve more difficult arithmetical processes, but it would indicate a more intelligent application of arithmetic to complete business situations. The entire absence of work of this character may indicate a need which the schools have not formerly met, and which can be adequately met only by definitely organizing large motivated business situations for public school work.

8. The present study is more extensive than necessary; the problems for a single week would have shown the same distribution. . . . If two weeks are used in such a survey, the second week should come at a different season of the year.

9. The study shows the arithmetic needed by the masses, the 95 per cent of the population. It does not attempt to analyze the specific requirements of different business and commercial pursuits.

10. Certain possible sources of error suggested by the author are: Parents may have invented problems to be accommodating, some parents did not contribute, pupils have not reported accurately in all cases, the parents contributing may have been too highly selected, the addition and subtraction problems may have been scored too high because of carrying ciphers when no cents were involved, and the scores had a constant probable error.

§6—DEPARTMENT STORE ARITHMETIC
(Study 27)

Department-store salespeople have presumably been taught the fundamental operations, fractions, and decimals in the elementary grades; but frequent errors are found in their computations. To discover exactly what operations are of importance for salespeople, several thousand sales checks were examined as follows by Charters:

In addition, 7337 charge checks (records of purchase transactions in which the goods are charged to the customers' accounts), selected at random, were examined.　In 75 per cent of the cases no addition was necessary because the customer purchased only one item.　In 16 per cent of the cases two items were purchased; in five per cent, three; in two per cent, four; in one per cent each, five, six, and seven items.　There were a few cases of purchase of more items up to the maximum of eighteen. In only one check out of twenty-five is it necessary to add more than three items.　Five places constituted the maximum ($456.00). The typical case then corresponds closely to that found by Wilson. In 90 per cent of the cases involving addition the problems are not more difficult than four places and four addends.

With this material at hand, it was possible to construct a review curriculum.　This was done by the preparation of "practice tests" in which drill upon all facts (as $9 + 8$) was given equally. Unfortunately, it was impossible to pay special attention to the relative difficulty of the combinations, and to give additional drill on those of greater difficulty.

For subtraction, 4304 cash checks were examined.　In 24 per cent of the cases the exact amount of the purchase was given by the customer and no subtraction was necessary.　In tabulating the remainder of the cases, the minuends (amount given in payment) were classified.　Eighty-three per cent of these were listed as follows:

Amount received	Frequency	Per cent
$1.00	725	22
5.00	701	21
2.00	385	12
10.00	331	10
.50	247	8
20.00	141	4
.25	110	3
3.00	99	3

A complete table of each actual transaction was arranged showing how many times, for instance, one dollar was presented in payment of a bill of 19 cents. From this table it was possible to determine exactly what subtraction facts (as, $16-9$), were involved in the operations.

At once it became apparent that salespeople in making change use only 45 of the possible one hundred subtraction facts. For instance, they never subtract 9 from 18. The reason for this limitation lies in the fact that change is always given in fives or multiples of five. Thus, if the bill is nine cents, the customer gives in payment 9 cents, 10 cents, a quarter, a ha f dollar, a dollar or some larger bill but never 18 cents. Obviously this limits the range of subtractions. It easily follows by analysis of all possible cases that the subtraction facts used are: 15 minus 9, 8, 7, and 6; 10 minus 9, 8, 7, 6, to 1; 9 minus 9, 8, 7, to 0; 8 minus 8; 7 minus 7, 6, and 5; 6 minus 6 and 5; 5 minus 5, 4, to 0; 4 minus 4, 3, to 0; 3 minus 3; 2 minus 2, 1, and 0; 1 minus 1 and 0; and 0 minus 0.

But it was found upon further examination that salespeople do not subtract at all; they add. If the purchase amounts to 9 cents and a dollar is tendered in payment, the salesperson calculates as follows: The amount necessary to make 10 is added. This, a penny, is taken in the fingers from the penny compartment of the cash register, then a nickel and a dime, bringing the total to a quarter. This is followed by the selection of a quarter and a half. His statements to himself as he manipulates the money are "nine, ten, fifteen, twenty-five, fifty, one dollar."

This being the case the amount of subtraction used by a salesman is negligible. A curriculum in subtraction was, therefore, made by the selection of quantities which would require the use of all compartments of the cash register and appeared as practice tests as follows:

Amount Received	Amount of Sale	$1	50c	25c	10c	5c	1c	Amount of Change
1.00	16		50	25		5	4	64

In studying multiplication the 7337 charge checks used in

studying addition were analyzed. On the checks appear items such as 6 collars at 25 cents, amounting to $1.50, a process commonly known in store terminology as an extension. In the checks were found 2771 extensions as against 1853 additions.

Classifying these first upon the basis of multipliers (number of like articles bought) it was found that in 54 per cent of the cases the multiplier 2 was used; in 18 per cent, 3; in 9 per cent, 4; in 5 per cent, 5; and 6 per cent, 6. These constituted 92 per cent of the cases. Multipliers within the limits of the conventional multiplication tables (from 2 to 12) constituted 97 per cent of the cases. Twenty-five was a multiplier in 19 cases and the remainder were under 20 except for a few multipliers ending in ciphers.

On the other hand the multiplicand (price per article) showed that 10 cents was the most common price of articles bought more than one at a time. A few of the more frequent ran as follows, constituting 67 per cent of the cases.

Price	Frequency	Price	Frequency
$0.10	276	$0.45	86
.25	253	.19	72
.15	239	1.00	64
.35	173	.20	63
.59	150	.39	55
.50	126	.08	54
.05	113	.09	51
.29	93		

There are 8 cases of four places in the multiplicand, 288 cases of three places, 310 cases of single-place numbers, and the balance, 2173 (78 per cent), consisted of two places.

From these facts it will be seen that in 97 per cent of the cases, at least, the multiplier is 12 or less, and the multiplicand three places or less.

A review course of study was constructed within these limits in the form of practice tests. In one of these, the hundred most common extensions were included. In others, systematic exercises with multipliers up to 12 were used. The value of the study lay in setting the limits of complexity.

No division is used by salespeople except in the form of fractions. Everything is done to relieve them of calculations. In mark-down sales the reduced price is usually given. In adding per cents for the luxury war tax, the amount is placed on the sales tag. With some goods sold by the yard measuregraphs are used on which pointers on dials may be set, a crank turned, and the exact length and price are both indicated. But notwithstanding this it was found that in the 7337 checks referred to twice before, there were 444 cases of common fractions. In addition 2458 sales checks were used to supplement the study. From both sources 1178 cases were obtained. The distribution is shown as follows:

Denominators	Pure	Mixed	Total	Per cent.
2	247	413	660	56
4	137	160	297	25
3	25	48	73	6
16	14	56	70	6
8	22	9	31	3
6	4	11	15	1
5	0	13	13	1
12	1	7	8	1
7	1	6	7	1
9	2	1	3	0
10	1	0	1	0
Total	454	727	1178	100

It will be observed that one-half constitutes 56 per cent of the cases, either as a pure fraction ($\frac{1}{2}$), or as a mixed number, ($4\frac{1}{2}$). Eighty-one per cent are halves or quarters. Sixteenths are more frequent than eighths. Obviously the range of denominators is very narrow.

Practice tests were constructed in which the fractions were drilled upon with equal attention to each denominator and with varying numerators. Mixed multipliers were not used because these are not more complicated than pure fractions except that addition and multiplication are necessary.

Decimal fractions were found to a very limited extent for reasons given above, and they consist of ten, fifteen, and twenty per cents in the stores studied. One "rule of thumb" method of computation is as follows: To get ten per cent of $11.73, for instance, "put your thumb over the three" and the part appearing, 1.17, is ten per cent. To get twenty per cent multiply this by two, and to get fifteen per cent divide it by two, and add the quotient to ten per cent. From this it is clear that decimals involve only "putting the thumb over the right-hand figure," addition, multiplication, and fractions.

The conclusion is obvious. In this one vocation of department-store selling the chances are nine out of ten that no problem in addition will be more complicated than the addition of four four-place addends; no subtraction is used in making change, and if it were, only forty-five out of one hundred subtraction facts would be used; the chances are ninety-seven out of one hundred that in multiplication the multiplier will be 12 or less and the multiplicand three places or less; in fractions only eleven denominators are found, all being under ten except ten, twelve, and sixteen; and by the simple device of using the thumb, decimals disappear.

§7—ARITHMETIC AND OTHER COMMERCIAL USES
(Study 28)

Mitchell* studied a standard cookbook, the payrolls of a number of artificial flower and feather factories, mark-down-sales advertisements, and a general hardware catalog.

He states his purpose as follows: "The following study is presented to illustrate the use the author is making of the statistical method in discovering and in determining the relative importance of the various content elements of the course of study in arithmetic. . . . An index of the relative importance, from the

*Part I, *Seventeenth Yearbook*, pp. 7-17, H. E. Mitchell.

standpoint of social usage, of the different content elements is found in the frequency of their occurrence and in the manner of their use, *i. e.*, whether used in computations or merely in descriptive terms." The four sources were analyzed and the arithmetical elements in each tabulated.

Summarizing the tabular display of the cookbook arithmetic we find the following units of measurement: teaspoonful, tablespoonful, cup, pint, quart, gallon, peck, ounce, pound, and unit. The quantities used were ⅛, ¼, ⅜, ⅓, ½, ⅔, ¾, ⅞, 1, and 32 other whole and mixed numbers with the same denominators as in the pure fractions, in their fractional portions. The integer one affixed to the denominate numbers occurred most frequently, 1836 times. One-half was next in importance, 1127 times, and 2 followed with a total of 1101. Then appeared 3 with a score of 484, ⅓ with 353 mentions, and 1½ with 300.

In the factory payrolls the dozen is the sole unit of measurement. The fractions are twelfths, sixths, fourths, thirds, and halves. The figures were obtained from the weekly payrolls of 100 piece workers selected at random from 300 records examined in ten factories. Sixty-nine different fractions, integers, and mixed numbers were tabulated. The number of greatest frequency was ½, which occurred 528 times out of a total of 2364 cases. Following this occurs 1 with a score of 476, 1/12 with 442, ¼ with 292, ⅓ with 130, and 2 with 101. No mixed number occurred oftener than 25 times.

"To compute accurately the earnings of any given worker, it is necessary to add to get the total number of dozens of articles made at each of the different rates per dozen, and then to multiply together each given rate per dozen and the total number of dozens of articles made at that rate. The arithmetical processes involved are, therefore, addition of all possible fractions with 12 as denominator to integers and mixed numbers. The fractional parts of the mixed numbers likewise include all possible fractions with 12 as denominator; multiplication by a fractional integral, or mixed number of dozens, of decimals in terms of dollars and cents; and addition of United States money."

In the 300 sales advertisements studied to find the nature of the arithmetical operations which the customer must know to understand the advertisements, both decimals and common fractions were found and tabulated together with the departments in which the discount applied. The 175 discounts, in per cents, were 10, 15, 20, 25, 30, 33⅓, 40, 50, 60, and 75. Of these the most common were 20 per cent (31 times), 10 per cent (26 times), 25 per cent (21 times), 10-50 per cent (16 times), and 50 per cent (13 times). The others probably ran less than ten in each case. The 125 fractional discounts were ¼, ⅓, and ½. Among these ½ occurred 57 times.

The general hardware catalog reveals the following units of measurement: inch, foot, yard, ounce, pound, quart, dozen, gross, hundred, square foot, hundred-foot, and hundred square feet. Fractional parts have denominators as follows: 2, 3, 4, 6, 8, 16, 32, and 64. Mixed numbers, with never more than two integral places, are more common than pure fractions but less common than integers. The dozen and gross were units of measurement in 1974 cases out of a total of 4075.

His conclusions are as follows:

1. The relative frequency of small numbers is great.

2. The prominence of the dozen as a unit of production and of trade suggests the importance of familiarity with the aliquot parts of 12.

3. Decimalization is much more important in school arithmetic than in production and trade.

4. Discount rates in advertisements of mark-down sales are most often worked in per cents.

§8—SERVICE MATHEMATICS
(Studies 29 and 30)

Williams* studied the mathematics used in Noyes, "A Textbook in Chemistry" (029) He was investigating the claim of a

---

*"The Mathematics Needed in Freshman Chemistry", L. W. Williams, *School Science and Mathematics;* Vol. XXI, No. 7; Oct., 1921.

chemistry department that their students needed more than two years of high-school mathematics. In studying the text he examined both the expository body and the problems of the text. In the expository portions of the text he determined what words and expressions were present which either were distinctly mathematical or implied mathematics. These were classified and the frequency obtained. The exercises were worked out by the simplest methods and both the operations and the quantities were tabulated.

In determining what to select as mathematics, the following rules were laid down:

1. Expressions giving dates, either specific or general, imply mathematics. Examples: 1844, last century.

2. Denominate numbers are distinctly mathematical. Examples: 50° F., 76 cm.

3. Expressions having several meanings or uses are distinctly mathematical if, from the context, a mathematical meaning is evident; if not, they are omitted. Examples: equivalent, constant.

4. Expressions having no use or meaning other than in a mathematical sense are distinctly mathematical. Example: volume and number.

5. Expressions not classified under Rule 4, but involving a use of mathematics, are considered as implying mathematics. Examples: rate of expansion, equilibrium, divisions of a scale.

6. Cardinal, ordinal, and numeral adjectives are distinctly mathematical. Examples: three, first.

7. Equations, formulæ, symbols, etc., are distinctly mathematical. Examples: $AB = 180, \dfrac{F\text{-}32}{180} = \dfrac{C}{100} = \dfrac{R}{80}$

In the body of the text, 124 mathematical concepts were used 1156 times of which per cent (310 cases) and volume (208) constituted nearly half. Denominate numbers to the extent of 73 were used 1937 times and of these, degree, °, was used 865 times. *First, second, once, twice, double,* and *triple* were used 301 times, *first* being used 116 times, *second,* 55 times, and *twice,* 20 times.

Fifty-five different fractions were used 242 times, and of these one-half occurred 47 times, one-fifth 32 times, one-tenth and one-third, 23 times each, and one-fourth 17 times. The denominators of the fractions were ten or less in all cases except 43 cases and among these eight were less than one hundred and twenty-four ended in hundreds or thousands. Only five denominators were mixed decimals.

In the body of the text 434 decimal fractions were used, of which 33 were one-place; 140 two-place; 125 three-place; and the remainder ran to eight places as the maximum. Mixed decimals occurred 1020 times. The most common form was found in 256 cases of two integers and one place, as 27.3. Other common forms were, two integers and two places, 186 times; one integer and two places, 173 times; three integers and one place, 154 times; and one integer and one place, 121 times. Integral quantities occurred 4120 times. One-place integers, such as 9, occurred 1545 times; two-place, 1189 times; three-place, 902 times; and four-place, 391 times. One twenty-place integer occurred.

In the problems, which were solved and the quantities and operations tabulated, 19 denominate-number units occurred 173 times, the most frequent being *gross*, 32 times; *liter*, 32 times; and *degree*, 17 times. Twenty-one operations are listed as occurring 962 times. In these, chemical equations occurred 134 times and multiplication with integers, 149 times, and with decimals, 118 times. Equations of first degree and one unknown occurred 7 times, and with two unknowns, twice. There were no equations of two unknowns. Fractional equations occurred six times, and algebraic addition, twice. Algebraic subtraction, multiplication, and division did not occur. There were nine cases of substitution in formulæ and 77 cases of ratio and proportion. No other algebra occurred.

In the problems, arithmetical addition is shown in its most complicated form, as for instance the addition of three numbers consisting of one integer and three decimals, such as 8.456, two integers and three decimals, and three decimals. The range of subtraction is very narrow, the most complicated being the subtraction of one six-place decimal from another. In the 235 cases of multiplication, 93 consisted of the multiplication of a two-place integer by a one-place integer. In 156 cases the operation involved nothing more complicated than a four-place integer by a six-place. In decimals 63 cases were found in which a decimal fraction or a mixed decimal is multiplied by an integer. Of these the decimal is never more extended than four places and the mixed decimal than five places in the integral portion and three places in the decimal portion. In 16 cases mixed decimals are multiplied by mixed decimals, the most complicated being 34.875 by 326.74. In 139 cases of division, 46 consist of the division of one integer by another, mostly two- and three-place integers. In 25 cases a decimal was divided by an integer. In 26 cases an integer was divided by a decimal. In 42 cases a mixed decimal was divided into another mixed decimal, the most complicated being 874362.73 divided by 847.2.

The study shows quite clearly that the mathematical information needed in freshman chemistry is limited to arithmetic and to simple algebraic processes with a wide range of denominate number units. The arithmetic is quite complicated and the algebra quite simple.

Mrs. T. T. Callaway (30) made a companion study* to that of Williams for the freshman clothing course. Using the same rules of procedure, she examined a freshman text, "Clothing for Women," by Laura I. Baldt, which is used in Stephens College. The report is summarized as follows:

The mathematical concepts, a reading knowledge of which is necessary for understanding the text, are 111 in number. Of these, 44 are geometrical terms chiefly included in simple mensuration, and all the others are arithmetical. The pupil may become familiar with all the facts by the time she has completed the eighth grade, except a few facts in geometry which are involved in pattern-drafting and which can be learned easily on the job.

*Unpublished.

The most commonly mentioned concepts are *line* (613 times), *equal* (447), *center* (311), *measure* (285), *width* (171), *length* (132), *point* (107). The total number of mentions of concepts was 3115.

The denominate numbers used are those which occur in ordinary grade arithmetic, with two exceptions, the *head* and the *skein*. Long measure and United States money are the two most important measures used in making clothing. The *inch* occurs 1122 times out of a total of 1723 uses of denominate numbers, while the word *foot* does not occur at all. The dollar sign occurs 454 times.

The order runs as follows: *inch*, 1122, the dollar sign, 454 times; the *yard*, 70 times; *head*, 14; *year*, 12; and the remainder below 12.

The common fractions occur as follows: *one-half*, 214 times, *quarter* 248 times, *sixth* 15 times, *eighth* 108 times, *tenth* 16 times, *twelfth* 5 times, and *sixteenth* 9 times. Only 59 cases included in the above list were given in figures. There were twelve cases of a decimal fraction (.5). There were 176 cases of fractions other than that of United States money, but distributed in about the same proportion among the various denominators.

Integers occur as follows: Of 532 words, 523 were one-place integers. In addition to this, there were eight two-place and one larger. In Arabic figures there were 1048 occurrences, of which 2 were zero, 566 were one-place, 161 two-place, 289 three-place, and 30 four-place quantities. There were 77 Roman numerals, of which 71 were one-place and 6 two-place.

"It did not seem necessary to make a table showing the operations and processes required in this text, for the reason that practically all the problems in which they are used are contained in the five chapters on the drafting and use of patterns. These are usually stated in the form of rhetorical algebraic equations, conveniently listed and accompanied by a small drawing of the pattern to be drafted. These equations represent arithmetical problems to be solved, geometrical constructions to be made, or, more frequently, a combination of the two. Relatively few processes are required in the solution of the problems, but every possible combination of these processes appears. Following are three illustrations of the equations representing the smallest, the most common, and the most complicated type:

"1. A C equals one-half neck measure minus two inches.

"2. A E equals one-sixth neck measure plus three-eighths inch.

"3. A B equals one-half hip measure minus one-eighth of one-half width around bottom (of skirt).

"The solution of these three problems requires nine processes at most, as follows: (1) Translating the rhetorical algebraic equation into a symbolic numerical equation. (2) Multiplying whole or mixed numbers by a fraction. (3) Subtracting a whole or mixed number from a whole or mixed number. (4) Adding a fraction to a whole or mixed number. (5) Finding a fraction of a fraction. (6) Reducing a mixed number to an improper fraction. (7) Reducing an improper fraction to a whole or mixed number. (8) Reducing yards to inches. (9) Drawing a line of a given length.

"Since each girl drafts a pattern to a standard set of measurements and then to her own measurements, every degree of complexity and difficulty is involved, but the numbers are not large. The greatest measurement of a school girl will probably never exceed 45 inches.

"The 430 equations of the type given above involve, besides the nine operations stated, the following six additional operations: (10) Reduction of inches to yards. (11) Division of whole numbers, mixed numbers, or fractions, by whole numbers, which are usually one-place numbers. (12) Drawing a line parallel to a given line. (13) Drawing a line perpendicular to a given line. (14) Drawing a circle or the arc of a circle, having given the center and radius. (15) Reading geometrical figures by means of letters representing points.

"Percentage occurs in just two chapters. The first is in the discussion of the family budget, and the second is concerned with the absorbent quality of fabrics. In the latter instance the pupil need only know the meaning of the term 'percentage.' In the distribution of the family income she is required to find a certain per cent of a given sum of money."

Chapter XIX

HISTORY
(Studies 31-35)

§1 — Introduction

In the field of history we encounter the most difficult type of investigation. To discover what history is necessary to understand modern customs and institutions presents almost insurmountable difficulties. The explicit references to history, historical facts, dates, and events, can easily be detected, but the history "necessary to understand" is quite a different matter.

The current studies have evaded the more subtle problem and have confined themselves entirely to a consideration of the historical items that are explicitly used in the material examined.

In the studies which follow, there are several cases of the consensus of experts. Wooters obtains the opinions of members of the American Historical Association, and Horn and Bassett consult with specialists in universities. Three of the investigations are studies in service history, where the historical content is derived from its use in other subjects. Two of them investigate the history found in the social sciences and the third the history explicitly referred to in poetry. Expert classification as well as expert opinion is used by all the writers. One study of the similarities and differences in content of American History textbooks published during a period of fifty years, is included in the chapter.

On the technical side we find frequency of occurrence measured by lines, inches, paragraphs, and selections. Studies are made with typical material which include a description of methods for determining trueness to type. Two full descriptions of method are found in the studies.

§2—DATES
(Study 31)

Wooters* collected the opinion of experts to determine the minimum essentials of dates that may be profitably memorized in seventh and eighth grade history.

A questionnaire submitted to 150 members of the American Historical Association reads as follows (after an introductory statement explaining the purpose of the investigation):

"Indicate the relative values of the following dates in the following way:

"1. Place before each date the numeral representing its value as compared with the others, marking the most important date as 1; the second, 2; and so up to 20.

"2. Dates, the thorough learning of which by the elementary school pupil would not in your opinion repay the time and effort involved, please mark 0.

"3. Please add any date or dates (each with its event) which you believe should be in the list, and indicate the rank of each.

"4. If two or more dates are of approximately equal value, give the same numerical rank to each."

Then follows a list of 52 dates (with the event) following Bourne's "Teaching of History." After this is given a list of four questions concerning the memorization of names of the Presidents and their terms, and the whole or parts of the Declaration of Independence and the Federal Constitution.

There were 86 replies, 73 of which were usable, from 25 States and the District of Columbia. Of these 3 were from authors, 28 from college teachers, 9 from normal-school teachers, 25 from high-school teachers, 4 from city superintendents, and 4 from others. Two individuals submitted new lists without marking them, to each item of which the value 1 was given; six marked no dates for elimination; six were unable to rank below 12; and ten were

*J. E. Wooters, Part I, *Fourteenth Yearbook*, pp. 139-141, and *School and Home Education*, December, 1914.

unable to rank below 5. Forty-nine ranked from 1–20 and marked eliminations, and these formed the basis for compilation.

In calculating the final ranking the highest date in each list was given the value 20; the next, 19; and so to 1. Each vote for elimination was arbitrarily given the value of 10, which was subtracted. The totals of the first twenty dates ran as follows, the numbers in parentheses following the date in each case indicating hundreds. For instance, 1776 (13) means that the total was over 1300 (1327, exactly):

1776 (13); 1492 (12); 1607 (11); 1789 (11); 1620 (9); 1803 (9); 1861, April 14 (9); 1787 (8); 1863, January 1 (8); 1820 (7); 1812 (7); 1765 (6); 1783 (6); April 14 (3), *sic;* 1850 (5); 1854 (5); 1775 (5); 1781 (5); 1823 (5); and 1846 (4).

Five dates, only, received no vote for elimination: 1492, 1607, 1776, 1789 and 1812. One date was given every rank and 53 additions were suggested. The vote for memorizing the names of the Presidents in order stood 49 *for* to 21 *against;* for memorizing the number of terms of each, 33 to 33; for memorizing parts of the Declaration of Independence, 37 *against* to 30 *for*; and for memorizing parts of the Federal Constitution 36 *for* and 29 *against*.

§3—The Content of Textbooks
(Study 32)

Bagley and Rugg* studied the content of twenty-three eighth-grade histories selected at random from those published in each of the following periods: 1865 to 1874; 1881 to 1888; 1890 to 1904; and 1906 to 1912.

"*Objective*. It is the purpose of the present paper to present facts and raise problems rather than to set forth conclusions or outline solutions. The following pages reveal fairly accurately the present content of this basic historical instruction and the significant changes that this content has undergone in the past century. Both the principal events and the characters associated with them

*The Content of American History as Taught in the Seventh and Eighth Grades, W. C. Bagley and H. O. Rugg, University of Illinois Bulletin, Vol. XIII, No. 51.

have been listed with reference to the relative emphasis which the different texts lay upon them in so far as this emphasis can be determined by proportions of space and frequencies of reference.

"*Method*. At the outset the following method was adopted: the number of words in each of the books was carefully computed by one person; each book was then assigned to an individual for analysis, with the expectation that the topics and the amount of space devoted to each could be determined for each book and the results be brought together later for comparison. A brief trial proved this method to be unsatisfactory, and the procedure was so modified that each member of the group was assigned a single period or epoch and asked to analyze each of the books with reference to this period, noting the topics and names common to all of the books, the topics and names common to at least three-fourths of the books, and the topics and names common to at least one-half of the books. The brief statement of preliminary results published in the *Fourteenth Yearbook* is based upon this analysis.

"At the conclusion of this work the results seemed to justify a careful 'checking' in order to reduce the error that is unavoidable when so many individuals collaborate in work of this sort."

An examination was made to show changes in the tendencies of the organization of the tests, appendices, references, and bibliographies; questions, outlines, and problems; style; anecdotal materials; pictures and maps.

The periods of American history were listed as the following: Discovery and exploration; Colonial development; Colonial wars; pre-Revolution; Revolution; 1783 to 1812; 1812 to 1861; Civil War; and 1865 to date of publication.

The percentage of space devoted to each period in each book was tabulated and from this tabulation tendencies were observed. Each of the periods was sub-classified and the average per cent of the total space of the period devoted to each was tabulated. For instance, the amount of space devoted to Spanish exploration in the period of discovery and exploration rose from 9 per cent in the books published between 1865 and 1874 to 37 per cent in the next later group of texts, and in the latest period it is 29 per cent.

Similar analyses and tabulations were made for each period. Relative emphasis was determined upon a word basis; as, for instance, in Goodrich's text it was found that 23.8 per cent of the words were devoted to a consideration of the Civil War. In some periods the presence of topics in all the books, in three-fourths, and in one-half was calculated.

For each period the persons whose names are mentioned in connection therewith in each book were enumerated. The names appearing in all the books, in three-fourths, and in one-half were determined. In some periods the division between civil and military leaders was observed. The proportion of space devoted by the latest group of books to the exploits and achievements of the persons in the period of discovery and exploration was calculated and, rating the one with the greatest amount of space devoted to him at 100, the others were evaluated and ranked. The distribution runs as follows: Columbus, 100; Raleigh, 26; Champlain, 20; etc.

A "Hall of Fame" was constructed by noting the "relative frequency of reference" of the names of each period. Two classes of leaders were made, civil and military, although some appear in both. The person obtaining the most frequent mention in each was rated at 100 and the others in their respective proportions. In the period from 1765 to 1865 among civil leaders Lincoln is rated at 100, Washington at 84, Jefferson at 82, Jackson at 49. Among military leaders the ratings run: Washington, 100; R. E. Lee, 83; Grant, 76; Sherman, 48; Cornwallis, 42; and so forth.

As a check upon the relative emphasis accorded these leaders in school texts, the relative proportion of space devoted to the same names among civil leaders in the "Encyclopedia Britannica" (11th Edition) was computed. The Pearson co-efficient was found to be .27, the most notable shift being Franklin, who was accorded eleventh rank in the school texts and second in the Encyclopedia.

A list of the topics common to all of the twenty-three books and a further list common to three-fourths of the books are summarized.* A few additional found in less than three-fourths are included, particularly where they coincide with the recommendations of the Committee of Eight of the American Historical Association. This list indicated by plus and minus signs whether the amount of space devoted to each topic has noticeably increased or decreased chronologically in the groups of texts. Asterisks indicate the topics recommended by the Committee of Eight.

The more important facts set forth in the preceding pages may be summarized as follows:

"(1) In so far as can be determined from the materials presented in the textbooks, elementary American history as taught in the seventh and eighth grades has been and still is predominantly political and military history.

"(2) Within the past fifty years, the emphasis upon military affairs as measured by the proportion of space devoted to wars has declined. In general, battles and campaigns are treated less in detail than was formerly the rule, while proportionately more space is devoted to the causes and the results of the wars. The lessening emphasis upon the details of the wars is first noticed in some of the textbooks published between 1881 and 1888, and the tendency has been general and decided since that time.

"(3) The later books give a perceptibly heavier emphasis to the facts of economic and industrial development than do the earlier books, although political development still constitutes the essential core of elementary historical instruction.

"(4) As regards the treatment of specific eras or epochs, the principal increases in emphasis are to be noted in connection with: (a) the period 1783–1812 (especially in the treatment of the so-called 'critical period' between the close of the Revolution and the adoption of the Constitution); (b) the non-military affairs of the period 1812–1861; and (c) European events preceding and during the periods of discovery, exploration, and settlement.

"(5) The persons whose names are most frequently mentioned in the elementary textbooks are very predominantly those

*Part I, *Sixteenth Yearbook*, pp. 143 to 155.

who have been most intimately associated with political development and with military and naval affairs.

" (6) Variations among the several textbooks in respect of persons mentioned are numerous and wide. Most of the books mention a very much larger number of names than the average pupil will be likely to remember. Certain names, however, are made to stand out through repetition. Whether these are the names that should in justice be perpetuated through the powerful agency represented by universal education is a question which it is not the province of this paper to consider.

" (7) Variations in the topics and events which constitute the chief content of elementary historical instruction are probably less numerous and less wide than variations in names of persons mentioned. In any case there is a rather distinct 'core' of topics common to most of the books, and these topics may be looked upon as constituting the present 'standardized' content of elementary American history. Again it is not the province of this paper to consider the right of these common topics to the important place that they now occupy as basic elements in the culture of the next generation.

" (8) Numerous changes have taken place in the construction of elementary textbooks in history during the past fifty years. The more important of these are: (a) a movement toward a simpler 'style' with larger emphasis upon clear statements of causal relationships; (b) the introduction and development of the 'problem' as a method of teaching history, and a consequent encouragement of 'judgment' as contrasted with rote memory — of rational as contrasted with verbatim mastery; (c) a marked decline in the employment of imaginative pictures as illustrations and an increase in the use of pictures that represent sincere attempts to portray actual conditions; (d) a marked decline in the use of anecdotal materials; (e) a larger and wider use of maps."

§4—SERVICE HISTORY FOR THE SOCIAL SCIENCES
(Studies 33 and 34)

Horn* assumed that the chief purpose of teaching history in the elementary school is "to make pupils more intelligent with respect to the more crucial activities, conditions, and problems of present-day life." The crucial problems were obtained from the heads of the university departments of political science and sociology and economics. The books in which each problem was given the most intelligent treatment were obtained from the same expert source. The following historical data were obtained from each book examined: (1) The percentage of historical material in each book. (2) The specific and approximate dates referred to in each book. (3) The historical characters referred to in each book. (4) The frequency of reference to each period in history (following Bagley and Rugg). (5) The frequency of reference to each of the most important phases of history (following Langlois and Seignobos). (6) Movements, events, conditions, problems, etc., used as check on the material collected under 5.

The investigator points out certain difficulties encountered, such as variations among scorers, unavoidable indefiniteness in the directions dealing with the phases of history, and the question as to whether the best books had been selected.

To check the study the historical material in thirty-eight topics of the International Encyclopedia was analyzed. Three-fourths of the dates compiled from both sources were census dates, and outside of these only one date, 1803, is included in the Wooters list obtained from members of the American Historical Association. Period reference was distributed under ancient, medieval, and modern, American, and modern history not American, by countries (showing the frequent mention of many small countries, such as New Zealand), and by periods in ancient history.

Persons were listed for each problem with which they were mentioned. Mention was tabulated first as the product of the number of mentions per problem and the number of separate

*Sixteenth Yearbook, Part I, pp. 156-172, Ernest Horn.

problems in which they were mentioned in the book; second, the same procedure was followed for the articles; third, a combination of these; and fourth, a ranking of the separate mentions in problems in encyclopedias and books. Sixteen hundred individuals were mentioned, most of them once. Two hundred and sixty-one occurred in both books and articles or in one or the other with a score of 6 (by products). Roosevelt receives most frequent mention among living or dead characters. Adam Smith and John Stuart Mill stand higher than Napoleon, Washington, or Jefferson.

References to phases in history were compared with the Committee of Eight report and the Bagley and Rugg study of modern textbooks. Naturally, the books and articles analyzed devote much more attention to social and economic phases of history than to military and political. The figures run in the books analyzed as follows: political, 18.7 per cent; military, 4.7 per cent; and social and economic, 76.3 per cent. In the Bagley and Rugg study they run 42, 40, and 18 respectively.

Bassett* (34) made a similar study, following Horn, and limited his investigations to the history "most necessary to the intelligent understanding of modern *political* problems, conditions, and activities." (*Political* is substituted for social, found in Horn's study.) The method of procedure was essentially the same with a few exceptions. Members of the staff in the department of political science in the University of Iowa were asked to make a list and indicate the books in which they were best treated. The Cyclopedia of American Government was substituted for the International Encyclopedia, and Small's outlines, found in his *General Sociology*, were used as a basis for classification instead of Langlois and Seignobos.

In checking and classifying these historical data, the following rules and regulations are observed:

"(1) Score only those references that are clearly historical.

"(2) In case of historical movements, events, and problems, indicate them in the specific terms of the author, and place the

*Seventeenth Yearbook, Part I, pp. 81-89.

reference under the main section of the outline where it seems most logically to belong. In case the reference clearly has a double significance it may be checked under two headings, as, for example, under 'Protection of Health' and under 'Achievements in Harmonizing Human Relations.'

"(3) Score any given item but once in a single paragraph.

"(4) Dates in parentheses are not to be checked.

"The analysis of a single paragraph may serve further to illustrate the classes of data desired, and the method used in checking the material. The following paragraphs taken from a contemporary writer upon 'Equal Suffrage' will serve as the basis of this analysis:

"'The movement for equal suffrage may be said to have begun in England toward the close of the eighteenth century. In 1792 Mary Wollstonecraft published a book on the Vindication of the Rights of Women which, though greeted with a storm of ridicule and abuse, gave the first considerable impulse to a discussion on the subject. In 1797 Charles Fox is quoted as saying that all the superior classes of the female sex in England must be more capable of exercising the elective suffrage with deliberation and propriety than the uninformed individuals of the lowest class of men to whom the advocates of universal suffrage would extend it. Bentham likewise remarked upon the injustice of refusing women the right to vote. In 1835 Bailey strongly advocated the extension of the suffrage to women in his treatise entitled 'The Rationale of Political Representation.' Likewise, Benjamin Disraeli, in 1848, declared in the House of Commons that he saw no reason for denying women the right to vote. But the most influential advocate of equal suffrage in England was John Stuart Mill, who espoused the cause with great power in his book on 'The Subjugation of Women,' published in 1869. Moreover, in 1867 Mill championed the cause of equal suffrage in the House of Commons by proposing it as an amendment to the Reform Bill then pending.'

"The specific items of historic interest in this paragraph are (1) Equal Suffrage, a subject to be classified under 'Achievements in Harmonizing Human Relations,' (2) the Reform Bill, likewise under 'Achievements in Harmonizing Human Relations' and (3) England, to be placed under 'Leading Foreign Countries.' Equal suffrage is mentioned three times, but since it is within a single paragraph, the subject is checked only once. England is mentioned twice, but is checked once.

"The specific dates occurring in this paragraph are 1792, 1797, 1835, 1848, 1867, 1869. The general period of the eighteenth century is also mentioned.

"The historical characters mentioned are Bailey, Bentham, Benjamin Disraeli, Charles Fox, John Stuart Mill, and Mary Wollstonecraft. Each of these persons is checked once, notwithstanding the fact that Mill's name appears twice.

In Bassett's study of twenty-two books, 653 names were found, 23 of which occurred in connection with three or more subjects. These were rated by products; that is, Roosevelt, being mentioned 25 times in connection with ten different problems, was given a rating of 25 times 10, or 250. Roosevelt occupies first rank with the score just mentioned; then come Cleveland, 63; Adam Smith, 55; McKinley, 45; Taft and Jackson, 44 each; and so forth. In the Encyclopedia of American Government seventy-nine names were found. Only five were mentioned in connection with more than one subject: Cleveland, Taft, Roosevelt, Wilson, and Francis Wright, rated in the order named.

In the books 214 dates, and in the Encyclopedia 89, were found. These show a marked divergence from Wooters' list. The dates 1492 and 1607 appeared only once; 1812, six times, and 1765 and April 14, 1861, not at all. More than 90 per cent were subsequent to 1812 as compared with 46 per cent in textbooks.

Comparisons were made with Bagley and Rugg for frequency of reference by periods with the observable difference that the history textbook devoted 25 per cent of its space to the period 1861–1916, while the figures in this study were 74 per cent.

§5—HISTORY IN POETRY

(Study 35)

Mrs. Dodd* studied the technique of determining the specific historical references contained in the 118 English poems required for entrance to the University of Illinois. To her the term "specific reference" means dates, institutions, persons, places, and written productions.

The plan to consider the historical references in each word and phrase was the first to present itself, but obviously such a plan would resolve itself into a study of the etymology of each word and the connotations which have grown up around it. It is difficult to determine what historical flavors and fragments of information are connoted in the phrase "ivy-mantled tower" when Gray speaks of "In yonder ivy-mantled tower, the moping owl does to the moon complain." Equally difficult is it to determine what history one should know to obtain the full flavor. Important as such a study would be, it was discarded because of practical difficulties, and the plan of collecting only specific references was decided upon.

The classification of the items was developmental, growing as the study progressed, rather than systematic, following an accepted expert classification. The classes were the following: character, event, place, social class, symbol, institution, date, document, people, principle, and established fact.

The second difficulty faced, when specific references are listed, was the determination of the historical background included in the thoughts, feelings, resolutions, beliefs, and customs of the individual characters and of the peoples treated in the selections. The lyrics and the drama are rich in feeling, but none of this adheres to the specific references. Furthermore, the historical references frequently lose their significance when taken out of their setting in the poem. In addition, literary references are likely to distort historical facts. These difficulties were not solved.

*Journal of Educational Research, Vol. IV, No. 4, Mrs. S. H. Dodd.

A third problem was that of scoring. A quotation of fifteen lines from "Alexander's Feast" will facilitate the discussion:

> "'Twas at the royal feast for Persia won
> By Philip's warlike son;
> Aloft in awful state
> The godlike hero sate
> On his imperial throne;
> His valiant peers were placed around,
> Their brows with myrtle and with roses crown'd,
> (So should desert in arms be crowned);
> The lovely Thais by his side
> Sate like a blooming eastern bride
> In flower of youth and beauty's pride:—
> Happy, happy, happy pair!
> None but the brave,
> None but the brave,
> None but the brave deserve the fair."

It would be impossible to score all references to Alexander, for instance. There are eight such references, including the title, as follows: Alexander; Philip's warlike son; hero; his (three times); pair (distributed as reference to Alexander and Thais); and, possibly, brave.

It is quite evident, however, that in a total summary of references to Alexander there would be a quite different significance attached to the importance of knowledge of Alexander if the eight references were gathered from eight different poems or from fifteen lines of one poem. In the former case he would be a character referred to frequently in literature; in the latter, only once, though frequently on that occasion. This line of reasoning led to the decision to score characters, places, dates, institutions, and written productions only once for each selection.

A fourth problem was connected with the scoring of dates. Take, for instance, the question of how to dispose of "Written in Early Spring" and "St. Cecilia's Day, 1687"; the first was discarded on the ground that it was not a specific reference to a date, and the second included because it was specific. So also was discarded for the same reason: December, Christmas, Martian Kalends, Marathon Day, and *One hundred fourscore* and *thirteen years* in the "Battle of Lake Regillus." Dates appearing in the titles of poems were included, while dates showing the year of publication were omitted.

Only twelve dates appeared in the 118 poems. These were Marathon Day, 490 B.C., in Browning's "Pheidippides"; St. Cecilia's Day, Nov. 22, 1687, in Browning's "A Song for St. Cecilia's Day"; Drummessie Day, April 16, 1746, in Burns's "Lament for Culloden"; 1692 and May 31, 1692, in Browning's "Hervé Riel"; 1746 in Collins's "Ode Written in MDCCXLVI"; 1802 in Wordsworth's "England and Switzerland, 1802"; 1802 in Wordsworth's "London MDCCCII"; Sept. 3, 1802, in Wordsworth's "Upon Westminster Bridge, Sept. 3, 1802"; 1803 in Wordsworth's "Yarrow Unvisited, 1803"; 1803 in Wordsworth's "Composed at Neidpath Castle, 1803;" and September, 1814, in Wordsworth's "Yarrow Visited."

A fifth problem arose in connection with specific references to persons including references to individuals and peoples. The characters fell naturally into four groups: historical, Biblical, legendary, and mythical, with shadowy lines between the groups. Historical characters were considered to be those appearing in "The Century Cyclopedia of Names." Brewer's "The Reader's Handbook", or in the editorial textual exposition of authors' writings found in special editions. To be tabulated as an historical character the person must have actually lived and must have a definite record in addition to that made in the poem. References to "brother" in "Snowbound" and to "doctor" and "sergeant" in "Macbeth" were not included on the ground that only specific names should be listed. Similar action was taken in the case of common nouns, such as "peers" in "Alexander's Feast." Where different names for the same person were used, they were included if they carry different connotations, as, Macbeth, Thane of Cawdor, and King of Scotland. Names of authors of poems were not included unless they appeared within the poems analyzed. Personal references by pronouns were not included.

One hundred and twenty-seven different characters appear in the 118 poems and none appear in more than one poem. Biblical characters are designated on the basis of their mention in the Bible. Of these there were twenty. Six Biblical peoples are listed: Christians, Hebrew-Jews, Ephesians, Midianites, Philistines, and Romans. Historical peoples are defined as those not now in existence and include references to clans (Clan Alpine), line of descent (House of Beaudesert), family groups (Douglas), religious groups (Druids), groups by nickname (Yankee), city-states (Athenian), and races (Angles). Proper adjectives were scored under the name of proper noun (Lydia for Lydian). References to persons in "The Lays of Ancient Rome" were, upon expert advice, not included among historical characters. Legendary characters—human beings of whose actual existence there is no authentic record (Robin Hood), — and mythological characters — superhuman beings conceived of as possessing divine characteristics (Apollo) — were not included.

Nine references to written productions were found: Bariffe's "Artillery Guide" and Goldinge's "Commentaries of Cæsar" in "The Courtship of Miles Standish"; Chalkley's "Journal" in "Snowbound"; Chapman's "Homer" in "On First Looking into Chapman's 'Homer'"; Sewell's "History of the Quakers" and "Arabian Nights" in "Snowbound"; and the Bible, the One Hundredth Psalm, and Proverbs, in "The Courtship of Miles Standish."

Mrs. Dodd's summary of technique is as follows:

"At best this investigation has secured only a partial amount of the historical content contained in the poems analyzed. In securing this content the following methods were used:

"1. To score only once each reference of a kind in a given poem.

"2. To collect only specific references to date, institution, person, place, and written production.

"3. To regard as historical only those references to date that are specific and definite in point of year.

"4. To collect references to political, religious, educational, industrial and social institutions that are not running after 1900.

"5. To regard as historical only those references to persons, meaning both character and people, who have actually lived, and of whom we have a definite record in addition to the poem in which mention is made.

"6. To regard as historical only those references to place that are associated with an historical event and character.

"7. To collect only references to written productions contained within the poems.

"8. To include all historical references to date, institution, person, place, and written production, that are unmistakably implied but not directly mentioned.

"9. To include all designations for the same person or people, which carry different connotations.

"10. To include references to historical character regardless of treatment by poet."

Chapter XX

GEOGRAPHY

(Studies 36-39)

§1—Introduction

Four quite distinct problems are attacked in the geography studies. One writer obtains a consensus of teachers' opinions concerning the relative rankings of countries for purposes of emphasis in geography instruction. This study is the earliest reported upon in the literature examined and consequently does not use rigorous methods. The second study is concerned with the technique of determining the content of geography from an examination of newspapers and magazines, proceeding on the assumption that the content of school geography will be determined by its use in current literature. Here again, as in history, explicit mention of geography was investigated and no further attention was paid to the problem of determining the geography "necessary to understand" the material read. The third study, of a comprehensive sort, seeks to determine the importance of countries by setting up objective, quantitative standards, obtained by composite ranking, according to area, population, exports, imports, etc. The fourth study uses geographical material as the basis for a technical study which seeks to determine short methods to obviate the drudgery of exact tabulation.

§2—Expert Opinion

(Study 36)

In 1913 Whitbeck* endeavored to assign values to geographical items which ought to be thoroughly taught and reviewed until their locations are permanently learned.

*Education, Vol. 31, pp. 108-116, R. H. Whitbeck.

The method used is that of obtaining a consensus. The details are as follows: Seventy-five teachers, principals, and superintendents in the geography class at Cornell University, from twenty or more states and representing all kinds of schools, were used as judges. The teachers were divided into committees and each committee was asked to decide upon what cities in the continent assigned to it are of primary importance — "cities that are so important that the American school teacher should teach their location rather accurately, teach why they are important, and for what they stand in world affairs. It was agreed that a city must stand for more than one important thing in order to be included in the list."

The findings of these committees were passed over to a committee of the faculty of geography consisting of three geographers, a professor of education, and two superintendents. By a method which is not clear it was found that two-thirds of the cities listed by the first committees failed of approval by the faculty committee. Any city in the United States which received two or more of the faculty votes was listed.

The cities of the United States obtaining full votes were: New York, Chicago, Philadelphia, St. Louis, Boston, Pittsburgh, San Francisco, New Orleans, Washington, and Minneapolis-St. Paul. Those receiving four votes were: Puget Sound cities and Galveston. Next in rank were Cleveland, Buffalo, Salt Lake City, Scranton-Wilkes-Barre, and Lowell. Those receiving two votes were: Baltimore, Cincinnati, Milwaukee, Louisville, Kansas City, and Indianapolis.

The outstanding cities of Europe were: London, Liverpool, Edinburgh, Glasgow, Berlin, Hamburg, Rome, Athens, Constantinople, St. Petersburg, and Paris. Cities of Asia receiving full votes were Bombay, Calcutta, Pekin, Jerusalem, Tokyo-Yokohama. On the Western continent, outside of the United States, cities included were Montreal, Quebec, Rio de Janeiro, Buenos Aires, Havana, and Mexico City. In the rest of the world were listed: Manila, Honolulu, Cairo, Cape Town, Melbourne, Johannesburg, Sydney, and Batavia.

§3—Newspapers and Magazines

(Study 37)

W. C. Bagley* made a preliminary study of newspapers and magazines to "record geographical references and determine from the frequency of these references the relative value of the different types of geographical information.

"A large number of newspapers and magazines were read by members of the seminary, the geographical . . . references were recorded and classified, and an attempt was made to evaluate the general procedure as a means of determining minimum essentials.

"The methods of counting references is an important detail in the technique of this work. Two methods were tried: (1) counting one for each term (such as the name of a place or of an historical event) or each statement with a geographical or historical content; and (2) taking as the unit the article in which the reference occurs, and counting one for each article containing a certain type of reference. (Thus, if London as a commercial center is referred to in an article, this group of references receives one credit, no matter how many times the word *London* may recur in the course of the article. But if in the same article London is referred to in another way, a separate count under its appropriate group is made for this reference.) A comparison of these two methods showed clearly that the latter is to be preferred, and this was used in two out of the three investigations reported."

Eighteen issues of *The Outlook* and *The Literary Digest* from 1906-13 yielded 2237 geographical references. The distribution was as follows:

Per cent

"References to facts of location, size, direction, etc., which may be assumed to require for their understanding a knowledge of 'place and location' geography........   53.5

*Part I, *Fourteenth Yearbook*, National Society for the Study of Education, pp. 133-36.

Per cent

"References to political divisions and facts of government, which may be assumed to require a knowledge of 'political' geography............................. 25.1

"References to industries, commerce, products, etc., which may be assumed to require a knowledge of 'commercial' geography.................................... 5.8

"References to people, customs, religion, education, etc., which may be assumed to require a knowledge of 'social' geography................................. 4.8

"References to places as scenes of historical events, which may be assumed to require a knowledge of 'historical' geography....................................... 1.7

"Other references primarily of local or transitory interest.. 8.9

"A grouping of this sort is obviously subject to the errors or peculiarities of individual judgment, but it may be said that the classification just presented is quite consistent with those furnished by other readers. Except for the absence of explicit reference to physiographical principles, this grouping represents fairly accurately the distribution of emphasis in the textbooks ordinarily used in the seventh and eighth grades. The physiographical principles, however, are precisely the 'general' principles to which we referred above; that is, their function is broadly interpretative and adaptive; they 'cover' a host of particulars too numerous in the aggregate, and too insignificant separately to warrant specific attention.

"Another suggestive grouping is based upon the frequency of references to the various continents. If one is to read intelligently the journals which formed the basis of this test, one will find occasion to apply one's knowledge of the continents in approximately the following proportions (the maximum frequency of reference being represented arbitrarily by 100):

North America	100	Africa	4
Europe	73	South America	3
Asia	13	Australia	1

"The principal European countries had an importance for the readers of the journals in question in the following proportions (giving England, as the country most frequently referred to, the arbitrary value of 100):

England	100	Italy	32
France	80	Turkey	30
Germany	70	Austro-Hungary	24
Russia	35	Spain	22

"The countries and colonies of Asia show the following proportions of references as compared with England: China, 55; Japan, 50; India, 19; Korea and Persia (typical of the less important divisions), 4 each.

This order of frequency in references to European and Asiatic countries is fairly constant in the two reports which furnish comparable data.

"The frequency of reference to cities is perhaps not so significant, although here, too, there is a goodly measure of similarity among the different reports. A combined rating, which may mean much or little, is given herewith:

Foreign Cities (New York, 100)

London	31	Constantinople	12
Paris	26	St. Petersburg	7
Berlin	15	Vienna	7
Rome	12		

American Cities

New York City	100	Chicago	26
Washington	27	Philadelphia	20
Boston	27		

"There is, in general, a direct, although not a perfect, correlation between the number of references to cities and the size of the cities — except, of course, that capitals of countries have an importance not always represented by their size.

"Compared with references to countries and cities, the references to physical and physiographical features are not numerous. For readers of the journals used in the investigation, information about the following rivers seems to be of the greatest importance and approximately in the order named for the first five: Mississippi, Hudson, Ohio, Missouri, Rhine, Nile, Danube, St. Lawrence, Potomac, La Plata, Seine, Niagara, Rio Grande, Columbia, Amazon, Congo. References to seas and gulfs follow the following order: Mediterranean, Ægean, Mexico, Black, Adriatic, Marmora, Red, and Caspian. The straits most frequently mentioned are the Dardanelles, Bosphorus, Magellan, and Bering."

Bagley "ventures the following opinions" as a result of this trial with geography and parallel study with history:

"1. A thoroughgoing application of the method might well result in a table showing the relative frequency with which certain geographical and historical references recur in the discussions of current problems, and this table might prove suggestive to teachers and administrators, and especially to textbook writers, as indicating the relative emphasis to be placed upon different topics.

"2. So far as the results of our initial test justify inferences, they suggest that the present content of history and geography in the elementary school is not radically inconsistent with the need for geographical and historical information as revealed by a study of current publications; that is, the historical and geographical references that seem to recur most frequently in current literature commonly involve types of information already well represented in the school program.

"3. If one were to take the newspapers and magazines of a single month as a basis for applying the method, one would be likely to get results that would make the materials taught in the school appear to be somewhat ill adapted to real needs; but when 'samplings' of these publications are taken representing periods of from seven to ten years the recurring references stand out distinctly. The actual facts to be taught in the schools should, in the writer's judgment, emphasize the kind of information represented by these recurring references. To provide a basis for interpreting the numerous non-recurring references the pupil should be supplied with geographical principles of general applicability and with general methods of procedure in finding and interpreting specific information. The recent developments in the teaching of geography have certainly emphasized this type of compromise — a compromise that is inevitable in framing curricula for the elementary and secondary schools. It is quite impossible to predict the precise type of particular knowledge that one will need in order to understand the current literature of ten years hence. To limit our instruction to the specific information that happens to be necessary at the present time would be a most short-sighted policy, but the particular facts that have been of outstanding value for the past decade may reasonably be predicted to retain their value for some time to come. Beyond a careful impressing of these — using them, indeed, as a basis — it is impossible to develop general principles and methods of work that will serve to adapt intelligence to the varying and non-recurring situations.

"4. It would be reasonable to infer that, in the material which they furnish to their readers, newspapers are somewhat limited by the basis of interpretative knowledge that they may assume on the part of their readers. This inference is strongly borne out by the results of our initial tests. In certain newspapers we found geographical and historical references very few and far between. In such papers the appeal is largely upon the basis of primitive interests (or instincts) which can be safely assumed to be common to all; hence the so-called 'sensational' character of such journals. On the other hand, there are journals that presuppose a large capital of interpretative information among their readers, and which are, for this reason, commonly limited in the number of their readers. This is strikingly illustrated by one periodical which was taken over by a publisher some years ago with the avowed intention of increasing its circulation. He succeeded admirably. We computed the number of historical, geographical, and literary references from an equal number of samplings over a period of five years before and five years after the magazine changed hands. As the circulation increased the number of references decreased, and for some classes of references the decrease was almost precisely in proportion to the increase in circulation.

"5. It would appear from these suggestions that any method that attempts to utilize current literature as a criterion for the selection of educational materials should be applied with a distinct understanding that it may simply result in a circular form of reasoning: current literature of a 'general' nature is likely to represent pretty accurately the level of 'general' education. In some respects it is just as valid to infer from the content of the school program what the character of current literature *will* be as to infer from the character of current literature what the content of the school program *should* be. Certainly, if there is a causal relationship, it is from the school to current literature, and not vice versa."

§4—Essentials Selected by Standards
(Study 38)

Branom and Reavis* assume the functions of geography teaching to be "to impart the more important facts of conventional or practical value; to secure on the part of the pupil ability to interpret properly the geographic factors that enter into problems of timely moment, and to develop an appreciation of the importance of the United States intrinsically, and its relational aspects to the world as a whole."

"The realization of these aims requires a general knowledge of (1) the relative location of the large land and water bodies, (2) the location of the more important countries of the world, (3) the location of the more important cities of the world, (4) the physical conditions of the more important countries, (5) the occupations of the people and the conditions of transportation, (6) our commercial relations with these countries, and (7) the fundamental relationships between the physical factors and human activities.

"In determining a minimal essential list of countries of the world, the following standards were employed: (1) the area of the

Seventeenth Yearbook, Part I, pp. 27-39, M. E. Branom and W. C. Reavis.

country in square miles, (2) population, (3) total value of imports, (4) total value of imports from the United States, (5) total value of exports, and (6) total value of exports to the United States. These criteria not only offer objective data of great significance in the study of a particular country, but also afford a means of measuring the relationships of the United States to other countries.

"The statistical data for each of the above criteria were secured from the 'Statistical Abstract of the United States' (1915) in which reports covering the latest year for which statistics were available, for the fifty-two more important countries of the world, were given. The countries were ranked according to their relative importance with respect to each of the six criteria.

"The fifty-two countries were then divided into quintiles under each of the six criteria previously discussed, and values were assigned to rank in the various quintiles as follows: (1) rank in the first quintile in each criterion received a score of 5 points; (2) rank in the second quintile, a score of 4 points; (3) rank in the third quintile, a score of 3 points; (4) rank in the fourth quintile, a score of 2 points; and (5) rank in the last quintile, a score of 1 point. The total score thus received by a country would serve as an index of the relative importance of that country among the countries of the world in area, population, import and export trade; and of its relative importance to the United States in import and export trade.

"In the selection of a minimal list of cities, several factors, such as import and export trade, advantages of location, importance of hinterland, and advantages of transportation, were tried as standards; but the lack of sufficient data for many cities rendered such work unsatisfactory. A very close correlation, however, was found to obtain between these standards in cases where such data were available and the single standard of population. It was decided, therefore, to use the standard of population as a criterion for determining the list of cities. After considering the list of cities determined by the single standard of population, it was believed that the largest city of each of the 21 'essential' countries of the world (as previously determined) should be included in the list, with the addition of all other cities of more than 200,000 population in the Western Hemisphere, of all other cities of more than 600,000 population in Europe, and of all other cities of more than 800,000 population in the rest of the world. This standard of population was established on the basis of American relations to the different regions of the world.

"This gives a list of 29 cities for the United States; 10 for the Western Hemisphere, exclusive of the United States; 18 for Europe; and 9 for Asia, Africa, Australia, and the scattered islands. . . .

"In selecting a minimal list of products, dependence has been placed upon the value of production in the United States, supplemented by the value of products imported into the United States. The aggregate value of a class of products may be large with large quantities in use, and a low price; or with small quantities in use, and a high price. Neither price nor quantity is an exclusive index of the importance of the products to man. Ranking products in the order of aggregate values has the advantage of taking both these factors into consideration.

"Ranking the products on the basis of the aggregate values of each product for all countries is desirable, but, because of unsatisfactory data, impracticable. Fortunately, from a somewhat different point of view statistics almost as satisfactory can be obtained. Recent world events have brought out in an emphatic manner the commercial dependence of every first-class power upon practically every part of the earth. The United States, consequently, either produces practically all important materials or imports them in important quantities from other producing areas. Hence, a consideration of the products of the United States and the products imported into the United States offers a comprehensive list of the world's industrial products. . . .

"In working out the relational material, it has been assumed that location, area, surface features, soils, climate, distribution of plant and animal forms, and distribution of minerals are the significant physical factors."

This analysis was utilized for the testing of pupils' information by a completion test given in the report.

The conclusions of the investigations are as follows:

1. The writers would place the minimum essentials at the lower limit of the second quintile and "these should receive a more comprehensive treatment than would be given to the remaining thirty-one countries." The countries included in the first two quintiles are as follows in order of rank: United States, Great Britain, Germany, France, India, Austro-Hungary, Russia, Canada, Italy, Japan, China, Brazil, Argentina, Netherlands, Mexico, Belgium, Australia, Spain, Sweden, Egypt, and Turkey.

2. The list of twenty-nine cities in the United States is: Baltimore, Boston, Buffalo, Chicago, Cincinnati, Cleveland,. Columbus, Denver, Detroit, Indianapolis, Jersey City, Kansas City, Los Angeles, Louisville, Milwaukee, Minneapolis, Newark, New Orleans, New York, Philadelphia, Pittsburgh, Portland, Providence, Rochester, St. Louis, St. Paul, San Francisco, Seattle, and Washington.

The list of ten cities in the Western Hemisphere is: Bahia, Buenos Aires, Havana, Mexico City, Montevideo, Montreal, Rio de Janiero, Santiago, Sao Paulo, and Toronto. The list of eighteen cities in Europe is: Amsterdam, Berlin, Brussels, Budapest, Constantinople, Glasgow, Hamburg, Liverpool, London, Manchester, Moscow, Madrid, Naples, Paris, Petrograd, Stockholm, Vienna, and Warsaw. The list of nine cities on the remainder of the globe is: Bombay, Cairo, Calcutta, Canton, Hankow, Osaka, Sydney, Tientsin, and Tokio.

§5—A SHORT CUT IN TABULATION

(Study 39)

An extended study of the items of place geography referred to in the first October number of *The Literary Digest* in alternate years from 1899 to 1913, inclusive, was made by Charters and members of a seminar. The object was primarily to examine methods of analysis.

For purposes of the study, advertisements, maps, and lists of places were omitted, while cartoons were included because they are essential parts of reading matter widely used to make ideas clear.

In this analysis geographic names (as *England*) were at once included. Then it was decided to add the names of people (as *English*) since to obtain a gauge of the importance of a country, mention of the activities of the inhabitants was as important as mention of the country, and in any event the name of the people could awkwardly, but logically, be changed to a statement of the name of the country, as by substituting *the people of England* for *the English*. Following this line of reasoning it was found that the people of a country were frequently referred to by nicknames, as Yankee, Hun, etc. It was further found that one could not omit proper adjectives (as *the American navy*); and, to make the list complete, pronouns would have to be included when reference was made to peoples or countries. For instance, in "The American nation and its associates," if *American* is included as a reference, obviously *its* would have to be in a complete enumeration of references.

One large source of difficulty was the disposition to make of "distributed terms." For instance, the term "Allies" and "Triple Entente" would necessarily need to be distributed among the countries included in the terms, because, if the term was important, the nations which constituted the groups were of enough importance in world affairs to receive a tally in the total findings. Terms such as the *Western States* required a careful reading of the context and the consultation of authoritative geographies, dictionaries, and encyclopedias before exact distribution could be made, and a few terms were so indefinite as to escape distribution by any methods which were found. Every reference was tabulated (in contra-distinction to one reference per paragraph or article as is the rule in some studies). This was done because of the effort to obtain a complete analysis. Places of the most minute sort, as the *Arc de Triomphe* in Paris, were included. Rivers, mountain ranges, lakes, bays, channels, gulfs, seas, and oceans were not included.

On the basis of this classification the totals for all numbers of *The Literary Digest* were calculated. The references by continents were: North America, 3112; Europe, 1835; Asia, 597; Africa, 190; South America, 38; and Australia, 28; total, 5800.

The most frequent references by countries were, for the first 20: United States, 2712; British Isles, 725; Germany, 257; France, 205; Japan, 202; China, 136; Russia, 121; Italy, 108; Turkey, 82; Canada, 78; India, 73; Mexico, 61; Russia, 57; Transvaal, 54; Turkey, 43; Orange Free State, 34; Spain, 33; Austro-Hungary, 32; Congo Free State, 23; and Greece, 23.

An attempt was then made to determine whether the same rankings of countries could be obtained by the use of fewer than six items: (1) geographical names, (2) names of people, (3) nicknames, (4) proper adjectives, (5) pronouns, and (6) distributed terms. To this end, several correlations were made, using the Spearman foot rule. The correlation between the rankings obtained by the totals with that obtained by the use of geographical names alone was .95; a second correlation between the total and the sum of geographical names and names of people was found to be .98; but in both of these correlations nine of the sixty-six countries did not appear. The correlations between rankings of all items and those derived from geographical names and distributed terms is only .90. Finally, a correlation between the rankings obtained in the totals with those obtained by combining geographical names, names of people and distributed terms was calculated and found to be .99 with all countries represented.

This is so nearly a perfect correlation that for practical purposes it appears that in making such an analysis to determine relative emphasis it is sufficient to include only the three items.

CHAPTER XXI

VOCATIONAL COURSES
(Studies 40-46)

§1—INTRODUCTION

The studies that have been made in the field of vocationa education are more varied than are those that have been made in any other field, and more complete than in any except spelling. They include investigations of the machinists' trade, the occupation of salesmanship, and that of sheep husbandry. A course in commercial engineering, based upon extensive job-analysis, has been made, and two studies into the objective bases of manual arts courses.

The studies in the machinists' trade include a complete course in the shop work and the subjects related thereto. For salespeople control elements are set up and the material is gathered from many sources. In sheep husbandry a cycle calendar of operations for the year is determined, and all the methods for handling them are gathered together, and to this are added the basic facts which give this information its scientific validity. In commercial engineering, job-analyses of executives' duties are made and the information necessary for performing them is derived, after which it is arranged in a four-year course with credit hours and a yearly program provided. One of the studies in manual arts lists all the construction projects that farmers carry out, while the second study does this for home repairs and takes the additional step of determining the tool processes involved in each project.

In accomplishing these results, service mathematics is worked out for the machinists' trade and service science for sheep husbandry.

One study provides an illustration of the complete process of deriving the topics of the curriculum through vocational analysis, collecting methods of solving the problems listed as topics, giving the basic sources for the solutions, arranging the material in instructional order, and teaching it to a class to verify the attempt to determine the working units. This is the one single study which carries the steps of curriculum construction through from beginning to end.

§2—JOB ANALYSIS AND THE DERIVATION OF RELATED SUBJECTS
(Study 40)

Allen* has derived curricula in mathematics, drawing, and science from an analysis of seven machine operations.

The method used is to analyze each process into its subordinate operations and determine for each subordinate part the information necessary to its performance. The plan of procedure can best be shown by a sample page of the Drilling Chart.

For our purposes attention needs to be paid to all the items. *Checking level* is meant to indicate the relative complexity of the operations, number one being simpler than number two. *Objective* describes what the operative can do when he has mastered item number one. *Type job specifications* is a description of the subordinate operations. *Auxiliary information* refers to the technical shop names of tools and operations. *Trade mathematics, trade drawing*, and *trade science* indicate the items of each necessary for carrying on the job in an intelligent manner.

It will be observed that in the column marked "Trade Mathematics," for instance, there is found a list of all mathematics needed for all the operations, and so for drawing and science. This gives the complete curriculum. It shows what denominate numbers are used, the fractions, integers, fundamental operations, and so forth.

*Outline of Instructions in Related Subjects for the Machinists' Trade, C. R. Allen, Federal Board for Vocational Education, Bulletin No. 52, 1919.

ANALYSIS OF MACHINISTS' TRADE

DRILLING

Checking Level	Type Job Specifications	Objective	Auxiliary Information	Trade Mathematics	Trade Drawing	Trade Science
1	Rough drilling and counter sinking to punch mark on all ordinary kinds of stock with or without oil where location is only approximate, with open holes, on relatively thin stock, and the machines set for speed by the instructor.	Man can do any ordinary job of rough drilling where no measurements are called for in locating the hole. He can run the machine and drill holes if the location of the holes is indicated and the machine is set up for him.	Names of parts of machine that are used on this grade of work. Operating terms, names of tools, safety precautions, knowledge of stock, working properties of all materials usually drilled in a machine shop, care of tools and equipment.	Trade technical mathematics: None.		Use of: (a) Lever for magnifying pressure (feed lever). (b) Rack and pinion for converting rotary to linear motion. (c) Worm gear for changing r.p.m. (d) Latch for locking (automatic feed). (e) Friction used to transmit power (if friction feed). (f) Heat due to friction (cutting lubricants).
2	Drilling open holes of one size: drilling holes not more than four times the diameter of the drill in thickness; holes quite accurately located with regard to each other either by measurements to punch marks or by use of a plate jig; job includes setting machine for proper speed and feed.	Man can do any ordinary job requiring holes to be laid out by ordinary measurements, or by the use of a jig.	Additional names of tools and additional operating terms.	Linear measurement — inches to $\frac{1}{4}$. Use of machinists' rule. Problem to find a drill that will make a hole of a given diameter. Device — diameter marked on shank of drill in fractions — 16th or 32ds (excluding reamer drills); Linear measurement — English decimal scale and conversion to nearest 64th.	To lay off work from sketch or detail drawing. Learn method of dimensioning holes as to: (a) Size of hole. (b) Location of hole.	(a) Friction, lubrication (bearings, etc.), oiling. (b) Lever for clamping (clamping down work). (c) Pulleys for changing one r.p.m. to another r.p.m. (cone pulley). (d) Heat due to friction (drill speed drawn temper). (e) Use of friction between surfaces F oo P (in clamping work).

To these applied items will be added other elementary items which are necessary for the understanding of each. Consequently the curriculum in each will consist of both applied items and elementary items which, when determined, will give a complete curriculum.

When these have been determined, the organization of the curriculum will be further modified by two methods of teaching. If the items are taught incidentally along with the operation by holding up the operation while the derived mathematical or scientific items are being taught, the curriculum will need no further modification. It is arranged in the proper order as it stands.

However, if the derived subject is taught at another time, antecedent to or parallel with the operations of the job, it is advisable and probably necessary to alter the order of the items in the interest of simplicity or logical relations. Instead of teaching linear measurement first it may be preferable or necessary to begin with the fundamental operations or at some other point.

This Allen has done in the case of each of the derived subjects. To illustrate, we may select the first item of General Trade Mathematics.

This unfortunately sets no definite limits to the operations which could be wisely done. It shows the relations to school methods; it gives special methods of calculation; it furnishes auxiliary information and suggestions for teaching.

The mathematics necessary consists of addition, as shown; subtraction of whole numbers by ordinary methods; multiplication of whole numbers with the aid of four-place logarithm tables and slide rule; division of whole numbers by the use of the four-place logarithm tables and slide rule; powers and roots, square, cube, and any root, with the use of the slide rule, logarithm tables and tables of powers and roots; addition of pure fractions and mixed numbers with fractional denominators of 2, 4, 8, 16, 32, 64, and 128, by the aid of a scale or foot rule, fractions by use of highest denominator and tables of equivalent fractions; subtraction of fractions by use of scale and of largest denominator; decimals to

FUNDAMENTAL ARITHMETICAL OPERATIONS

NOTE.—While set forth here as a specific block on general trade content, the requirements of good teaching indicate that these operations should be treated in so far as possible as incidental to the trade technical computations and should be taught in that connection; abstract drill problems should be avoided.

Operation	School Method	Special Method or Device	Auxiliary Information	Remarks
Addition of whole numbers.	Assumed to be known, so far as a command of the mechanics of the operation is concerned.	Use of mechanical adding machines either by demonstration sufficient to show that such machines exist and are commonly used or with enough practice to give ability to use. As a checking device some other special methods could be given, such as adding 10s and subtracting for 9s and 8s.	Some special methods for adding, such as "throwing out tens" and "double addition" might be included largely for the arousing of interest. Example of "double addition." To add: 7,945 847 2,648 6 48 Add th. 9,000 Add hds. 2,300 Add tens 160 Add units 34 Add total 11,494	It can be fairly assumed that the learner who comes into any vocational course has been taught the processes of arithmetical addition, subtraction, multiplication, and division so far as doing the work in a purely mechanical way goes. It can also be fairly assumed that he can not use these operations with intelligence as tools for the solution of given problems. He does not need further drill on the operations, but requires training in the intelligent use of these operations in the solution of actual problems.

.001; decimal equivalents; a slight amount of factoring; approximating; and multiplication of fractions.

This shows the comparatively narrow range of the mathematics required, a characteristic common also to drawing and science.

§3—DETAILED DERIVATION
(Study 41)

A considerably greater amount of detail is shown in the following excerpts from an unpublished study by B. W. Noel of St. Louis. While Allen gives a general description of what is done, Noel in the following three fragments indicates what the operations are in detail sufficient for the description to carry itself without teaching.

(1) In machine-shop operations one of the minor objectives is the computation of the revolutions per minute (R. P. M.) for cutting stock of different diameters and of different materials. In this case the first step is the analysis of the processes involved, which are as follows:

"Use formula R. P. M. $= \dfrac{K}{d}$, where R. P. M. $=$ revolutions per minute, $K =$ a constant, and $d =$ diameter of the part of the material being cut.

"A. Find K.

    "I. Select cutting speed of the tool.

        "(a) Depends upon the material being cut, kind of tool, depth of cut, amount of feed, etc.

            "(1) Consult handbook for tables of cutting speeds for different materials.

        "(b) Reduce cutting speed in feet to cutting speed in inches.

        "(c) Find the circumference of a piece of stock 1″ in diameter.

        "(d) Divide the cutting speed in inches by 3½, the circumference of a piece of steel 1″ in diameter.

"Answer =

"B. Find R. P. M.

"I. Substitute value of K and of d in the formula

$$R. P. M. = \frac{K}{d}.$$

"II. Divide the value of K by the value of d.

"The degree of accuracy in the result requires only a whole number."

If from these operations we draw off the mathematics required we find the following: To understand the first item the student needs to have enough acquaintance with substitution formulas to know what they are and to understand the meaning of a constant. None is needed for A I a. For A I b he must know how to reduce feet to inches. For A I c he must know the meaning of 1″ and of 3.1416, and the more erudite fact that the circumference is 3.1416 times the diameter. For A I d he must know how to divide a whole number (the cutting speed) by 3.1416, or, as an alternative, how to reduce 3.1416 to its equivalent (for shop purposes) 3⅐, and then to divide a whole number by 3⅐. For B I he must know how to substitute arithmetical quantities for the symbols, and for B II he must know how to perform the necessary division.

No ability to speak or write English correctly is necessary for this operation, and in "science" only a few elemental facts are necessary. For A I he needs to know the kinds of steel, and for A I a 1 he must have some familiarity with the arm speed. Finally, the formula $R. P. M. = \frac{K}{d}$ is based upon the fundamental fact that the R. P. M.'s of two wheels having the same surface speed vary inversely as their diameters.

In this case the last of these items is basic in the negative sense that the operation could be carried on without any knowledge of it by the operator and in the positive sense that the formula is based upon it. All of the other items are necessary for the successful completion of the operation.

As an illustration of the method by which the items of the fundamental subjects are derived from the analyzed processes involved in controlling the objective, the following will serve. As said above, it differs from Allen in the greater detail with which the exact range of content is described so that curriculum limits may be set concerning the degree of complexity of operations which must be taught.

In this process of derivation the items of the related and fundamental subjects are drawn off one by one without organization within the subjects. The order in which the mathematics was drawn off in the illustration above was first a substitution formula and a constant, then the reduction of feet to inches, followed by the determination of the circumference, the diameter being given, and so forth. Obviously, this is neither a logical nor a pedagogical organization. As a result of this it is necessary to collect all the items and classify them in some adequate order. For instance, in turning a cylinder (1 inch in diameter and 6 inches long between centers) a classification of the mathematics involved is made in Table I:

If a course of study in mathematics were constructed to show exactly what of the foregoing material should be taught, it would consist of items found in Table II. (This constitutes the raw material of a course based upon this fragmentary job. That it may be taught efficiently it is still necessary to arrange it in proper instructional order.)

TABLE I

A SUMMARY OF THE MATHEMATICAL ELEMENTS APPEARING IN THE ANALYSIS OF A JOB

Trade: Machinist

Job: Turning a Cylinder

(1″ Diameter, 6″ Long between Centers)

Mathematical Element	Number of Times appearing in the job
1	4
6	3
7	1
9	1
60	1
90	2
$\frac{1}{32}$	1
$\frac{1}{16}$	1
⅛	1
⅜	1
$1\frac{1}{32}$	1
1⅛	2
1½	1
(′)	1
(″)	18
(°)	3
Straight line	1
Parallel lines	2
Perpendicular	2
Angle	7
Bisector	2
Circle	6
Diameter	4
Concentric circle	2
Cylinder	1
Element	1
Radius	2
Vertical	4
$6\frac{1}{16}$″	1
Addition of whole numbers and common fractions	3
Addition of mixed numbers and common fractions	1
Measuring linear magnitudes	4
A point lying in the bisector of an angle is equidistant from the sides of the angle	2

TABLE II

A COURSE OF STUDY IN TRADE MATHEMATICS BASED ON THE
ANALYSIS OF A JOB

Trade: Machinist
Job: Turning a Cylinder

(1″ Diameter, 6″ Long between Centers)

Mathematical elements that are found in the job, and that can be taught with this job.	Mathematical elements that must be supplied to solve the problems according to traditional methods.	The traditional mathematics the mechanic does not need to know because he uses a short-cut method.	Method used by the mechanic.
The digits 1, 2, 3, 6, 7, 9, cipher 0.			
	The value of a digit due to its position, as in 16, 32, 60, 90.		
The numbers 16, 32, 60, 90.			
	Addition of two whole numbers, one containing one digit, and the other one or two digits.	*Need not be taught.	Steps off distances on a two-foot rule.
	Multiplication of two whole numbers. Multiplicand contains one or two digits. Multiplier contains one digit.	Need not be taught.	
	Division of two whole numbers. Dividend contains one or two digits. Divisor contains one or two digits.	Need not be taught.	
Meaning and notation of the common fractions: $\frac{1}{32}$, $\frac{1}{16}$, $\frac{1}{8}$, $\frac{3}{8}$, $\frac{1}{2}$.			
	Definition of Numerator Denominator	Need not be taught.	
	Equivalent fractions.	do	
	Common denominator.	do	

*Note: The topics marked "Need not be taught" are used only when the mechanic does the work of addition mentally or with pencil and paper. The type of addition entailed in this job is often performed, by the mechanic, by stepping off the values on a two-foot rule.

TABLE II — (Continued)

A COURSE OF STUDY IN TRADE MATHEMATICS BASED ON THE ANALYSIS OF A JOB

Trade: Machinist
Job: Turning a Cylinder

(1″ Diameter, 6″ Long between Centers)

Mathematical elements that are found in the job, and that can be taught with this job.	Mathematical elements that must be supplied to solve the problems according to traditional methods.	The traditional mathematics the mechanic does not need to know because he uses a short-cut method.	Method used by the mechanic.
	Change common fractions to equivalent fractions having a common denominator.	Need not be taught.	
Meaning and notation of the mixed numbers: $1\frac{1}{32}$, $1\frac{1}{8}$, $1\frac{1}{2}$, $6\frac{1}{16}$.			
Addition of whole number and one fraction.		Need not be taught.	Step off values on a two-foot rule.
	Notation of an improper fraction.	Need not be taught.	
	Change of a mixed number to an improper fraction.	Need not be taught.	
	Change whole numbers to improper fractions having denominators containing one or two digits.	Need not be taught.	
Addition of one whole number and one fraction.			
Definitions of: Straight line Parallel lines Perpendicular Angle Bisector Circle Diameter Radius Concentric circle Cylinder Element Vertical (The definitions may be given in this order, and they may be given at any time in the course.) Symbol (″)			

Table II —(Concluded)

A COURSE OF STUDY IN TRADE MATHEMATICS BASED ON THE
ANALYSIS OF A JOB

Trade: Machinist
Job: Turning a Cylinder

(1″ Diameter, 6″ Long between Centers)

Mathematical elements that are found in the job, and that can be taught with this job.	Mathematical elements that must be supplied to solve the problems according to traditional methods.	The traditional mathematics the mechanic does not need to know because he uses a short-cut method.	Method used by the mechanic.
The meaning of (″) may be taught at any time after the number characters have been learned.			
The meaning of (°) may be given any time after the definition of an angle, and the meaning of the whole numbers, 60 and 90, have been given.			
Measurement of linear magnitudes may follow any time after the (″) sign, and the notation of mixed numbers have been taught.			
A point lying in the bisector of an angle is equidistant from the sides of an angle. This theorem should be stated as a fact, and need not be supported by a rigorous proof.		Need not be taught. If it is taught in a more complete course, the center square should be made the application of it.	

§4—MERCHANDISE INFORMATION

(Study 42)

The problem of collecting merchandise information to be made available for the use of salespeople was studied by Miss Elizabeth Dyer and the writer. The question to be answered is, What information should salespeople have about the merchandise which they sell? The practical difficulty faced is that of the proper selection of information so that enough will be given to meet the needs of the salespeople, but not more than enough.

In order to answer this question, it was necessary to set up control elements, delimit the field, and collect the information. The methods used can be illustrated from a textile study.

(1) The first step taken was to list all the articles made of textile fibers which are carried in seven department stores. This constituted a very large number.

(2) The second step was to examine the articles and list the different raw materials (fibers) and fabrics used in each article. This list was found to contain sixty-four fabrics of one kind or another. These two steps provided the investigators with the materials to which attention needed to be given.

(3) The third step was to determine the values which customers looked for when they were purchasing textile fabrics. These were discovered by several methods. One method was that of collecting many hundred questions which customers ask when they are buying. The second method was to interview customers, of whom some seventy were seen. The majority of these were married, kept house, and had children. There were also included stenographers, secretaries, teachers, and some students. As a result of this it was found that consumers are interested in the following six classes of values: They are concerned about the beauty or appearance of the material, or article; about the style; the becomingness; the serviceability or durability; and the comfort, as, for instance, the use of cotton in summer and wool in winter. Finally, they are interested in sentiment, by which is meant the satisfaction which a customer obtains from knowing

that she owns something which is imported, rare, and expensive, although the difference between such articles and others more common may not be apparent to most other persons.

Superficially it would seem that the customer is also interested in price, but fundamentally this is not accurate, for the reason that she wants to obtain the largest amount of the values which she considers to be most important for the least amount of money. If, for instance, she is more interested in serviceability than in any other quality, she then seeks to purchase materials which possess the greatest amount of value for the money which she feels that she can spend.

(4) When these values had been classified, a study was made to determine the classes of merchandise information upon which these values depend. This revealed five important classes. One or another of these values is dependent upon the fiber, the character of the yarn, the construction of the cloth, the finishing process, and supply and demand.

The following chart shows the problem graphically:

MERCHANDISE FACTS UPON WHICH VALUES ARE DEPENDENT

Values Looked for in Textiles	Fibers	Yarn	Construction of Cloth	Finishing Processes	Style, Supply and Demand
1. Beauty or Appearance					
2. Style					
3. Becomingness					
4. Serviceability (Durability)					
5. Comfort					
6. Sentiment					

This merchandise chart, which shows the merchandise facts upon which values are dependent, has the six *values* running down the left-hand margin and the five *classes of information* across the top.

(5) In collecting merchandise information, all facts concerning fibers, for instance, which had a bearing upon style were inserted

in the rectangle formed by the intersection of the columns headed "Fibers" and "Style." All facts concerning the relation of yarn to serviceability were likewise inserted in the rectangle formed by the intersection of the columns under the headings "Yarn" and "Serviceability." In this way it was possible to obtain the minimum essentials of merchandise facts which are useful in explaining values to salespeople and to customers.

The information was collected from several sources, as follows: textbooks, buyers, assistant buyers, expert salespeople, mills, factories, home-economics teachers, advertisements, and experienced customers.

(6) The material was then organized for use; this meant that it had to be divided according to departments, because the salesperson in the suit department must have different information from one of the people in the yard goods. As a result a basic manual was prepared for use by high school students who have not yet selected the departments in which to work, and merchandise manuals for specific departments were drawn off from this master manual. This resulted in a general manual and in several departmental manuals.

(7) After the material was collected and organized in this form, it was checked by experts in textiles in order to see that the information was correct.

(8) For instructional purposes in the stores the material was then thrown into the form of question and answer, because of the fact that salespeople are not "eye-minded" and will not read material if they have to dig out the ideas for themselves. Finally, it was used and checked to see whether it was within the comprehension of salespeople and reached the level of their working units.

§5—A SHEEP HUSBANDRY CURRICULUM
(Study 43)

J. H. Greene, in an unpublished thesis, The Construction of a Project Curriculum in Sheep Husbandry (University of Illinois), constructed a project curriculum following the annual cycle of sheep husbandry. The cycle was divided into the following problems:

(1) Should I raise sheep? (2) Location, selection, and purchase of breeding stock. (3) Getting the animals into breeding condition and breeding them. (4) Preparing winter quarters and laying in a stock of feed. (5) Caring for pregnant ewes. (6) Preparing for lambing. (7) Caring for the ewe and the lamb at lambing time. (8) Starting the lambs on feed, docking, and castrating them. (9) Providing early pasture; shearing the flock and caring for and selling the wool. (10) Caring for the flock on pasture. (11) Weaning the lambs and selling the surplus stock.

Each problem is subdivided into "sub-problems" of which the following is typical:

Problem: Docking and castrating lambs and starting them on feed.

Sub-problems: 1. Docking lambs
2. Castrating male lambs
3. Starting lambs on feed
4. Keeping records.

The sub-problems are solved one by one and basic facts upon which the solutions depended are given. Table I is a complete tabular statement of sub-problems 3 and is typical of the treatment of all problems. It will be noted that the column headed Solutions gives information about the procedure, while the column headed Basic Facts gives the reasons for the procedure. In some cases there is no reason except consensus of sheep experts, while in others experimental evidence is available.

From the column "Basic Facts" Greene has selected all those in the whole study which can be labeled chemistry, physics, and zoölogy. He finds six in zoölogy; life history of stomach worm, sheep louse, sheep tick, maggot fly, tape worm, and sheep bat fly. Six are included in chemistry: carbon dioxide cycle, nitrogen cycle, classes of food nutrients, carrying of oxygen by the blood, use of litmus paper in testing soil, and sodium chlorate. Physics is represented by five items: osmosis, heat conduction, adhesion, capillarity, and vaporization.

In addition to determining the content of the curriculum he taught it to see whether he had reduced it to the level of the work-

TABLE I

OUTLINE OF CURRICULUM MATERIAL

Sub-Problems	Solutions	Basic Facts
3. To start lambs on feed.	1. When lambs are from 8 to 16 days old the following mixture is recommended: a. Ground corn, 2 parts Crushed oats, 2 parts Linseed oil meal, 1 part Wheat bran, 1 part Only a very small amount of grain mixture should be placed in bottom of trough at first.	a. It is better to give them (lambs) about the amount of feed they will clean up in a day than to place a large quantity before them to nose over and spoil. The wheat bran is very essential to this mixture because it contains the mineral matter the growing lamb needs, and being somewhat like a roughage it adds bulk to the ration and aids in developing capacity for feed. The hulls from the oats serve the same purpose.—Coffey,—Prod. Sheep Husb., pp. 272 and 274. "In experiments at the Wisconsin Station it was found that lambs fed grain up to ten months old reached a given weight four to seven weeks sooner than when no grain was fed before weaning time, and the lambs were ready for the market at any time during this period, so that advantage might be taken of favorable market conditions. In experiments with different grain feeds for unweaned Shropshire lambs, for periods averaging ten weeks, 0. 3 to 0.4 pound of grain was eaten daily, with resulting average gains of about one-half pound per head daily. The following amounts of different grain feeds were required per 100 pounds of gain in body weight: wheat bran, 71 pounds; corn meal (4 trials), 74 pounds; whole oats, 78 pounds; and cracked peas, 81 pounds. Unweaned lambs that go into the breeding flock should receive feed like oats and peas, wheat or bran, while corn is preferable for lambs intended for the butcher, as it tends to produce a fat carcass." Woll, Productive Feeding of Farm Animals, p. 324.
	b. Also some leguminous hay should be fed.	b. This adds bulk and protein to the ration.

TABLE I — (Continued)

OUTLINE OF CURRICULUM MATERIAL

Sub-Problems	Solutions	Basic Facts
	2. Feed these feeds in a lamb creep placed in the sunniest, most comfortable part of the barn.	2. Lambs like to frequent a sunny, comfortable spot, and hence will come and be tempted to feed.
	3. Troughs and racks should be cleaned daily. Scrub them with lime water when they become soiled. Feed surplus feed taken from racks and troughs to ewes.	3. Sheep are dainty feeders and will not touch tainted food. "Lime is employed outside of the body to destroy putrefying organic matter by combining with water and forming slaked lime, which absorbs many of the products of decomposition." Winslow, Veterinary Materia Medica and Therapeutics, p. 148.
	4. Change to whole corn and oats when lambs are 5 to 6 weeks old.	4. "Experiments conducted at the Illinois Agricultural Station indicate that western lambs six months old or past will make more gain from whole shell-corn than they will from ground corn." Coffey, Prod. Sheep Husb., p. 271.
	5. Lambs which are to be marketed should receive ration largely of corn. Lambs which are to be retained for breeding purposes should receive ration not more than half of which is corn and the other half consisting of oats and possibly bran and oil meal.	5. See Wisconsin Experiments cited under 1a above.
	6. Lambs on forage should be fed about one-half the grain that those in a dry lot receive. Feed what will be cleaned up readily.	6. Forage will take the place of part of the grain ration.
	7. Graze lambs on grass, old clover and rye before regular grazing season for about 2 to 4 hours daily.	
4. To keep records and accounts of the project.	1. The same accounts will be used as heretofore. Records on results of docking and castrating should be made in miscellaneous notes.	

ing units of a group. The procedure was as follows: A group of farmer boys in the ninth and tenth grades was selected in a small high school which by mental test was found to consist of pupils of average intelligence, the boys representing a fair sampling of the school. To give the curriculum a thorough test he wrote up the tabular material, a sample of which is given above, in textbook form, and placed it in the hands of the students. Before each problem was presented the students were formally tested by prepared questions to see what they already knew about the subject. The problem was then raised and the chapter in the text given to the pupils. At the close of the treatment of each major problem a test of equal difficulty was given and the improvement noted.

To obtain an additional check, the students were put into a hypercritical attitude after the test was given and asked to carefully criticize the text for difficulties and obscurities, to see if it had been reduced to their working units. This criticism, with the criticism of the author as he taught, was used to modify and clarify the text.

To assist in the criticism the pupils were asked to keep a diary in which they recorded facts according to the following outlines:

"Members of the class are to write a book on sheep husbandry, based on study and practical experience. The instructor will help to supply some facts; others will be found in books and be obtained from the practical experience of sheep men and of students.

"A. Be sure you understand *every word* in the text as you read. Underline all words you do not understand.

"B. Be sure you record:

"1. Every word you do not understand.

"2. Every additional explanation found in another book or explained by a sheep man, a farmer, or the instructor.

"3. Every observation as to how the 'Solutions' succeed."

The study of the text showed that very little material of consequence had been omitted in its original construction. In getting back to working units, the life history of the stomach worm and some practical facts concerning the economic returns from western ewes were found necessary in helping the pupils to solve the problem: "The Kind of Breeding Ewes to be Purchased." In the preparation of the test the discussion of the phenomenon of birth seemed to render prerequisite a preliminary treatment of the anatomy of the reproductive organs of the ewe, a discussion not included in the original curriculum, and a threatened outbreak of hemorrhagic septicæmia made this consideration actually necessary. The foregoing modifications were practically the only important ones made. Many words were used which were not intelligible to the class and a glossary would have been a very valuable and necessary addition.

§6—A COMMERCIAL ENGINEERING CURRICULUM
(Study 44)

Strong* bases a curriculum for executives of production, building construction, and printing upon a job analysis.

"Let me trace for you the steps which have been employed during the last seven months in working out the contents of certain curricula designed to train men to become executives in the three fields of building construction, printing, and production.

"A staff of fourteen men spent the summer in making careful job analyses of six production companies, five printing companies, and twenty-seven building construction companies. Most of the latter were very small, involving only one, two, or three executives each. In nearly all of these companies a job analysis was made of the duties of each executive from foreman to president, inclusive. The companies were selected so as to represent as wide a variety of features as possible. Thus we studied in each of the three fields the largest company in this district and one of the smallest; we studied companies with mass production and with specialized production; companies truly typical of the field and companies on the boundary line; etc.

"Our job analyses contained six parts. First we listed the

*E. K. Strong, "Analyzing Industrial Educational Requirements", *C. I. T. Technical Journal*, Jan., 1921; "Job Analyses of the Manager in Industry", *School and Society*, April 16, 1921.

duties of the position—what the executive did. Second, we noted the essential qualifications—that is, what he had to know in order to perform those duties. Third, we added the qualifications not essential but of value. Here were recorded such groups of information as the executive himself pointed out that he ought to possess to handle his job better, or such as appeared to the investigator to be of value to the executive. Command of English was a frequent entry under this heading. Fourth, the route to the job the official had himself pursued. Fifth, the probable line of promotion. In most cases this was not known to the executive, and in many cases it was not clear to anyone in the company. Sixth, recommendations and notes of any sort.

"Let me illustrate these six points by giving the first three or four items under these six headings from a job analysis of a superintendent of a pattern shop.

"'1. Duties of Position:

"'(a) Supervises the work of about seventy men and takes the responsibility for the correctness and accuracy of both the pattern-maker and the checker.

"'(b) Selects work to be given men according to their natural ability and training.

"'(c) Studies drawings sent in to see that the principles embodied are sound from the standpoint of pattern construction, moulding, and casting. For example, areas of sections may be so proportioned that undue shrinkage stresses will be set up during the cooling of the casting.

"'(d) Secures cost estimates from jobbing pattern shops and decides whether it is more economical (considering here the time element) to have patterns made outside or in own department, etc.

"'2. Essential qualifications:

"'(a) Must be a first-class pattern-maker.

"'(b) Must know the traits and abilities of each man, whether always inclined to work slowly and accurately, or whether able to judge when accuracy may be sacrificed without detriment for the sake of speed. (May get into difficulty with the cost office through assigning the wrong man to a particular piece of work.)

" '(c) Must be expert in reading drawings in order to visualize patterns in detail, the relationship of parts, the placement of cores, and the appearance of the mould when finished.

" '(d) Must be able to calculate cost of construction of pattern, etc.

" '3. Qualifications not essential but of value:

" '(a) Calculation of weight of castings from drawings.

" '(b) Some knowledge of chemistry and metallurgy for information during discussions in conferences, etc.

" '4. Route to the job:

" '(a) Finished eighth grade.

" '(b) Worked in foundry about eight months.

" '(c) In drawing room about three months.

" '(d) In pattern shop, chiefly on loam sweep work, about five years.

" '(e) During this time attended school at night taking drawing and mechanical engineering. Also did a great deal of home study, particularly on drawing, receiving instruction from his father, who was a superintendent of a pattern department.

" '5. Line of promotion:

" '(a) Not definitely marked.

" '6. Recommended by executive:

" '(a) Since the average age of men finishing a four-year technical course is twenty-two years, they are too old to train the memory for the details connected with the work. They should start at not later than about sixteen years of age.'

"So much for how we gathered our data. Now how are we using the data to improve our existing curricula?

"We have gone through all our job analyses and noted down every item that pertains, for example, to the subject of English. All of these details have been carefully studied and finally summarized. Here is our conclusion as to the function of English in our Production Course.

"'English is to be taught in order that the student will be enabled to do five things:

"'1. To express more or less technical ideas in a form which will secure the attention and action of another executive. (This seems to require, among other things, training in the handling of topic sentences, avoidance of ambiguous expressions, the expression of ideas in their logical order, and the emphasis and forceful expression of important points.)

"'2. To write letters of all kinds, such as acknowledgments, inquiries, claims, and complaints.

"'3. To express himself orally in conversation with workmen, officials, customers, and the general public.

"'4. To express himself orally in conferences and public meetings, either from the floor or in the capacity of presiding officer. (This seems to require, among other things, practice in extemporaneous speaking and drill in "Robert's Rules of Order" so that the presentation of ideas will not be interfered with through lack of confidence or the inability to cope with parliamentary technicalities.)

"'5. To write technical specifications according to established standards so that they may briefly, but fully, cover the subject and be easily understood.'

"In addition to these five objectives which we should like to hold the English Department responsible for putting over, we have three other objectives somewhat closely related but yet outside any existing English Department today. These three are:

"'1. To compile statistics in economical ways and to evaluate statistical results and present conclusions in a clear and interesting manner. (This seems to require, among other things, familiarity with methods of statistical tabulation, such as the Hollorith machine, with conceptions of probability and correlation, and the like.)

"'2. To express statistical facts in the form of curves, diagrams, and charts, as well as to understand and interpret them. (Much of this should be established in college algebra, in drawing, and in the writing-up of laboratory notes.)

"'3. To take an assigned problem, collect proper data, draw valid conclusions, express facts and conclusions in concise and interesting form, and fit the whole into a report so as to meet the idiosyncrasies of an executive or the interests of the general public.'

"These eight objectives make up very clearly and without question the second most important and second most common function of all executives from foremen to president, whether in building construction, printing, or production. The most common and most important function, I might say in passing, is that of handling men. These two stand head and shoulders above all other functions. Yet there is scarcely a course in the country on the handling of men and very little attention is given to English in our technical curricula — that little hardly meeting any one of these eight objectives outlined above."

The material so collected was presented to a central committee composed of all faculty members concerned and was referred to the departments which would deal with each of the subjects — mathematics to the mathematics department, chemistry to the chemistry department, etc. These departments were asked to organize or reorganize a course to meet the objectives revealed by the job analysis, and to report their results to the central committee. The content of all the subjects has been determined, the number of hours to be devoted to each, and the year in which each shall be taught. In other words, the study has been carried through all the stages from job-analysis to schedule-making.

§7—A FARM SHOP COURSE
(Study 45)

Struck* investigated four questions as follows:

" 1. What kinds of construction work do farmers perform in wood, concrete, and iron and steel?

"2. What kinds of repair work do farmers perform in the same materials?

"3. What kinds of construction work in the materials mentioned do farmers leave to expert mechanics such as carpenters, concrete workers, and blacksmiths?

"4. What kinds of repair work in the same materials do farmers leave to expert mechanics?

"The data for Part I of the study were secured from four hundred farmers who are distributed in thirty of the thirty-three communities of the State in which rural community vocational schools and vocational agricultural departments in high schools were in operation during the school year 1918–1919.

"It was deemed advisable to secure the data desired from the farmers through the pupils in the schools concerned. In order to accomplish this, personal visits were made to all of the schools. These visits were made in the course of two months, at the rate of four or five schools per week. In two cases slightly less than half a day was spent in the schools; in two other cases two days were spent in the schools; in the remainder the time spent varied from a half to a whole day. Owing to the topography of the State, and to distances traveled, it was not feasible to visit more than five

*Farm Shop Work in Pennsylvania, F. T. Struck, Pennsylvania State College, School of Agriculture, Rural Life Department, Special Bulletin No. 1.

schools per week. During the visits, printed questionnaires were distributed among the pupils, and were then carefully explained to both teachers and pupils. Pupils were asked, provided they lived on farms, to take the questionnaires to their fathers or to friends who were farmers. The pupils were further asked to explain the questionnaires to whoever was to fill them out and to render assistance where it seemed advisable in the mechanics of scoring the questionnaires. Upon being filled out, the latter were in all cases first returned to the respective schools, in order that they might serve as a basis for discussion and for action in connection with the educational work affected. Later the questionnaires were sent to the writer."

Unfortunately, no statement is given of the method of obtaining the original lists or of the form of the questionnaire.

"The information secured from the farmers was grouped in three distinct ways:

"1. In view of the fact that over 70 per cent of the farming in the State is of the general farming type, it was thought advisable to group all of the data secured in the first classification; namely, on the basis of all farms studied. It is believed that the facts brought out in this classification closely fit conditions in the entire State. It may be argued that poultry-raising is quite different from dairying, but the former, as a distinct type of agriculture, is found on only half of one per cent of the farms.

"2. The data secured were next grouped on the basis of the ages of the farmers, giving the information in order to show a possible relationship between age and the kind or variety of repair and construction work performed.

"3. The information was grouped according to the type of farming pursued, in order to see if this has a material influence on the kind or variety of repair and construction work undertaken by farmers.

"In presenting the data secured from the farmers, the following distinctions have been made:

"1. Construction work in a given material is taken to mean 'making' work. It also includes repair work when performed on the objects originally constructed by farmers, as it is assumed that with a possible few exceptions more skill is required to make an object than to repair it.

"2. 'Repair work' includes only the repair work done on objects not made by farmers. It will be kept in mind that the actual amount of repair work done is greater than shown in this classification as explained in the preceding paragraph.

"3. Work done by expert mechanics is that work which farmers leave to men who follow vocations such as that of carpenter, concrete worker, and blacksmith."

The ten most common kinds of construction work with their frequency per thousand farms were: wire fence (710), nests for laying hens (672), chicken coop (645), milking stool (642), nest for setting hens (640), farm gate (612), jockey stick (517), hammer handle (512), feeding trough for chicks (452), pig pen (445).

The ten most common kinds of repair work in wood with their frequency per thousand farms were: door screen (235), wheelbarrow (232), rail fence (185), window screen (185), horse manger (182), cattle manger (182), bins for grain (172), wire fence (170), wagon box (167), horse barn (160).

The ten most common kinds of work in wood done by expert mechanics with their frequency per thousand farms were: combination barn (192), kitchen sink (152), poultry house (132), dairy barn (122), horse barn (97), kitchen cabinet (90), door screen (87), kitchen table (87), privy (85), hog house (82).

The eight most common kinds of construction work in concrete done by farmers with frequency per thousand were: Floor (310), foundation (270), walk (220), cellar (170), steps (170), watering trough (135), gutter (117).

The nine most common kinds of repair work in concrete were: Cellar (47), floor (45), foundation (40), steps (32), walk (30), silo (30), cistern (25), fence post (25), gutter (20).

The five most common kinds of construction work in concrete done by mechanics were: Cellar (130), cistern (122), walk (102), floor (92), silo (87).

The seven most common kinds of work done by farmers in iron and steel with frequency per hundred were: Chain link (7), gate hook (7), chain hook (6), singletree hook (6), clevis (6), ring (6), staple (6).

The material was further classified according to the kinds of construction and repair done by farmers of different ages and upon different types of farm.

No analysis of the jobs into processes as in Fuller's study was made, probably because the investigator assumed that the work would be taught by the project method.

§8—Manual Arts Based on Home Repair
(Study 46)

Fuller* undertook "to determine what problems and processes would be involved in a manual arts course, based upon work which is done or may be done around the home by a handy man with a common carpenter's and painter's tools. The problems of investigation were: first, to discover the jobs; second, to list and classify them; and third, to determine what processes were involved.

"The method of procedure in the investigation was as follows:

"1. By personal interviews with fifty people, I made a preliminary list of the things which they in their own experience had had to do or have done about the house. These people consisted of housewives of Columbia, Missouri, school teachers from various sections of the State who were attending summer school, real estate and rental men of Columbia, and business men. In conduct-

*"Manual Arts Based on Home Repair", L. D. Fuller, *Journal of Educational Research*, March, 1921.

ing these interviews I explained what I wanted and asked the people to take twenty or thirty minutes to go into the matter in detail. At first I helped a little by asking if this or that had ever needed repairing and usually they took great pains to recall everything. When we had gone as far as we could, I asked specifically about other things which were mentioned previously by someone.

"2. I supplemented these interviews by personal inspection of twelve houses — in many cases the dwellings of the people I had interviewed. Using a list of two hundred items, I made a complete survey, in a small rural community of Missouri, of the problems of household construction and repair. In this way I reached the point where additional inspection or additional conversation added only an occasional item to the list.

"3. All the items were then grouped under general headings of painting, furniture repair, house repair in general, house repair inside, doors, windows, screens, general repair, shoe repair, sharpening, plumbing and metal work, and new things made for the house. In all there were 328 items. These were printed with the following directions. (The first section in painting is also included to show the form used.)

"'DIRECTIONS

"'Name.............City.............Date..........

"'Have you had any work in Manual Training?.............

"'*Our purpose*

"'To find out what has to be done about the house, the doing of which requires the use of tools.

"'*What you are asked to do*

"'First: Examine carefully the following list of things which are suggested as possible things to be done.

"'Second: Take the list and with the help of your parents or the landlady examine the house in which you live. Underscore all things which need to be done. Also underscore all things which you, your parents, or landlady recall have been done in this house or any other house with which you, or they, have been acquainted.

"'Third: Write in the blank space provided all those things which need to be done or have been done, which are not found in this list. This is especially important, as we wish to make this list as complete as possible.

"'Fourth: Please fill this out tonight. Mark as directed above. Have sheets fastened together. *Bring them to your first class tomorrow.* Lay them on the teacher's desk as you enter.

"'*Painting*

"'Paint house, paint outbuildings, paint repairs, paint screens, paint interior woodwork, paint floor, paint gutter, paint tin roof, tint walls, enamel bed, varnish furniture, stain furniture, patch scarred varnish, remove varnish, varnish woodwork, varnish floors, shellac floors, oil floors, wax floors, clean and oil furniture, polish furniture, apply wood filler.'

"These questionnaires were presented in person to the students at assemblies in the Columbia High School, the University High School, and to the college students in the university shops. In all 430 blanks were used and returned. The frequency of mention of each job was then determined as shown in Table I for the first 54 jobs.

"Assuming for purposes of study that these jobs would determine the content of a manual arts course, two alternatives presented themselves. First, the course might be taught as a project or home-project course, and the students might be given the jobs to do at home or in the shop. Or, second, the tool processes necessary to perform these jobs might be drawn off the jobs and the tool processes might be taught systematically or by the problem method. Of these two the second alternative was selected; and a type of analysis is shown in Table II.

TABLE I

THE 54 JOBS WITH A FREQUENCY OF MENTION OF 150 OR OVER.

CLASSIFIED ACCORDING TO TYPE OF JOB

Rank	Frequency	Job	Rank	Frequency	Job
		PAINTING			PUT HANDLE IN TOOLS
1	271	Paint house	36	169	Rake
5	222	Paint floors	39	163	Hammer
7	219	Paint screens	41	161	Ax
9	211	Paint outbuildings	50	152	Hatchet
13	197	Paint interior woodwork			
11	208	Varnish furniture			SHARPEN TOOLS
43	157	Varnish woodwork			
45	156	Varnish floors	2	253	Knives
27	183	Polish furniture	4	224	Scissors
48	154	Clean and oil furniture	9	211	Skates
31	176	Wax floors	14	195	Ax
			49	153	Lawn mower
		FURNITURE REPAIR			
7	219	Tighten screws in furniture			PLUMBING
16	194	Put knob on drawer			
33	171	Tighten belt on sewing machine	31	176	Stop leaks in faucets
36	169	Clean and adjust sewing machine	41	161	Thaw frozen pipes
52	151	Reseat chair	48	154	Clean oil stove
					GENERAL REPAIR
		SCREEN REPAIR	4	224	Put up clothes line
			11	208	Paper room
12	198	Make fly swatter	16	194	Mend locks
16	194	Put new wire on old frames	18	193	Re-putty glass
24	188	Put new spring on screen door	20	190	Build fence
26	184	Rehang screen door	20	190	Hang shades
37	167	Put new hook on screen door	20	190	Plane tight door
45	156	Screen in porch	23	189	Stop rat holes
45	156	Hang window screens	23	189	Build chicken coop
52	151	Mend torn screen wire	26	184	Make hen's nest
			28	182	Fit and lay linoleum
			29	177	Make swing
			32	172	Put shelves in closet
			34	170	Make sled
			38	165	Set fence posts
			41	161	Mend window shades
			52	151	Set glass
			54	150	Make yard gate

This table should be read as follows: Painting the house ranked first in frequency and was mentioned 271 times.

The eleven highest frequencies were: painting the house (271); sharpening knives (253); sharpening scissors (224); putting up clothes lines (224); painting floors (222); painting screens (219); tightening screws in furniture (219); painting outbuilding (211); sharpening skates (211); varnishing furniture (208); and papering rooms (208).

In ranking, when two jobs had the same frequency both were given the lower rank and the higher omitted; when three jobs had the same frequency the middle rank was used.

TABLE II

DETERMINING THE TOOL PROCESSES

A. Tool Processes Used in Woodwork

Number	Process	Number	Process
1	Planing	17	Laying-out
2	Scoring	18	Chamfering
3	Sawing	19	Beveling
4	Boring	20	Modeling
5	Sandpapering	21	Carving
6	Scraping	22	Mortising
7	Bowsawing	23	Mitering
8	Gauging	24	Fitting
9	Nailing	25	Superposing
10	Screwing	26	Doweling
11	Glueing	27	Inlaying
12	Countersinking	28	Assembling
13	Spokeshaving	29	Dadoing
14	Chiseling	30	Grinding
15	Gouging	31	Whetting
16	Finishing	32	Filing

B. Processes Other than Woodworking Used in the 54 Projects

Number	Process	Number	Process
33	Plumbing or leveling	47	Cutting glass
34	Scribing to irregular service	48	Fastening with glazer-points
35	Stapling	49	Applying putty
36	Mixing paint	50	Puttying nails, staples, tacks
37	Puttying holes	51	Removing old wall paper
38	Filling		
39	Applying paint	52	Mixing paste
40	Removing paint	53	Cutting paper
41	Applying varnish	54	Applying paste
42	Removing varnish	55	Hanging paper
43	Polishing	56	Brushing paper smooth
44	Applying wax	57	Tinkering — (general adjusting not reducible to processes)
45	Digging postholes		
46	Setting posts in ground		

TABLE III

PROCESSES USED IN 54 JOBS OF HIGHEST FREQUENCY

Rank	Frequency	Job	Process by Number (Table II)
1	271	Paint house....................	36, 37, 38, 39, 40
2	253	Sharpen knife.................	30, 31
4	224	Sharpen scissors..............	30, 31, 32
4	224	Put up clothes line............	57, 35, 9, 45, 46
5	222	Paint floor...................	36, 37, 38, 39, 40]
7	219	Paint screen..................	36, 39
7	219	Tighten screws in furniture......	10
9	211	Paint outbuilding..............	36, 37, 38, 39, 40
9	211	Sharpen skates................	30, 32
11	208	Varnish furniture..............	41, 42, 43
11	208	Paper room...................	51, 52, 53, 54, 55, 56
12	198	Make fly swatter..............	1, 3, 5, 9
13	197	Paint interior woodwork........	36, 37, 38, 40
14	195	Sharpen ax...................	30, 31
16	194	Put knob on drawer............	10, 57, 4
16	194	Put new screen wire on frames...	9, 35, 57
16	194	Mend locks...................	57, 32, 10
18	193	Reputty glass.................	48, 49
20	190	Build fence...................	9, 3, 45, 46, 57
20	190	Hang shades..................	10, 57, 25
20	190	Plane tight door...............	10, 1, 25, 34
23	189	Stop rat holes.................	9, 57
23	189	Build chicken-coop............	1, 3, 9, 28, 35
24	188	Put new spring on screen door...	10, 57
26	184	Rehang screen door...........	1, 10, 57
26	184	Make hens' nest...............	1, 3, 9, 24, 28
27	183	Polish furniture...............	43
28	182	Fit and lay linoleum...........	34, 2, 17, 24
29	177	Make swing..................	1, 2, 3, 4, 5, 9, 10, 14, 16, 17, 18, 24, 25, 28
31	176	Wax floor....................	44, 43
31	176	Stop leak in faucet............	10, 57, 24
32	172	Put shelf in closet.............	1, 2, 3, 24
33	171	Tighten belt on sewing machine	57
34	170	Make sled...................	1, 2, 3, 4, 7, 9, 10, 13, 14, 17, 22, 25, 28, 24
36	169	Clean, adjust sewing machine...	10, 57
36	169	Put handle in rake............	57, 13, 6, 24
37	167	Put new hook on screen door....	10, 57
38	165	Set fence post................	45, 46
39	163	Put handle in hammer.........	3, 6, 13, 24, 57
41	161	Put handle in ax..............	3, 6, 13, 24, 57
41	161	Thaw frozen pipes............	57
41	161	Mend window shades..........	57, 9
43	157	Varnish woodwork............	38, 42, 41, 43
45	156	Screen porch.................	9, 17, 28, 57
45	156	Varnish floors................	42
45	156	Hang window screen..........	1, 3, 9, 10
48	154	Clean oil stove...............	57
48	154	Clean and oil furniture........	57, 43
49	153	Sharpen lawn mower..........	30, 32
50	152	Put handle in hatchet.........	57, 13, 6, 24
52	151	Mend torn screen wire.........	57
52	151	Reseat chair..................	9, 10, 24, 25
52	151	Set glass.....................	47, 48, 49
54	150	Make yard gate..............	1, 2, 3, 9, 10, 14, 17, 24, 28

TABLE IV

FREQUENCY OF THE PROCESSES INVOLVED IN THE REPAIR JOBS
LISTED IN TABLE I

Number	Job	Frequency	Number	Job	Frequency
1	Planing	10	31	Whetting	3
2	Scoring	5	32	Filing	4
3	Sawing	11	33	Plumbing or leveling	0
4	Boring	3	34	Scribing	2
5	Sandpapering	3	35	Stapling	3
6	Scraping	4	36	Mixing paint	6
7	Bowsawing	1	37	Puttying holes	4
8	Gauging	1	38	Filling	5
9	Nailing	14	39	Applying paint	5
10	Screwing	15	40	Removing paint	4
11	Gluing	0	41	Rubbing varnish	2
12	Countersinking	0	42	Flowing varnish	3
13	Spokeshaving	5	43	Polishing	5
14	Chiseling	3	44	Applying wax	1
15	Gouging	0	45	Dig post hole	3
16	Finishing	1	46	Set posts in ground	3
17	Laying-out	5	47	Cutting glass	1
18	Chamfering	1	48	Fastening with glazer-points	2
19	Beveling	0	49	Applying putty	2
20	Modeling	0	50	Puttying nails, etc.	0
21	Carving	0	51	Remove old wall paper	1
22	Mortising	1	52	Mix paste	1
23	Mitering	0	53	Cut paper	1
24	Fitting	12	54	Apply paste	1
25	Superposing	5	55	Hang paper	1
26	Doweling	0	56	Brush smooth	1
27	Inlaying	0	57	Tinkering (general adjusting not reducible to processes)	23
28	Assembling	6			
29	Dadoing	0			
30	Grinding	5			

"In Table II a standard is found for judging the practical value of the common manual arts course for the communities studied. That there is little similarity between the two is remarkably clear. As one runs over the list it is noticeable that fewer than half the processes are taught either as projects or in elementary form in the present courses. If home repair and construction were the objectives of the manual arts course, then present courses would need to be radically changed. For instance, painting, including puttying holes, filling, mixing, applying, and removing paint, should be taught.

"In Table III are shown the processes involved in performing the 54 jobs listed in Table 1. In order that all processes listed be determined, all the jobs are analyzed in terms of processes not only of woodworking, but also of painting, etc.

"When these have been derived it is possible to determine the relative frequency of each process. This has been done in Table IV, which shows that planing occurs ten times in the 54 jobs. Upon such a basis it would be possible to determine the more or less commonly used processes so that relative emphasis might be determined. It should be noted that the first 31 processes are those commonly taught in school shops. The remainder are not usually found in any manual arts course now in use. It is apparent that if home repair and construction be made the basis for a course in manual arts, it is not necessary to use the project method. For once the processes have been derived, it is a matter of choice as to whether they be taught systematically and in isolation from practical jobs as projects at home, or as problems in the shop. The important point to bear in mind is that it is entirely practicable to draw off the processes from home projects and determine which of them to teach and emphasize."

For purposes of curriculum construction Fuller's advance in analysis over that of Struck is significant. By Fuller's method it is possible to determine the frequency of the technical processes and thereby to safeguard the selection of projects which will provide skill in a desirable variety of tool processes.

To determine the amount of attention which should be given to each process, a definite standard of difficulty should be arrived at for each in terms of the amount of repetition which each requires Then when the importance of the process is combined with its difficulty of learning, an index is obtained which will guide in the selection of projects where less than a complete list of home repairs is selected. For instance, if screwing requires 50 repetitions and nailing 75, in order that the standard of efficiency may be reached, the selected projects when analyzed must provide this amount. If a few projects were selected which, however valuable, did not involve either of these processes which stand first in frequency of use on jobs, the projects would be poorly selected.

Chapter XXII

MISCELLANEOUS STUDIES

§1—Civics Based on Political Platforms

(Study 47)

Bassett* sought to derive a course of study in civics from a study of political platforms.

Method.—This, according to Bassett, is an appeal to experts for a definition of political problems, since the politician is an "expert" in politics and particularly in sensing the problems of the state.

Six classes of data were examined. First, an analysis of the national platforms of all political parties since 1832; second, an analysis of state party platforms in non-Presidential years since 1889 so far as they deal with national issues; third, an analysis of all state platforms of the major parties in the year 1910; fourth, an analysis of all the platforms of major parties in California, Indiana, and New York since 1850; fifth, an analysis of all platforms of the parties in Iowa since 1889; and, sixth, an analysis of the platforms of one Southern state.

Three measures were used: the linear inch; frequency of mention (the number of platforms in which the topic occurs); the number of distinct proposals falling under each topic. A list of twenty-six major topics was drawn off by trial and these were further subdivided as necessity demanded.

The usual tabulations occur, showing the linear inches devoted to the twenty-six items by the various parties issuing platforms in 1900; the linear inches in the Iowa state platform of 1914, devoted to the items by the parties issuing platforms; and the proposals in state platforms in 1910 by the Republicans and

*Part I, *Seventeenth Yearbook*, pp. 63 to 80, B. B. Bassett.

the Democrats. Tables also are shown showing the summary of ranks of each item by years in the national party platforms from 1844 to 1916.

This tabular information was given further treatment by assigning to the lowest item the value of one, to the next highest the value two, and so on. On this basis *Public Finance* made the highest score of 440 and *Public Office* the second with 449 (?). *Industry* with a score of 202, and *Health* with 32, were the lowest.

This was checked by giving the highest ranking topic in each campaign a value of five, the next four, etc. The relative rankings in this case were similar to those described in the preceding paragraph.

A further tabulation was made to show by years the number of inches devoted to each topic in the National platforms.

"1. Certain problems, in their broad outlines, are necessarily persistent, since they are inherent in the structure or constituent functions of government, *e. g.*, public finance, public office, foreign relations, and national defence.

"2. Certain other problems are persistent from the economic organization of society, *e. g.*, corporations (representing the capitalist), labor (representing the producer), and natural resources (representing the third factor of production).

"3. A third group of problems, which the writer has classified under 'moral reform', is necessarily persistent so long as there are men and women who are forward-looking, and subject to humanitarian impulses; and so long as a democratic form of government renders all social problems potentially political. The term 'moral reform' has been used in lieu of the more commonly employed term 'social reform,' for the reason that a moral judgment rather than an economic or administrative judgment is the determining factor in the voter's decision.

"4. Certain other problems are relatively persistent as corollary to our governmental or economic organization and status; *e. g.*, immigration (a result of better economic opportunities in this country than obtain in other parts of the world), foreign commerce (a result of our power of economic production), state rights (a result of the historic origin of the Federal government), constitutions (fundamental limitation of governmental action), and political parties (arising from the problem of registering the popular will).

"5. The responsibility for the solution of these various problems has been distributed among the three most important units of government in this country—*viz.*, national, state, and municipal (or local) government. For example, foreign relations belong exclusively to the Federal government; conduct of elections and suffrage qualifications largely to the states; education is delegated largely to the local units.

"6. There are certain tendencies evident from a careful study of the data: the problems of strict or liberal construction of the Constitution, state rights, personal rights, etc., tend to become of less importance in political discussion; while labor, corporations, and foreign relations tend to become of more importance; still other problems like public finance, commerce, and defence, about hold their own; health, industry, and justice appear to be gaining in importance; all topics of discussion are fundamentally affected by the two general trends which the writer believes he discovers beneath the surface of our national life — the trend toward more efficient nationalism and that toward more complete democracy, through the socialization of industry and the democratization of parties.

"7. From all that has gone before, it is safe to assume that any course of instruction whose purpose is to prepare for intelligent suffrage through the exercise of civic judgments upon concrete problems should contain at least the following topics: finance; federal, state, municipal, and school district; office, elections, civil service, etc., including the related topics of parties and suffrage as applied to the locality; corporations; labor, foreign relations, including relations to defence and commerce; natural resources, conservation, and reclamation; monetary system — money, banking, and credit; and the present moral issues of nation, state, and community."

§2—A Social Studies Curriculum

(Study 48)

H. O. Rugg and Emma Schroeppe in the Lincoln School are working upon a social-studies curriculum along lines presented in outline in an informal bulletin of information for visitors to the school. This report runs as follows:

"We are attempting to make a course of study which will deal with the important phases of the economic, industrial, social, and political world to-day, and how it came to be. We believe that in each of the twelve grades the children should study the importance of modes of living, activities and problems of contemporary life on as mature a plane as their mental growth permits. In each grade, along with the study of contemporary matters, sufficient historical background should be given to make clear the consideration of current affairs.

"We are incorporating in a single continuous course of study the essential and socially worth-while materials which have heretofore appeared in the separate subjects of history, geography, community civics, government, and economics. This material is taught in a fifty-minute class exercise each day in the fifth and sixth grades, and three times a week in the ninth grade. In addition, new materials are being incorporated from the study of industry, sociology, economics, primitive man, and the like.

"In 1921-22 we are writing and teaching daily the details of a new curriculum in the fifth, sixth, and ninth grades. In addition, and in order that our materials in these three grades may be placed in a total graded scheme, we are tentatively assigning materials to the other grades. Eventually, the curriculum research in the social studies should include the construction of a continuous course of study from the lowest grade through the senior high school.

"There are two such tasks. The first is to assemble and select such materials as will deal definitely with the social, economic, industrial, and political activities in which the masses of the people actually engage. The second is to organize this material in such order and form that (to the limit of their mental capacities) children shall develop:

"(1) A scientific attitude toward the economic, social, industrial, and political problem situations which they meet.
"(2) Skill in meeting problems of various degrees of complexity.
"(3) A clear acquaintance with established modes of living.
"(4) Active recognition of, appreciation of, and interest in, the great 'issues' of contemporary civilization.

"We are now carrying along, together, two sets of investigations: one that will reveal the present teaching of the social studies, and another that will enable us to construct a new course of study. The former task consists of the tabulation and the evaluation of material which we are collecting from schools throughout the country. This includes question blanks on the purpose and scope of course, time allotments, the evaluation of printed courses of study and of school textbooks, the critical study of existing experimental curricula, and the like.

"On the hypothesis that children shall deal only with materials that concern actual activities of people (with the crucial historical backgrounds), investigations are being made to determine what activities, modes of living, and problems are of sufficient importance to be incorporated in the course.

"A tentative statement of some 75 major contemporary problems—economic, social, industrial, and political—has been prepared from the careful analysis of about 140 books of outstanding prestige in the different fields. Four steps were taken to select this list of problems:

"1. About 80 leading authorities (economists, students of government, business and labor experts, editors, and men of academic prestige) gave their judgments as to the very outstanding books in each field, from which the deepest statement and analysis of contemporary problems could be obtained.

"2. A tabulation was made of the reviews of all books in respective fields, published since 1915, which dealt with any of these contemporary problems.

"3. The reviews in six weekly journals have been read for 18 months for the purpose of selecting only those books which, irrespective of faith, were regarded by reviewers as thoroughly fundamental discussions of contemporary matters.

"4. Each book on the shelves of Columbia University Library which dealt with any one of those problems (some 11,000) was examined. The title of any one book which was regarded by our group as crucial was included in our complete bibliography. This bibliography consists now of 1100 titles.

"From these four steps the list of 140 books has been compiled.

"We have selected tentatively the fundamental generalizations, principles, 'laws', which need to be used in order to discuss the crucial contemporary problems. These generalizations are now being distributed according to the problems to which they apply. They are so arranged as to be dealt with through the consideration of concrete materials.

"We are working on the principle that the consideration of problems and the utilization of principles and generalizations shall grow out of the study of specific incidents in human experience. In our course, therefore, hundreds of definite and concrete episodes are being incorporated. One principle controlling these episodes is that they shall deal with concrete descriptions of events and experiences which fit naturally into the lives of the children in the respective grades.

"An elaborate tabulation of allusions in magazines and newspapers is being made by Dr. Carleton Washburne, Superintendent of Schools in Winnetka, Illinois. Our episodes will be checked against the conclusions of this investigation to make sure that the minimum essential reading vocabulary of historical and geographical reference is incorporated in the course. In addition, we ourselves are making a tabulation of the current activities which are set forth in condensed form each week in some six weekly journals — *The Outlook, The Independent, The Literary Digest, The Nation, The New Republic,* and *The Survey.*"

§3—An Extensive Vocabulary Study*

(Study 49)

Thorndike has prepared "The Teacher's Word Book"** of 10,000 words according to methods described in *Teachers' College Record*, September 21, 1921, pages 334–370. This material was obtained from counts of over four and one-half million words, from forty-one different sources. In material read by children, counts were made in part or in whole from such books as "Black Beauty," "Little Women," "Treasure Island," and "The Legend of Sleepy Hollow," from ten primers, twenty readers, and textbooks in arithmetic, geography, history, and Spanish. In standard literature, counts were made in concordances of the Bible, Shakespeare, Wordsworth, Tennyson, and several other poets. Counts were made of books dealing with common facts and trades, such as books on carpentry, *The Garden and Farm Almanac*, and the *Army Trade Tests;* two newspaper counts were made. The correspondence studies of Anderson and of Cook and O'Shea were also used. A value was given to each word according to the number of times it appeared in each unit. For instance, in the reading of "Black Beauty," chapters 10–19, all those words which showed a frequency of 1–4 were given "source value" of one. Those occurring from 5–9 times were given a value of two. Those occurring 10–19 times were given a value of three; those from 20–29, a value of four; and to those occurring over 29 times a value of five was attached.

In tabulating the words, plurals in *s* were not counted separately. Usually words in which *y* was changed to *ies* were not

---

*Two other studies, by Knowles and Eldridge, which are frequently referred to in spelling literature, are not included here. Eldridge attempted to determine a common vocabularly for an international speech by a count of the words in the Sunday supplements of Buffalo papers. The Knowles study, which is referred to by Eldridge, but is seemingly not otherwise available, counted the words in certain passages of the Bible and "other literature." The Eldridge study is used by Thorndike as one of the sources for his vocabulary study.

**E. L. Thorndike, Teachers' College, Columbia University.

counted separately, nor were adverbs formed by *ly*, comparatives by *er* or *r*, superlatives by *est* and *st*, or verb forms ending in *s*, *ed* or *d*, *n* or *ing*, "in cases where the derived form would probably be easily read and understood by the pupil when he experienced it, if he knew the primary word." Adjectives formed from proper nouns by the addition of *n* were usually not counted. Every word and abbreviation in the investigator's own lists was counted. Of these there were some 20,000, with a credit of one or more. Rare names were omitted.

A credit sum for all words was obtained by adding all the credits. For instance, the word *and* received a credit of five from the Bible, four from Wordsworth, four from Cowper, etc., with a credit sum of 210, while the word *angel* receiving five from the Bible, three from Wordsworth. and two from Cowper, etc., had a total of 40.

The word receiving the. highest value, that of 211, was *in*. Words with a value of 200 or over were such as *for*, *it*, *on*, etc. Words with credit sums of 180-199 were such as *one*, *an*, *no*, *or*, *some*, etc. The investigator presents calculations to show the theoretical placing of the words in an infinite count and demonstrates the close approximation of his count to a true list.

The "Teacher's Word Book" contains about 10,000 words alphabetically listed, with key, showing the credit sum of each word and its position in the list. For instance, the word *a* is followed by the symbols 208 and 1a1. 208 indicates the credit sum and 1a1 means that it is in the first thousand, the first one-half, and the first hundred. The symbols 23 and 3a which follow the word *adopt* indicate that it has a credit sum of 23, and that it belongs to the first one-half of the third thousand.

The following are the practical uses to which, in the opinion of the author, the book can be put. It helps the teacher to decide quickly the proper treatment of a word by telling her just how important it is. It provides the less experienced teacher with that knowledge, both of the importance of words and their difficulty, which the expert teacher has acquired by years of experience with pupils and with books. It also provides a convenient place to record any useful facts about these words by which teaching can be guided and improved.

§4—GRADING SUBJECT MATTER BY INTEREST

(Study 50)

Uhl* investigated the selection and grade classification of reading material according to the interests of children, as reported by teachers and pupils. This very thorough study consists of several steps, described as follows by the author.

"*The procedure.*—The following outline shows the form of procedure followed in obtaining the reactions from teachers and pupils to reading matter:

"1. Reactions to basal reading matter.
   "(a) From teachers.
      "Questionnaire I: Analytical questions on the content of basal readers.
      "Questionnaire II: Classified lists of titles of selections sent to teachers for their comments.
   "(b) From pupils.
      "Representative selections presented directly to pupils.
      "Pupils' interest in the selections measured by asking them to state whether they liked or disliked each selection and why.
      "Pupils' comprehension of the selections measured by questions on the selections read.

"2. Reactions to new informational literature.
   "(a) From teachers.
      "Questionnaire sent to teachers who had used this literature.

Scientific Determination of the Content of the Elementary School Course in Reading, W. L. Uhl, University of Wisconsin Studies in the Social Sciences and History, Number 4.

"(b) From pupils.

"Informational selections presented to pupils with the request that they state whether they liked or disliked them and why."

Questionnaire I, which was answered by 2,253 teachers from 80 cities, is as follows:

"READING INVESTIGATION FOR THE COMMITTEE ON ECONOMY OF TIME IN EDUCATION

"To Teacher: Fill blanks carefully. Return to Superintendent's office by October 10th.

"City.......... School.......... Grade..........

"Name the one reader used most frequently in your grade

....

"Name selections in this reader which prove most successful for use in your grade as outlined below. Name same selection more than once if necessary.

"1. Name two selections which pupils ask to reread most. What reasons do they give for their choice?

"(a) Title........... Reason for choice............

"(b) Title........... Reason for choice............

"2. Name two selections which the pupils discuss most enthusiastically. Name the point of special interest in each.

"(a) Title........... Point of interest............

"(b) The same.

"3. Name the slection most effective in stimulating pupils to do independent thinking. Give reason.

"Title.................. Reason..................

"4. Name the selection which you think proves most satisfactory from every point of view. Give your reasons very briefly.

"Title.................. Reason..................

"Name the selections in this reader proving most unsatisfactory for use in your grade as outlined below.

"1. Name two selections which your pupils say they dislike.

What reasons do they give?

    "(a) Title............   Reason for dislike............

    "(b) The same.

   "2. Name two selections about which you are unable to provoke discussion. State cause of difficulty.

    "(a) Title............   Cause of difficulty............

    "(b) The same.

   "3. Name one selection which the pupils cannot understand because the thought is too mature.........................

   "4. Name the selection with which you secure poorest results. Why?

    "Title..............   Reason for choice..............

    "Signature.............................."

After the returns from the first questionnaire had been tabulated, it was found that many standard selections had been named by large numbers of teachers. The questions were so worded, however, that selections with outstanding good or bad qualities were most likely to be mentioned. Also, the mentioning of a selection depended upon its occurrence in a reader. Consequently, many standard selections were mentioned only a few times. In order to obtain more judgments on these standard selections, and to obtain the judgments of many teachers of each of the successive grades on the same material, another questionnaire was prepared.

The second questionnaire, which was sent in February, 1917, was based largely on the results of the first. It consisted of titles of selections arranged in lists of about fifty for each of the eight grades. In order to obtain a uniform terminology, a descriptive list of desirable and undesirable terms used in the responses to Questionnaire I was included with the directions for judging the selections.

The choice of selections to be submitted in the second questionnaire was determined on the basis of several considerations. Although close agreement existed in Questionnaire I upon some selections, there was either disagreement or a paucity of responses upon other widely used selections. The second questionnaire was planned with a view to obtaining (1) confirmatory evidence upon certain selections which the earlier questionnaire had indicated as either desirable or undesirable — the lists were not so representative of inferior as of superior selections; (2) more ample comments upon selections regarding which the responses to Questionnaire I were divided; and (3) judgments upon standard selections which were seldom or never mentioned in Questionnaire I. The descriptive list of qualities together with other directions was as follows:

"DIRECTIONS FOR JUDGING READING SELECTIONS

"1. On the following page is a list of selections which are widely used in your grade. The Committee on Economy of Time is desirous of securing the judgments of a large number of teachers with reference to each selection.)

"2. Rank by numbering from one to fifteen in order of merit, the fifteen selections which you regard as being the best ones for use in your grade. Do this independently of the following work.

"3. Below is a list of qualities which are to be used by you in giving your estimate of each of the selections. (You will need to write only the underscored part of the quality

"4. Below each selection with which you are familiar write the names of qualities which you consider as being uppermost in the selections. Be as specific as possible. When you name more than one quality in describing a single selection name the most important quality *first*.

"5. On the back of the next sheet make a more detailed analysis of two selections with reference to your own grade. Use the selection which the pupils like best and the one which they dislike most. In this analysis use the following terms or other ones to designate the qualities which make the selection desirable or undesirable for your grade. Return the sheet by March 10. Keep this sheet.

"Desirable Qualities

" (1) *Interesting* because of *humor; variety* of style or of material; *dramatic* — that is, exciting; *interesting action*, though not exciting; *interesting repetition*, as in tales for lower grades; portrayal of *home life* or *child life; personification; interesting people* described or taking part in the action; *interesting problems* for class discussion, or because the story is *well told*. (State which of these qualities make the selection interesting to your pupils.)

" (2) *Within grasp* because of the *familiar subject matter*, the *diction*, the *form of expression*, or *easy content*. (State which.)

" (3) A story of *adventure, knighthood, romance*, or *heroism*. (State which.)

" (4) A valuable lesson for your grade because it *cultivates expression* in oral reading; *enlarges vocabulary* by giving new words which are within grasp of the pupil; *stimulates thought* on account of *interesting information* or *character study;* presents *good moral* teaching; *imagination* stimulated. (State which.)

" (5) *Rhythm* or *rhyme particularly attractive* or because your pupils *like rhythm* or *rhyme*. (State which.)

" (6) *Festival element* as in Christmas selections.

" (7) *Nature* — the selection is good for use in nature study.

" (8) *Dramatization* — appropriate for dramatizing.

" (9) *Animal play* or *about animals*. (State which.)

" (10) *Fairy element, magic*, or *supernatural*. (State which.)

" (11) *Faithfulness, kindness*, or *sympathy* portrayed. (State which.)

"Undesirable Qualities

" (1) *Too mature* because of *hard words, hard* or *unfamiliar subject matter, too abstract* material, *hard symbolism*. (State which.)

" (2) *Uninteresting* because it has *no story;* too much *repetition;* is *too long; not well told; unreal; too childish; monotonous;* because *poetry is disliked* by your pupils; pupils are *tired of it; scrappy;* — not enough of the story is told; *characters disliked;* or *too didactic.*

" (3) *Moral teaching bad* or *moral too obvious*. (State which for No. 2 and No. 3.)

"(4) *Too sad* or *too depressing* for pupils to enjoy. (State which.)"

Returns were received from 741 teachers in 49 cities. In order to obtain a different kind of data, the selections were presented directly to 529 pupils of four different schools. The selections were chosen because of their use in nearly every city responding to either questionnaire, the variety of appeals to children as stated by teachers, and their common use in more than one grade. To provide a uniform appearance they were printed in seventy-page booklets. Before the selections were presented to the pupils the teachers were personally consulted so that the nature of the problem and of the work already done would be understood. The directions given to the teachers are as follows:

"PLAN FOR THE STUDY OF READING SELECTIONS

"This study of reading selections is being made in order to supplement the judgments of a large number of teachers who have already reported upon them. It is desired, therefore, that the real likes and dislikes of pupils be shown in the responses. Before beginning their reading, the children should have the general plan and purpose told to them in words about as follows:

"'One of the teachers at Northwestern University is anxious to find out just what kind of stories and poems children like. He has already asked many hundreds of teachers about this. The teachers made out their lists from the readers which the children used. There may be many others which were not included, but these could not be judged because they were not in the readers which the children used.

"'This teacher from Northwestern has gathered together the selections receiving a large number of votes and had them printed in this little volume.

"'You may each have a copy to read over. Perhaps you may recall having read some of them before. If so, reread to refresh your memory. Later you may tell on paper which ones you like best and why; also which ones you like least and why. Be very frank in expressing your opinions, because you can help most by describing fully and truly your likes and dislikes.'

"1. Ask pupils to read the selections for their grade without aid or discussion. All reading is to be done at school.

"2. After the reading has been done, ask the pupils to state on paper whether they liked or disliked each of the selections and why. Ask them to be as definite in replies as possible. The pupils should have their books for this work.

"3. Have a brief class discussion of the selections or parts of selections which seem most in need of such discussion.

"4. Ask the pupils to write responses to the mimeographed questions. Ask them to reply as briefly as possible. After the pupils finish their replies to each of the selections, ask them to state again whether or not they liked the selection.

"The pupils should have the books before them for all of the exercises. All of the work is to be done in school. If they want to use dictionaries of their own accord, allow them to do so. The purpose here is merely to find out what the pupils can do with these selections. In the class discussions as directed under 3, try to avoid influencing the pupils' judgments."

In addition to this, a fourth test was given upon material drawn from the set of national selections published by the United States Bureau of Education in the Community and National Life Series.

Fifty-nine teachers were asked to state their opinions of them according to the following directions:

"Please indicate in the columns headed 'Grade Actually Tried' the grade or grades where you personally used the lesson named in the preceding column. (For this purpose call the first grade of the high school the ninth grade, and so on).

"Rate the exercise in the column headed 'Degree of Success' so as to indicate your judgment of how the particular lesson succeeded, using letters defined as follows:

"A = highly satisfactory and understood by pupils.
"B = usable but not excellent.

"C = poor.

"D = complete failure.

"In the column headed 'Grade Recommended,' put a figure giving your judgment as to the grade for which the lesson is appropriate.

"In the column for remarks, indicate a word or two for each exercise which you rate A or D the chief characteristics which contributed to the result. Notes on others will also be welcome."

Lists of selections mentioned ten or more times in Questionnaire I, together with the percentage of favorable responses, are presented by the investigator. Of these, the list for Grade I is typical.

Selections	Frequency	Per cent Favorable
GRADE I		
Gingerbread Boy	33	100
Little Red Hen	33	100
Little Boy Blue	22	100
Three Little Pigs	17	100
Christmas Story	14	100
Cinderella	14	100
The Squirrels	13	100
Playing In Snow	12	100
Who Is It? Santa Claus	10	100
Christmas Morning	10	100
My Dream	10	100
Santa Claus	28	96
The Caterpillar	30	93
The Bee	18	67
The Star	11	46
Clever Jackal	11	27
Old Woman and Pig	11	27
The White Lily	17	12
Rose, Daisy, and Lily	15	0

The responses of teachers to Questionnaire II are tabulated

and show the amount of appeal that each selection makes to children so far as this can be judged by the reporting teacher.

The returns from the other studies are not available at the present time.

The investigator concludes by setting up standards and guiding principles for the selection of reading material for each grade.

§5—A CURRICULUM FOR CORRECTING PHYSICAL DEFECTS
(Study 51)

Todd* studied the problem of giving attention to physical defects in arranging the curriculum in the high school. The problem was two-fold: first, to collect correctives for defects and, second, to arrange a high school program so that attention could be given to special cases.

His first step was to select items for measurement. These were those commonly used in physical examinations, as follows: standing height, sitting height, weight, chest girth, expansion, grip of right and grip of left hand, and to the less definite items of bad posture, under-developed legs, under-developed arms, abnormal heart, uncleanliness, bad teeth, adenoids, chronic throat trouble, deformed feet, and eye strain.

For the first group it was necessary to procure standards for each by years. Some of these were found in Porter's tables and the remainder were obtained by Todd by the examination of 250 boys of each age. Standards for the second group are less definite.

The standards for the first group were prepared, not on the basis of averages, but on that of eleven percentiles. That is to say, chest expansion standards, for instance, showed the expansion of the upper five per cent of those examined, the upper ten per cent, the upper 20 per cent, and so forth. This, obviously, is a better standard than the average or median because of the fact that it provides an incentive for improvement which is not obtained if only the average is given. If a boy of thirteen has an

---

*"Provisions in the High School Curriculum for Correcting Physical Defects", E. M. Todd, *Journal of Educational Research*, Vol. III, No. 1.

expansion of 2.8 inches where the median is 2.5 inches, he is up to median standard; but if he knows objectively that he is in the upper forty per cent and that if by exercise he adds .4 inches to his record he becomes a member of the upper 30 per cent, or that if he adds a full inch he belongs to the upper five per cent, he has an added incentive for improving this very vital characteristic.

The table for expansion (in inches) is as follows:

Percentile	Rank	Age								
		12	13	14	15	16	17	18	19	20
95	1	3.1	3.8	4	5.1	4.9	5.1	5.3	5.7	6
90	2	3	3.7	3.8	4.7	4.7	4.9	5.1	5.4	5.6
80	3	2.8	3.5	3.7	4.6	4.5	4.6	4.9	5	5.3
70	4	2.6	3.2	3.5	4.2	4.1	4	4.4	4.8	4.9
60	5	2.3	2.8	3.1	3.6	3.8	3.4	4.1	4.3	4.5
50	6	2.2	2.5	2.6	3.4	3.2	3	3.7	4	4.4
40	7	2.1	2.3	2.4	3	2.8	2.9	3.2	3.8	4.3
30	8	2	2.2	2.3	2.6	2.4	2.5	2.8	3.5	4.1
20	9	1.8	1.9	2.1	2.3	2.3	2.3	2.1	3.3	3.8
10	10	1.6	1.6	1.8	2	2	2.1	2	3	3.6
5	11	1.3	1.5	1.6	1.8	1.9	1.9	1.9	2.8	2.9

The students are then examined and their cases recorded on a Data Card which shows their ranking in the first group in September, January, and May, and their defects in the second group.

With these records before the physical instructor he divides his boys into three groups: (1) Class A, or normal boys; Class B, or those found to be organically and mechanically sound but with poor general musculature; and Class C, or those boys in need of special corrective attention.

Class A boys participate in the usual athletic games, Class B boys are placed in a special gymnasium class to develop them and stimulate interest in physical development. Class C boys can be divided into three groups and handled upon that basis. In the first group Todd included those with flat feet, sub-normal heart, very poor expansion, and permanent or temporary cripples. Not more than ten can be handled in this group at one time and only about one in forty in a high school student body will be found in it. The second group is composed of those with postural faults, those needing especially development of the shoulders, arms, and chest. In the third group are placed those needing development of the legs, those with digestive troubles, the extremely fat, and the extremely thin. The second and third groups are not limited in numbers.

For each defect the exercises useful for correction are collected from the body of exercise material available.

Todd studied the problem of programming these classes and arranged a suggested schedule for the high school which will make it possible, on the one hand, to utilize the full time of the physical director and, on the other hand, permit the special cases scattered throughout the student body to be programmed in classes and sections.

This study is of interest as showing a method of determining and displaying standards for detecting defects and stimulating the desire for improvement, collecting correctives for defects, grading students on the basis of athletic efficiency, and so programming them as to group together those with like defects.

§6—Information for Bank Depositors
(Study 52)

Miss Camerer* studied the problem of determining what bank employees think depositors ought to know about banking.

Method. — Questionnaires were mailed to fifty bank employees and replies were received from thirty-five, representing the States of Illinois, Indiana, Iowa, Kentucky, Missouri, Nebraska, North Dakota, Oregon, and Texas. To obtain still further information the same questions were submitted to parents of children in the elementary school of the University of Iowa. The questionnaire,

*Part I, *Seventeenth Yearbook*, pp. 18-26, Alice Camerer.

which included fifty items in its list (method of selection not stated), was as follows:

"Questionnaire

"What, from your experience, do you think the citizens of your community, or of any community, ought to know about the following items? Please state after each item."

A list of banking facts followed, relating to making and endorsing checks, letters of credit, and so on. Directions for checking these were as follows:

"1. If knowledge of the item is *very* important, put a double check (xx) before it.

"2. If knowledge of the item is less important, yet of some value, put a single check (x) before it.

"3. If knowledge of the item would be of no value, cross it out."

Tabulations show the items listed in the order of their importance as finally determined by the number of double cross checks given them by bankers. (The method of giving two units to double crosses and one to single crosses was tried out but did not decidedly affect the rankings.)

The order of the items was as follows for the first five: How to write a check; How and why to fill out the stub; When check should be cashed; How to stop payment of a check; How to sign your name when endorsing a check. The five least important in ascending order were: How to secure a letter of credit; How to secure traveler's checks; How to use a letter of credit; How to write a produce note; Purpose of days of grace.

The returns from parents resulted in a ranking which had a very low correlation of r = 32 by the Spearman Footrule method.

Proceeding to the formation of a curriculum Miss Camerer prepared a composite answer made from ten replies to the question of what knowledge was necessary for the depositor to have. The information is presented in the following typical form:

"1. How to endorse a check in full.

"A check is endorsed in full by the payee's making it payable to the order of some bank or individual and then signing his name."

§7—Studies in Women's Education

(Study 53)

The organization of women's education upon the basis of a job analysis is under study for Stephens College by the writer. While the investigation has not gone far enough to produce results, a description of the methods being used may prove interesting. In general the method of attack involves some sort of job analysis of women's activities. This means, essentially, that a list of the physical routine activities must be made, and that to these must be added, obviously, those mental activities which may be included in the term "what she thinks about." Lists of interests and activities of an avocational sort need to be checked.

While this task seems superficially to be impossible of accomplishment because so complex, it may be affirmed with conviction that the broad outlines of women's activieies can be obtained with illuminating details and without undue difficulty.

The methods used in the study are based fundamentally upon the keeping of many hundred diaries with supplementary exhaustive check-lists of activities and interests.

On the following pages are given graphs for (1) the fundamental investigation, (2) the method of arriving at a vocational curriculum, (3) collecting material upon politico-social problems, and (4) the derivation of the fundamental service subjects.

Chart I, Column 1, shows the methods which are being used in the primary analysis. It will be noted that numerous diaries kept for a week by college graduates are being analyzed to find what college women do and think about after graduation. A number of more extensive diaries are being kept by a selected group of women, and still more intense analyses of physical and mental activities are being secured by expert investigators. Accompanying this procedure an exhaustive check-list of possible interests of women was submitted to a very large number of college graduates, to determine the trend of their interest for a number of years after· graduation. In addition to this, certain vocations for which training may be given with the facilities which the college possesses,

CHART I

FUNDAMENTAL INVESTIGATION

① **Activities**

Obtained in detail by analysis of what college women do and think about.

Through

(a) Numerous diaries carried on for a week.
(b) A number of more extensive diaries kept after training by a selected group of women.
(c) Use of psycho-analysis by an expert on 100 cases.
(d) Supplementary personal interviews on widest possible range of evaluated interests.
(e) Job analysis of certain vocations suitable for Stephens College, including housekeeping and secretarial work.

② **Classification of Activities**

Vocational
(a) Homemaking.
(b) Rearing of children.
(c) Teaching certain subjects.
(d) Secretarial work.
(e) Religious work.
(f) Etc.

Social
(a) Political.
(b) Organized social.
(c) Unorganized social.
    1. In home.
    2. Outside.

Personal
(a) Religious.
(b) Athletic.
(c) Health.
(d) Intellectual.
(e) Miscellaneous interests.

Determination of those which can be best learned on the job in view of curriculum time allotment.

③ **Controlling Ideals**

These are to be determined in connection with the sub-analysis of ② by expert opinion of college teachers and outstanding women and men who have given thought to the problem in the various fields.

④ **Sub-Studies**

From ① will be obtained a mass of activities which when classified as in ② will provide a picture of what the curriculum should present.

This picture will present a mass of detail useful in giving direction to the determination of the curriculum content.

At this point the study will be broken up into individual problems for study, such as politico-social and secretarial work in the two following charts.

The fundamental subjects are considered in Chart IV.

CHART II

POLITICO-SOCIAL ACTIVITIES

① Problems	② Controlling Ideals	③ Subject Matter	④ Teaching Objectives	⑤ Technic of Teaching	⑥ Public Service
Obtained by (a) Listing problems found in magazines, newspapers, programs of political parties, women's clubs, standard texts. (b) Evaluation of items by expert opinion to determine which to omit if list is too long for time allotment.	Ideals to control in political activities (*e. g.*, active participation and open-mindedness) in connection with *each* problem determined by expert opinion of college teachers, political leaders of high type, men and women.	Collected to show setting of each problem, solutions advocated in past (historical) and in present, with advantages and disadvantages of each, with interpretations in terms of fundamental subjects of political science, economics, and sociology. Collected and systematized by expert.	Developing in students of controlling ideals in each problem. Reaching personal decisions on merits of solutions. Participation in solution of problems in practical politics (where practicable), etc. These objectives are to be drawn from columns 1, 2, and 3.	Problem and project method. Reaching working units. Discussions. Study of textbooks, etc. Determined by teacher on basis of collected methods and experimental teaching.	Publication of (a) Methods of investigation used in this study. (b) Text for students' use in colleges. (c) Studies in methods of teaching.

CHART III

SECRETARIAL WORK

① Duties	② Controlling Ideals	③ Subject Matter	④ Teaching Objectives	⑤ Technic at Instruction	⑥ Public Service
Obtained by an expert who trains three teams of workers to make job analysis of duties of secretaries in type jobs selected. Determination of duties best learned on job —by opinion of those making analysis and other experts who train secretarial workers.	Qualifications of efficient secretaries in performing each duty determined by (a) Opinions of employers. (b) Opinions of experts in training secretarial workers. (c) Opinion of those who make job analysis.	Best methods of fulfilling duties with related ideals, collected by expert in charge of department. Fundamental material necessary to understand these is derived from the body of methods collected.	Developing ideals which control. Developing intelligent understanding of methods of performing duties. Developing skill in performing duties. (a) In class. (b) On the job. These objectives are to be drawn from columns ①, ②, and ③.	Determining instructional order. Class instruction. Project instruction. Study of texts. Developing skill. Developing ideals, etc. By expert teacher who directs ①, ②, ③, ④. Uses collected methods and experimental teaching.	Publication of (a) Methods and results of investigation used in this study. (b) Textbooks for students' use in college. (c) Studies in methods of teaching.

CHART IV

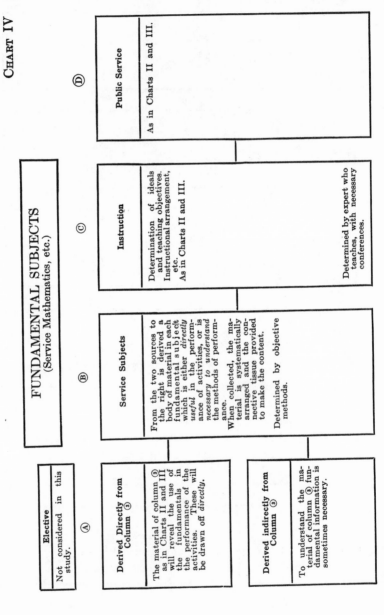

FUNDAMENTAL SUBJECTS
(Service Mathematics, etc.)

Ⓐ

Elective

Not considered in this study.

Ⓑ

Service Subjects

From the two sources to the right is derived a body of material in each fundamental subject which is either *directly useful* in the performance of activities, or is *necessary to understand* the methods of performance.

When collected, the material is systematically arranged and the connective tissue provided to make the content.

Determined by objective methods.

Derived Directly from Column Ⓓ

The material of column Ⓓ as in Charts II and III will reveal the use of the fundamentals in the performance of the activities. These will be drawn off *directly*.

Derived indirectly from Column Ⓓ

To understand the material of column Ⓓ fundamental information is sometimes necessary.

Ⓒ

Instruction

Determination of ideals and teaching objectives. Instructional arrangement, etc.
As in Charts II and III.

Determined by expert who teaches, with necessary conferences.

Ⓓ

Public Service

As in Charts II and III.

will be analyzed and courses of study built up on the basis of the analysis. In Column 2 is shown a tentative analysis of the activities revealed in Column 1. The ideals which should dominate graduates of Stephens College, and upon which major emphasis will be placed during the college course, are obtained by expert opinion of the college faculty and checked by the opinions of outstanding men and women with national perspective.

When the ideals and activities have been determined a number of sub-studies are ready, such as those connected with political and social life, the maintenance of health, the decoration of the home and person, etc.

Chart II shows the method by which a course in political and social activities is being constructed. Column 1 indicates the methods by which the list of fundamental current problems will be obtained. These will be evaluated, and in the most important, instruction will be given. The ideals which should control in carrying on all political activities will be determined by expert opinion. When these have been obtained, the possible solutions to current problems will be presented. An appeal to historical material will be made, and the advantages and disadvantages of each solution will be shown, in order that the ideal of open-mindedness may be developed.

After the subject matter has been collected, the problem of the teaching of the material emerges. This is divided into two minor problems. Teaching objectives must first be determined upon the basis of the ideals and subject matter. The technique of teaching, by which instruction can most efficiently be given, will be investigated. Then when the task has been completed in the college, it is the intention of the administration to have all findings of more than local interest published as a service to the teaching profession.

Chart III shows the method by which a vocational course will be determined. This follows Chart II so closely that no additional explanation is necessary.

The fourth type of study will be made in connection with the fundamental subjects, which are to be derived from the primary activities. It will be noted that no attention will be paid to elective subjects. Only the service phases of the fundamental subjects will be considered and these will be derived from the material found in Column III in all the studies of which Charts II and III are examples. When this material has been arranged in instructional order, it will be taught and later published.

It should be noted particularly that the courses in the service subjects are determined only after the primary subjects have been derived from the analysis; they cannot be determined beforehand. Only after the courses in foods and hygiene have been set up is it possible to discover what chemistry, for instance, is needed to master them. This is also true of such subjects as biology, physics, or mathematics. Each subject, after it has been set up, can be made to reveal the content of its service subjects. When the material of the service subject as derived in small portions from all superior subjects, is gathered together, the composite can be organized, and this with its connective tissue will constitute the total content of each service subject. Whether the program of studies will include all of a service subject in one course, as a course in service mathematics, or in a group of courses, such as service mathematics for chemistry or service mathematics for textiles, etc., is a matter of pedagogical administration. As a practical probability, the single general course is more likely to prevail under ordinary circumstances.

§8—COLLECTING UNRECORDED METHODS IN VARIOUS FIELDS

(Studies 54 and 55)

By interviews. — The writer has experimented with methods of collecting information to solve problems of teaching, of retail salesmanship, and of administration of departments in department stores.

In the first of these* a group of inexperienced instructors in college made a simple job analysis of their duties as instructors

* "Improving College Teaching," *School and Society*, April 23, 1921.

and checked their difficulties. This resulted in the listing of fourteen problems as follows: (1) Learning to know students, (2) Apportioning material to time, (3) Preparation of lessons, (4) Handling discussion, (5) Getting students to think, (6) Securing interest, (7) Testing (daily and session), (8) Grading papers, (9) Grading students, (10) Getting students to work consistently, (11) Making assignments, (12) Training students to use what they know, (13) Training students to memorize and form habits, and (14) Kinds of examinations.

The topics of the curriculum in methods of teaching thus obtained do not include all difficulties; but all topics were difficulties for the seminar group and were sufficient in number to occupy the full time of instruction.

To obtain the subject matter of the course, the method used was that of interviewing expert teachers. The members of the seminar were trained to interview by having each interview a different successful teacher and write up the answers to the fourteen points and then have this material criticized.

The methods of training are so important that they may be described in detail. At the first meeting of the group after the interviews had been written, the answers to each question were read in class. It was found that the interviewer can improve his report by a few devices. He should continually ask "How?" to make sure that he is obtaining all the methods used by the teacher; for the tendency is to forget that the methods are important and to accept generalities. Illustrations should be asked for; when the teacher makes a statement, the interviewer may often say "For instance — " or "Give me an illustration" with good results. Our interviewers found difficulty in realizing that they must *write* everything that they would *say* in reporting. For instance, we had to check the tendency of the interviewer to read a sentence from his report and then supplement it orally. This was done by asking him when he looked up from his paper and talked, "Is that down in your report?" Jocular insistence upon sticking to the written text produced good results. Occasionally it is found that supplementary questions have to be framed to get information because the original question does not open a lead. Care has to be observed by the interviewer not to rest content with the answer "I don't know how I do it." The teacher should be encouraged to talk, for, as his mind plays upon the topic, he begins to reveal his methods so that the interviewer is able to obtain significant fragments and jot them down. The interviewer must, also, write very rapidly, as the teacher talks, to get all that he can whether strictly on the point or not, and then select what he wants during the write-up. Considerable ability is rapidly developed by the interviewers in keeping the teacher on the point and in keeping him from talking too much; but this is a difficult task for a young instructor when interviewing an august and dignified senior colleague. Finally, the interviewer must preserve the exact language of the teacher so that vivid and effective expressions can be preserved.

When these criticisms had been made the interviewers visited other teachers until the results from about forty selected teachers had been obtained.

For mechanical ease each topic was answered on a separate half-sheet so that the forty answers to the first topic could be segregated. These answers were then read by an editor, who summarized the material with the purpose in mind of preserving all suggestions. Care was taken to avoid the editor's own more or less stereotyped expressions and to keep the language of the reports, which presumably were in the language of the persons interviewed.

The summarized material was then interpreted in terms of the underlying principles of teaching and of psychology. But it was found that some of the methods described were based on principles not to be found in textbooks, and consequently new principles had to be formulated to cover them.

The same plan was followed in handling the problems of retail selling. In this case the difficulties were obtained from three or four sources. Salespeople were asked to state their difficulties, but this yielded disappointing results because salespeople are not highly analytical. Executives were asked to list the difficulties of salespeople, but for the same reason little came of the effort. The best results were obtained by sending one of the faculty into the store to sell and watch the sales and note difficulties. This was checked by having her read a number of books on salesmanship.

After the difficulties had been listed, interviewers were trained, and the material was treated as in the teaching methods already discussed.

It will be of interest to learn that about seven to ten topics are enough for one interview on selling, and that thirty is the most satisfactory number to interview on any one topic, since we get no more suggestions from sixty than from thirty, above which number repetition begins to appear. In this way a great mass of information was obtained from 300 expert salespeople. The answers to about sixty questions from 300 salespeople, when digested and summarized, provided about one hundred thousand words of written material on selling methods.

In securing the difficulties of heads of departments three sources were canvassed. The salespeople were asked to state "the difference between a good head of a department and a poor one." Heads of departments were asked the same questions, and executives above the heads were invited to give their opinions. The collection of difficulties obtained from all these sources was thrown into a series of twenty-three questions, and one hundred of the best handlers of people in the stores of several cities were interviewed, after which the material was digested and summarized.

It must be recognized that the subject matter so collected is uneven in quality. We may feel quite sure that some of the methods described are better than others, although we have no means of objective measurement. The same plan of collecting information about agriculture or medicine would bring to light the common practices of expert farmers and doctors, yet it might well happen that a single farmer or doctor would have a better method than most experts as measured in crops or cures. Obviously, then, the material so collected is worth while only because it is better than *a statement of principles without illustration.* And such a body of material affords the basis for the scientific evaluation of the methods used by experts.

Furthermore, such a body of methods is more useful in teaching, in selling, and in other inexact arts than are the mere statements of principles whose application is left to individuals. It is better for salespeople to know the eleven methods of keeping the temper with disagreeable customers than to be told merely that one way of becoming efficient is to learn to keep one's temper.

By a central agency. — The following method for the collection of curriculum material is presented by the "Committee of Social Studies in the High School" of the National Association of Secondary School Principals (Study 55).

"A further broad matter which we wish to present with emphasis is the necessity of coöperation in the organization of the material for instruction in the social sciences. The field is broad and we shall develop very slowly if we depend on the purely personal initiative of authors and publishers to try out various lines of possible work. There must be coöperation in creation. When a teacher finds some topic which works well he must make his experience available for use by all. When there are criticisms of existing material which will serve to guide revision, these criticisms must be formulated in such a way as to advance the course in other centers.

"The suggestion just made is not an easy one to carry into practical operation. American teachers and principals are not in the habit of working on the course of study in a creative way. There are no agencies which are able easily to collect experience and make it available to many. Committees can indeed be appointed and can be told to find out something, but committees are like the rest of the world — slow to create.

"We believe that American schools are in need of any agency which will seriously attack the problem of coöperative making of materials of instruction. The members of this association are able, if convinced, to do more than almost any other group in the American school system toward such an organization. Our recommendation is that a group of principals of high schools who will volunteer for this service undertake to do, each at his own school, some definite constructive work. This shall be of three types: first, the preparation in full detail of five lessons in any aspect of social studies which appeals to him; second, a trial of these lessons with a view to determining whether they work and in what grade they work best; and third, the exchange of such prepared and tested material with other members of the group. This third obligation involves the duplication in some form of the five lessons to be exchanged and the assumption of the small expenses for postage and correspondence necessary in effecting the exchange.

"The business of the Central Committee of this Association would then become merely the business of preparing and circulating lists of volunteers, of receiving one copy of each lesson prepared for exchange, and of serving as a central repository for the experience accumulated during the experiment. It should be noted that the Central Committee would not be responsible under this arrangement for the creation or even the criticism of the material.

"The Central Committee could serve another useful purpose if such a group of volunteers really began work. It could be a center to which reports might come of progress made in the direction of really introducing this kind of work into schools."

§9—JOB ANALYSIS OF TEACHING
(Study 56)

A. J. Jones, as Chairman of a committee of the Society of College Teachers of Education,* reports upon a job analysis of the duties of teachers.

The method used by the Committee in arriving at the duties of teachers is as follows:

"Each one of a group of graduate students, all actively engaged

*Educational Monographs, Society of College Teachers of Education, No. 10.

in teaching, made out a list of the things he actually did in connection with his teaching job. This covered a period of several days and ranged from giving advice to pupils regarding choice of occupations, through conduct of the recitation to answering the telephone and inspecting toilets. These were listed with no attempt at organization and with no presuppositions about whether any training would be necessary to prepare for these activities, or, if training were necessary, what it should be. These were then placed in the hands of one member for combination and organization in order to facilitate the study. The next step was a careful and detailed study and discussion by the group, and the addition of activities overlooked and of those which came at frequent intervals. This list was reorganized, printed, and distributed as a questionnaire to teachers in various parts of the country in order to correct, supplement, or verify it and to find to what extent the activities listed were common in the life of the teacher."

A list of 139 duties was obtained by this means, and the returns from the questionnaire are now in process of being compiled to show the amount of participation, the frequency, the presence or absence of professional preparation, and the presence or absence of assistance from superiors. These are obtained by the following directions:

"In Column 1, marked PARTICIPATION

"Place a double cross (xx) before each activity in which you have actually taken part during the present school year.

"Place a cross (x) before each activity in which you have NOT taken part so far this year, but in which you have taken part during the past four or five years in your capacity as a teacher.

"Place a circle (o) before each activity in which you have NOT taken part within the past four or five years, or never.

"In Column 2, marked FREQUENCY

"Write D before each activity which you perform daily or nearly so; W for weekly or nearly so; M for monthly or nearly so.

"Write R before each activity which you perform (or performed) rarely — not more than three or four times a year.

"In Column 3, marked PREPARATION

"Place the letter U before each activity listed for which you can definitely demonstrate that you have received assistance in the course of your professional training in normal school or college (UNDERGRADUATE).

"Place the letter G before each activity for which you can definitely demonstrate that you have received any assistance in graduate professional courses.

"In Column 4, marked ASSISTANCE

"Place a check ($\sqrt{}$) before each activity in which you feel that you have received real assistance from superintendent, principal, or supervisor since you began to teach.

"In advance of the report of the results of this study we may properly consider the steps which must be taken in the preparation of curricula, utilizing the facts obtained.

"1. After the complete list is obtained the first step will be to determine the activities for which no formal preparation is necessary, and to eliminate these from the professional courses. Great care must here be taken to find whether teachers, as they are, can really perform these activities effectively without help. These activities would include those which can safely be left to the teacher, where no help is needed, and those in which help can best be given by principal or supervisor to teachers after they have begun to teach.

"2. When this step has been taken there will presumably be left those activities for which formal preparation is necessary or helpful. These must then be subdivided into activities, preparation for which should be given to inexperienced undergraduates and those which should be given to experienced teachers. The latter should probably be again divided into undergraduate and graduate groups.

"3. The usual problem is not the mere separation of activities into these subdivisions, but the determination of what part of the preparation for certain activities can best be given to inexperienced teachers and what part should be left until after experience has been gained.

"4. The next step is the organization of courses and curricula to give the preparation necessary. To do this effectively a further refinement of job analysis will be necessary. We must distinguish between different teaching jobs; e. g., first grade, second grade, fifth grade, high-school English, composition, high-school algebra, etc. We must determine the elements common to all or to certain groups and the elements peculiar to each.

"After this has been done we must determine the groupings of activities that will be most convenient and effective for teaching purposes. These should be organized into courses and curricula with three aims in view: (1) To prepare undergraduates to begin teaching. (2) To improve the teaching of teachers now in service. (3) To broaden and liberalize the work of teachers. These three aims are usually confused in the plans for professional curricula, and this is largely responsible for the ineffectiveness and pointlessness of our work. We have failed to keep clearly in mind the steps necessary in the professional training which are, in a measure, comparable to those taken in the preparation of the master workman in industry. These steps are, roughly: (1) Definite preparation for doing those specific things that will make up the large part of the teacher's time. These will include facts, habits, and skills which are definitely related to specific situations. (2) Such training as will enable the teacher to do better the things he is doing — to improve his methods and provide the basis for meeting new situations successfully. (3) Such training as will give the teacher an intelligent understanding of and appreciation for the reasons for those activities, for the place of the teacher in the school, the place and function of the school in the social order, and the meaning and purpose of education in a democracy. While these need not be taken absolutely as serial steps in the preparation of teachers, yet they do afford a point of view from which such steps should be planned. They are arranged in the order of most immediate need. The usual method of procedure is to reverse the order and either to leave out altogether the preparation for specific activities or to reduce greatly the relative amount of time given to it. We have signally failed to recognize elements of preparation that are appropriate to the *apprenticeship* stage of teaching, and have attempted to prepare *master workmen* all at once out of those who have had little or no experience on the job.

"If the analysis thus far made is correct the best general plan for courses and curricula would be as follows:

"1. Courses for inexperienced undergraduates.

"These should center very largely around the practical work.* Just what these should be must be left for a later study. How much background, perspective, or 'liberalizing' elements it is wise to include must also be left to later investigation. This would depend, in part at least, upon the intelligence level of the group of undergraduate students preparing to teach. It seems probable that we are now presupposing too high a degree of intelligence on the part of the average undergraduate and too extensive a background to profit by much of this work, especially when it is divorced from the practical work above mentioned.

"2. Courses for experienced teachers.

"These should take the form of:

"(1) Practical courses based primarily upon the actual, specific needs of the teachers constituting the group. These should be organized around their needs and not around the stereotyped divisions of the field of education, methods, history of education, school administration, etc. They should begin with actual conditions, point the way to improvements in procedure, and attempt to give the fundamental principles underlying the best practices. When this can be done it will give the teacher a basis for self-improvement and superior adjustment not otherwise possible. We must, however, not blind ourselves to the fact that many teachers will fail to get the underlying principles, no matter how

---

*Practical work is here used to include observation, supervised practice teaching, and any other exercise or activity which places the prospective teacher in actual touch with teaching situations and conditions.

hard we try. In other words, the ability to grasp these principles is one of the marks of the master workman, or at least of the journeyman stage.

" (2) 'Fundamental' or liberalizing courses, such as history of education, principles of education, educational sociology, etc. Indispensable as these courses are to the superior teacher, the master workman, their value is certainly much lessened when they are made basic for the practical work and given to immature, inexperienced undergraduates. They should be recognized as the *culmination* of the professional training of the teacher rather than the *beginning* of such training. It is only thus that they can have their full value and that time may be given for the more immediately necessary courses needed by the prospective teacher."

INDEX

Activities, analysis of, 34-40; as factors in the curriculum, 9, 10; breadth of content of, 29; dependent upon individual nature and environment, 29; exhibited in the form of a chart, 53; for normal child and for normal adult, 151; governed by ideals, 32, 33; influence of satisfaction and dissatisfaction upon, 27; less fluid than ideals, 31; motivated by failure to realize ideals, 30; partly independent, 29; relation of, to school subjects, 148; relative rank of, 101; Spencer's attempt to analyze, as a basis for construction of curriculum, 10; vocational and nonvocational, 48

Aim of education, 10; a prerequisite to both selection and use of material, 5; as expressed by Comenius, 8; as outlined in Plato's *Republic*, 7; changes in theory concerning, 3; "information" and "conduct" as, 76, 77, 143-145; historically considered, 41; must be stated in terms both of ideals and activities, 11; no ultimate objective, 65; present-day objectives, 42; tardy changes in, 3; varying emphases on, 41

Allen, C. R., 36, 71, 99, 105, 116, 119, 120, 155, 274, 276, 278, 280

American Historical Association, 67, 68, 244, 245, 249, 251

Analysis, approximations in, 60; distinction made between expert and lay operations in, 131; of ideals and activities, 34-40, 94; of the machinist's trade in a drilling operation, 275; limits of, 56-62; perfect, 60; Spencer's 59; study to examine methods of, 270-272; zones in, 57 *See* Informational analysis, Job analysis

Anderson, William N., 114, 124, 128, 129, 133, 173, 179, 314

Applied psychology, 21

Aristotle, 3

Arithmetic, a study in, 162, 163

Art, a study in, 165, 166

Ashbaugh, E. J., 99, 119, 173, 188

Authorship of textbooks, 61

Ayers, L. P., 87, 99, 114, 118, 119, 171, 173, 175, 181, 186, 187, 193, 224

Bagley, W. C., 24, 62, 68, 72, 116, 130, 262

Bagley and Rugg, 69, 88, 116, 127, 246, 251, 252, 254

Ballou, F. W., 99

Barnes, W., 115, 194, 195, 196, 198, 207

Bassett, B. B., 62, 67, 68, 69, 70, 72, 88, 116, 117, 123, 127, 244, 252, 254, 308

Betz, Annette, 115
See Betz and Marshall

Betz and Marshall, 115, 195, 201

Bobbitt's principle, 81; qualifications of, 81, 82

Bonser, F. G., 11

Boston (spelling) list, 187

Botany, beginnings of, 14; varying emphases in, 17

Bourne, H. E., 67

Branom, M. E.,
See Branom and Reavis

Branom and Reavis, 116, 267

Brewer's *Reader's Handbook*, 69, 257

Brilliance, prestige of, 12; *versus* use, 13

Buckingham, B. R., 99, 119, 173

California speller, 187

Callaway, Mrs. T. T., 70, 106, 116, 119, 212, 241

Camerer, Alice, 62, 67, 68, 70, 117, 129, 133, 326

Capps, A. G., 114, 118, 123, 128, 129, 133, 188

Century Cyclopedia of Names, 69, 257

Chancellor, W. E., 175, 186

Charters, W. W., 70, 115, 116, 117, 119, 190, 195, 208, 212, 231, 270, 285, 328, 334
See Charters and Miller

determine the arithmetic actually used by adults in their social and business relations," 223-231
Studies in spelling, Ayre's measuring scale for ability in spelling, 172, 173; extensive study of letters to parents, 179-186; graded list, 186-188; intensive study of family letters, 173-176; interesting investigations in, 170, 171; "one hundred spelling demons," 178; other spelling scales, 173; spelling errors in the high school, 188-193; vocabulary of children's themes, 177-179; vocabulary of personal and business letters, 171-172
See Spelling, Spelling vocabulary
Studley, C. K.
See Studley and Ware
Studley and Ware, 186
Subject material,
See Subject matter
Subject matter, determined by analysis of life activities, 140; elements of difficulty as affecting, 98; for the elementary school, based on the layman's need, 132; grading of, 94-102; incidental and systematic presentation of, differentiated, 110, 111; interest as basis for grading of, in reading material, 316-324; methods for determining ideals which dominate instruction, 44; relationship of difficulty, interest, and use in grading, 99, 100; theories of gradation: based on children's interests and needs, 97; based on utility, 98; culture-epoch theory, 95; genetic stages, 96
Subjects of the curriculum, 103-113; combined as general service subjects, 111, 112; derived, 104; differentiation from specialists' problems, 103; place of "connective tissue" in, 107; primary, 103; systematic organization in, 106
Survey, The, 313
Systematic knowledge, acquisition and application of, 18; and unorganized fields, 20; constantly changing in organization, 17, 18; contribution of, to mental morale, 15; criticism of, as content of the curriculum, 16, 21; difficult to motivate unless useful, 19; effect upon the practices of civiliza-

tion, 15; organization of, facilitates instruction, 16; prestige of, 12, 14

Table, for chest expansion, 325; giving Greene's outline of curriculum material in sheep husbandry, 287-292; indicating the course in trade mathematics, based on the analysis of the job of turning a cylinder, 282-284; of frequency of jobs in home repair work, 305; of frequency of mention of jobs of home repair work, 303; of frequency of processes in home repair work, 304; of fundamental arithmetical operations, 277; of investigations in language and grammar, 195; of processes in home repair work, 304; on drilling in analysis of machinist's trade, 275; summarizing the mathematical elements appearing in the analysis of the job of turning a cylinder, 281
Tabular list of investigations, 114-117
Teacher's Word Book, 314, 315
Textbooks, 20; authorship of, 61; conformed to a "general level," 60
Thompson, O. S., 14, 195, 196
Thorndike, E. L., 24, 117, 314
Todd, E. M., 71, 117, 324, 326
Transfer of training,
See Formal discipline
Trilling, M. B., 155
Trivium, 3, 151

Uhl, W. L., 97, 117, 316
Units of achievement, 56; importance of, determined by concensus of opinion, 66; expert classification, 68; expert opinion, 66; verdict of history, 66; reason for selection of, 63, 64; relative importance of, 63, 65
See Units of mention
Units of instruction, method of selecting and grading, 101, 102
Units of mention, errors, 70; inches, 70; scoring each item, 71; short cuts, 71, single mention, 71; specific mention, 71, topics; 70; words, 70
See Units of achievement
Usefulness, as a standard in curriculum construction, 4

Vocabulary, of children's themes, 177; of family letters, 173; of letters to

AMERICAN EDUCATION:
ITS MEN, IDEAS, AND INSTITUTIONS
An Arno Press/New York Times Collection

Series I

Adams, Francis. **The Free School System of the United States.** 1875.

Alcott, William A. **Confessions of a School Master.** 1839.

American Unitarian Association. **From Servitude to Service.** 1905.

Bagley, William C. **Determinism in Education.** 1925.

Barnard, Henry, editor. **Memoirs of Teachers, Educators, and Promoters and Benefactors of Education, Literature, and Science.** 1861.

Bell, Sadie. **The Church, the State, and Education in Virginia.** 1930.

Belting, Paul Everett. **The Development of the Free Public High School in Illinois to 1860.** 1919.

Berkson, Isaac B. **Theories of Americanization: A Critical Study.** 1920.

Blauch, Lloyd E. **Federal Cooperation in Agricultural Extension Work, Vocational Education, and Vocational Rehabilitation.** 1935.

Bloomfield, Meyer. **Vocational Guidance of Youth.** 1911.

Brewer, Clifton Hartwell. **A History of Religious Education in the Episcopal Church to 1835.** 1924.

Brown, Elmer Ellsworth. **The Making of Our Middle Schools.** 1902.

Brumbaugh, M. G. **Life and Works of Christopher Dock.** 1908.

Burns, Reverend J. A. **The Catholic School System in the United States.** 1908.

Burns, Reverend J. A. **The Growth and Development of the Catholic School System in the United States.** 1912.

Burton, Warren. **The District School as It Was.** 1850.

Butler, Nicholas Murray, editor. **Education in the United States.** 1900.

Butler, Vera M. **Education as Revealed By New England Newspapers prior to 1850.** 1935.

Campbell, Thomas Monroe. **The Movable School Goes to the Negro Farmer.** 1936.

Carter, James G. **Essays upon Popular Education.** 1826.

Carter, James G. **Letters to the Hon. William Prescott, LL.D., on the Free Schools of New England.** 1824.

Channing, William Ellery. **Self-Culture.** 1842.

Coe, George A. **A Social Theory of Religious Education.** 1917.

Committee on Secondary School Studies. **Report of the Committee on Secondary School Studies, Appointed at the Meeting of the National Education Association.** 1893.

Counts, George S. **Dare the School Build a New Social Order?** 1932.

Counts, George S. **The Selective Character of American Secondary Education.** 1922.

Counts, George S. **The Social Composition of Boards of Education.** 1927.

Culver, Raymond B. **Horace Mann and Religion in the Massachusetts Public Schools.** 1929.

Curoe, Philip R. V. **Educational Attitudes and Policies of Organized Labor in the United States.** 1926.

Dabney, Charles William. **Universal Education in the South.** 1936.

Dearborn, Ned Harland. **The Oswego Movement in American Education.** 1925.

De Lima, Agnes. **Our Enemy the Child.** 1926.

Dewey, John. **The Educational Situation.** 1902.

Dexter, Franklin B., editor. **Documentary History of Yale University.** 1916.

Eliot, Charles William. **Educational Reform: Essays and Addresses.** 1898.

Ensign, Forest Chester. **Compulsory School Attendance and Child Labor.** 1921.

Fitzpatrick, Edward Augustus. **The Educational Views and Influence of De Witt Clinton.** 1911.

Fleming, Sanford. **Children & Puritanism.** 1933.

Flexner, Abraham. **The American College: A Criticism.** 1908.

Foerster, Norman. **The Future of the Liberal College.** 1938.

Gilman, Daniel Coit. **University Problems in the United States.** 1898.

Hall, Samuel R. **Lectures on School-Keeping.** 1829.

Hall, Stanley G. **Adolescence: Its Psychology and Its Relations to Physiology, Anthropology, Sociology, Sex, Crime, Religion, and Education.** 1905. 2 vols.

Hansen, Allen Oscar. **Early Educational Leadership in the Ohio Valley.** 1923.

Harris, William T. **Psychologic Foundations of Education.** 1899.

Harris, William T. **Report of the Committee of Fifteen on the Elementary School.** 1895.

Harveson, Mae Elizabeth. **Catharine Esther Beecher: Pioneer Educator.** 1932.

Jackson, George Leroy. **The Development of School Support in Colonial Massachusetts.** 1909.

Kandel, I. L., editor. **Twenty-five Years of American Education.** 1924.

Kemp, William Webb. **The Support of Schools in Colonial New York by the Society for the Propagation of the Gospel in Foreign Parts.** 1913.

Kilpatrick, William Heard. **The Dutch Schools of New Netherland and Colonial New York.** 1912.

Kilpatrick, William Heard. **The Educational Frontier.** 1933.

Knight, Edgar Wallace. **The Influence of Reconstruction on Education in the South.** 1913.

Le Duc, Thomas. **Piety and Intellect at Amherst College, 1865-1912.** 1946.

Maclean, John. **History of the College of New Jersey from Its Origin in 1746 to the Commencement of 1854.** 1877.

Maddox, William Arthur. **The Free School Idea in Virginia before the Civil War.** 1918.

Mann, Horace. **Lectures on Education.** 1855.

McCadden, Joseph J. **Education in Pennsylvania, 1801-1835, and Its Debt to Roberts Vaux.** 1855.

McCallum, James Dow. **Eleazar Wheelock.** 1939.

McCuskey, Dorothy. **Bronson Alcott, Teacher.** 1940.

Meiklejohn, Alexander. **The Liberal College.** 1920.

Miller, Edward Alanson. **The History of Educational Legislation in Ohio from 1803 to 1850.** 1918.

Miller, George Frederick. **The Academy System of the State of New York.** 1922.

Monroe, Will S. **History of the Pestalozzian Movement in the United States.** 1907.

Mosely Education Commission. **Reports of the Mosely Education Commission to the United States of America October-December, 1903.** 1904.

Mowry, William A. **Recollections of a New England Educator.** 1908.

Mulhern, James. **A History of Secondary Education in Pennsylvania.** 1933.

National Herbart Society. **National Herbart Society Yearbooks 1-5, 1895-1899.** 1895-1899.

Nearing, Scott. **The New Education: A Review of Progressive Educational Movements of the Day.** 1915.

Neef, Joseph. **Sketches of a Plan and Method of Education.** 1808.

Nock, Albert Jay. **The Theory of Education in the United States.** 1932.

Norton, A. O., editor. **The First State Normal School in America: The Journals of Cyrus Pierce and Mary Swift.** 1926.

Oviatt, Edwin. **The Beginnings of Yale, 1701-1726.** 1916.

Packard, Frederic Adolphus. **The Daily Public School in the United States.** 1866.

Page, David P. **Theory and Practice of Teaching.** 1848.

Parker, Francis W. **Talks on Pedagogics: An Outline of the Theory of Concentration.** 1894.

Peabody, Elizabeth Palmer. **Record of a School.** 1835.

Porter, Noah. **The American Colleges and the American Public.** 1870.

Reigart, John Franklin. **The Lancasterian System of Instruction in the Schools of New York City.** 1916.

Reilly, Daniel F. **The School Controversy (1891-1893).** 1943.

Rice, Dr. J. M. **The Public-School System of the United States.** 1893.

Rice, Dr. J. M. **Scientific Management in Education.** 1912.

Ross, Early D. **Democracy's College: The Land-Grant Movement in the Formative Stage.** 1942.

Rugg, Harold, et al. **Curriculum-Making: Past and Present.** 1926.

Rugg, Harold, et al. **The Foundations of Curriculum-Making.** 1926.

Rugg, Harold and Shumaker, Ann. **The Child-Centered School.** 1928.

Seybolt, Robert Francis. **Apprenticeship and Apprenticeship Education in Colonial New England and New York.** 1917.

Seybolt, Robert Francis. **The Private Schools of Colonial Boston.** 1935.

Seybolt, Robert Francis. **The Public Schools of Colonial Boston.** 1935.

Sheldon, Henry D. **Student Life and Customs.** 1901.

Sherrill, Lewis Joseph. **Presbyterian Parochial Schools, 1846-1870.** 1932.

Siljestrom, P. A. **Educational Institutions of the United States.** 1853.

Small, Walter Herbert. **Early New England Schools.** 1914.

Soltes, Mordecai. **The Yiddish Press: An Americanizing Agency.** 1925.

Stewart, George, Jr. **A History of Religious Education in Connecticut to the Middle of the Nineteenth Century.** 1924.

Storr, Richard J. **The Beginnings of Graduate Education in America.** 1953.

Stout, John Elbert. **The Development of High-School Curricula in the North Central States from 1860 to 1918.** 1921.

Suzzallo, Henry. **The Rise of Local School Supervision in Massachusetts.** 1906.

Swett, John. **Public Education in California.** 1911.

Tappan, Henry P. **University Education.** 1851.

Taylor, Howard Cromwell. **The Educational Significance of the Early Federal Land Ordinances.** 1921.

Taylor, J. Orville. **The District School.** 1834.

Tewksbury, Donald G. **The Founding of American Colleges and Universities before the Civil War.** 1932.

Thorndike, Edward L. **Educational Psychology.** 1913-1914.

True, Alfred Charles. **A History of Agricultural Education in the United States, 1785-1925.** 1929.

True, Alfred Charles. **A History of Agricultural Extension Work in the United States, 1785-1923.** 1928.

Updegraff, Harlan. **The Origin of the Moving School in Massachusetts.** 1908.

Wayland, Francis. **Thoughts on the Present Collegiate System in the United States.** 1842.

Weber, Samuel Edwin. **The Charity School Movement in Colonial Pennsylvania.** 1905.

Wells, Guy Fred. **Parish Education in Colonial Virginia.** 1923.

Wickersham, J. P. **The History of Education in Pennsylvania.** 1885.

Woodward, Calvin M. **The Manual Training School.** 1887.

Woody, Thomas. **Early Quaker Education in Pennsylvania.** 1920.

Woody, Thomas. **Quaker Education in the Colony and State of New Jersey.** 1923.

Wroth, Lawrence C. **An American Bookshelf, 1755.** 1934.

Series II

Adams, Evelyn C. **American Indian Education.** 1946.

Bailey, Joseph Cannon. **Seaman A. Knapp: Schoolmaster of American Agriculture.** 1945.

Beecher, Catharine and Harriet Beecher Stowe. **The American Woman's Home.** 1869.

Benezet, Louis T. **General Education in the Progressive College.** 1943.

Boas, Louise Schutz. **Woman's Education Begins.** 1935.

Bobbitt, Franklin. **The Curriculum.** 1918.

Bode, Boyd H. **Progressive Education at the Crossroads.** 1938.

Bourne, William Oland. **History of the Public School Society of the City of New York.** 1870.

Bronson, Walter C. **The History of Brown University, 1764-1914.** 1914.

Burstall, Sara A. **The Education of Girls in the United States.** 1894.

Butts, R. Freeman. **The College Charts Its Course.** 1939.

Caldwell, Otis W. and Stuart A. Courtis. **Then & Now in Education, 1845-1923.** 1923.

Calverton, V. F. & Samuel D. Schmalhausen, editors. **The New Generation: The Intimate Problems of Modern Parents and Children.** 1930.

Charters, W. W. **Curriculum Construction.** 1923.

Childs, John L. **Education and Morals.** 1950.

Childs, John L. Education and the Philosophy of Experimentalism. 1931.

Clapp, Elsie Ripley. Community Schools in Action. 1939.

Counts, George S. The American Road to Culture: A Social Interpretation of Education in the United States. 1930.

Counts, George S. School and Society in Chicago. 1928.

Finegan, Thomas E. Free Schools. 1921.

Fletcher, Robert Samuel. A History of Oberlin College. 1943.

Grattan, C. Hartley. In Quest of Knowledge: A Historical Perspective on Adult Education. 1955.

Hartman, Gertrude & Ann Shumaker, editors. Creative Expression. 1932.

Kandel, I. L. The Cult of Uncertainty. 1943.

Kandel, I. L. Examinations and Their Substitutes in the United States. 1936.

Kilpatrick, William Heard. Education for a Changing Civilization. 1926.

Kilpatrick, William Heard. Foundations of Method. 1925.

Kilpatrick, William Heard. The Montessori System Examined. 1914.

Lang, Ossian H., editor. Educational Creeds of the Nineteenth Century. 1898.

Learned, William S. The Quality of the Educational Process in the United States and in Europe. 1927.

Meiklejohn, Alexander. The Experimental College. 1932.

Middlekauff, Robert. Ancients and Axioms: Secondary Education in Eighteenth-Century New England. 1963.

Norwood, William Frederick. Medical Education in the United States Before the Civil War. 1944.

Parsons, Elsie W. Clews. Educational Legislation and Administration of the Colonial Governments. 1899.

Perry, Charles M. Henry Philip Tappan: Philosopher and University President. 1933.

Pierce, Bessie Louise. Civic Attitudes in American School Textbooks. 1930.

Rice, Edwin Wilbur. The Sunday-School Movement (1780-1917) and the American Sunday-School Union (1817-1917). 1917.

Robinson, James Harvey. The Humanizing of Knowledge. 1924.

Ryan, W. Carson. Studies in Early Graduate Education. 1939.

Seybolt, Robert Francis. The Evening School in Colonial America. 1925.

Seybolt, Robert Francis. Source Studies in American Colonial Education. 1925.

Todd, Lewis Paul. Wartime Relations of the Federal Government and the Public Schools, 1917-1918. 1945.

Vandewalker, Nina C. The Kindergarten in American Education. 1908.

Ward, Florence Elizabeth. The Montessori Method and the American School. 1913.

West, Andrew Fleming. Short Papers on American Liberal Education. 1907.

Wright, Marion M. Thompson. The Education of Negroes in New Jersey. 1941.

Supplement

The Social Frontier (Frontiers of Democracy). Vols. 1-10, 1934-1943.